YOUR PROBLEM, OUR STORY

A management guide to handling emergencies and the media

PHILIP ALGAR

Matfield Books

HD49
A54
2008

First published 2008

Published by:
Matfield Books, Southern Lights, Foxhole Lane,
Matfield, Kent TN12 7ES

www.matfieldbooks.com

Copyright © Philip Algar 2008

ISBN 978-0-9540595-2-1

A catalogue record for this book is available from the British Library.

Printed and bound by T.J. International Ltd.,
Trecerus Industrial Estate, Padstow, Cornwall PL28 8RW, England.

Designed by Beechwood,
The Crow's Nest, 2 Acre Road, Kingston-upon-Thames, Surrey KT2 6EF.
www.beechwood.uk.com

Text set in Sabon 10.75/14 pt.

YOUR PROBLEM, OUR STORY

A management guide to handling emergencies and the media

Contents

FOREWORD

Organisations must be insured for many different potential problems and may carry out regular safety checks or drills. Consequently, they may believe that this and regular reappraisals will prevent an unfavourable incident but that feared emergency can still happen. How will those organisations explain themselves to the outside world, to minimise damage to their business and reputation? The media can help to mitigate the effect and, of course, bad publicity can destroy a company. Creating and regularly testing media-related procedures and relevant personnel can be as important as those original safety checks. Effective communications can be critical to a company's survival.

This essentially practical book is not about "spin", nor is it relevant only to large corporations. Its purpose is to advise organisations of all sizes why it is desirable to plan against a potentially serious event, then how to communicate with the media if that event occurs. Although the book concentrates on dealing with emergencies, much of the advice on how to secure advantages from good communication with the media is equally applicable to day-to-day situations.

There will be a little repetition as some basic facts apply to many forms of media response, and, within reason, each chapter is intended to be self-contained. There are no detailed case studies, which soon date, but some brief examples of problems are included to allow readers to identify with the incident. Some are based on what happened to large companies but, although this book is written for a wide audience, the big group incidents have been chosen because they will be familiar. Similarly, as most onshore incidents do not last long, as far as the media are concerned, this is not true of problems at sea so some examples of unfolding incidents are based on difficulties encountered by energy or shipping companies. This concentration, however, does not mean that only large companies are at risk from bad publicity!

Much of what follows may be common sense, yet a big part of emergency planning is precisely that. Common sense often flees when all the phones ring at the same time and nobody has been confronted before with the challenge of coping simultaneously with an emergency and maintaining routine business. This book is based on many hundreds of days of participation in training and exercises around the world as well as involvement in genuine crises, as a company employee, journalist and consultant. Finally, although many excellent executives and responders are female, the phrase "he or she" has been omitted in the interests of space.

INTRODUCTION: JUST IMAGINE

Shock, chaos, confusion and panic can overtake organisations, large and small, suddenly confronted with a problem. A fine reputation can be lost in hours. What follows conveys some of the uncertainty that can overtake an unprepared company when an incident occurs and the media become involved.

Roger Fisher, the inexperienced new general manager, was awaiting a call from his chauffeur saying that he was ready to spirit him to lunch. Apart from his chief executive, most senior managers were out of the office, so Fisher could anticipate a quiet, relaxing afternoon and an early departure. The phone rang. It was a colleague from one of the company's depots. He was in a panic. "It's awful. We've had an explosion and the bloody great fire's out of control. The fire crews aren't here yet and we've got dead and injured. It's chaos." Had everyone been evacuated? The local man did not know and asked for immediate help before saying that he had to go.

What should Roger do? No crisis plans existed. He had hoped that there would not be a serious accident, especially after his predecessor had reduced staff numbers dramatically and some important maintenance had been postponed. Suddenly, the office of the second most senior employee in the building resembled a London underground station in the rush hour. Both phones jangled discordantly, increasing the sense of drama. Roger, who realised that he must tell his chief executive, as soon as possible, picked up one phone.

It was the contact from the depot. "It's getting worse: it's Armageddon. I'm ringing from the Country Hotel because we've all been evacuated. The depot's ablaze. We think seven guys have been killed, six are injured and at least 12 are missing." Apparently, the emergency services, which had been delayed by traffic, were now on site. There were new problems. There was a purple cloud drifting towards the nearest town. The regional airport had been closed and local radio was claiming that some chemicals had entered a shipping canal. "The press are swarming all over the place and one junior employee's told local television that we reduced maintenance and fired so many people he's not surprised that there's been an accident."

Roger interrupted and asked for the hotel's phone number. He noted it and then asked for details of the dead and injured to be emailed to him immediately, as well as an update every 15 minutes. "Sorry, no, we can't cope. We need help, especially with the reporters, who are interviewing anyone they can find. It's absolute hell."

The general manager said that he would try but even if he could find someone, they would not be at the depot for hours. Nobody within the company had been nominated or trained for such work and no contemporary timetables were available. His office was full of very agitated colleagues who wanted answers to questions that nobody had anticipated, let alone solved in advance. The company was being besieged by the outside world. Roger did not know what to do. One colleague asked how to react to demands for broadcast interviews. This had never been discussed and the general manager did not know who would be any good in front of a camera or microphone. How could the company deal with the vast number of phone calls from next of kin and friends and, of course, the media? The investment manager sought Roger's advice on how he could stop the plunge in the group's share price and the local MP, angry not to have been told about the incident, was demanding information. Roger's secretary told him that "the Secretary of State for Business wants a one-page report of what has happened and what you are doing about it, to be sent within the next half hour".

Around the building, his colleagues were trying to respond to myriad other calls from contacts, other companies, health, safety and environment officials, Brussels bureaucrats, financial analysts, journalists and companies offering their services to help mitigate the impact of the disaster. Downstairs, some journalists, unable to glean any information from the company by telephone, were mingling with relatives who lived in the London area and who, like the scribes, unable to find out what was happening, were now surrounding the lone receptionist who did not know what had happened...Another note was placed on Roger's desk. The telephone exchange was jammed so normal business had ceased.

Roger turned on the television to hear the latest news. An elderly lady, standing in front of her old cottage, now lacking a front door and windows, sobbingly revealed that her Jack had been blown up and that he always said that it was a dangerous place to work because nobody cared about safety. Apparently, hundreds of local people were being evacuated to the nearest village hall where they would have to stay overnight. All those close to the site, and whose windows were still in place, should stay indoors, because of the smoke, and boil all water because chemicals leaking from the site had penetrated the watercourse. Roger turned off the television to take a call on his mobile phone from a non-executive director who angrily demanded an update on what had happened. Everyone seemed to think that they had a divine right to be fully apprised. What Roger did not know was that an active pressure group concerned with industrial safety was organising a boycott of the company's petrol stations and that the leading trade union had called out its members at other locations in protest against cuts in the maintenance budget.

The phone rang again. It was the chief executive who had been told of the emergency by another colleague. He wanted to see Roger immediately. "We've got a major crisis. Crisis management is in your patch, so find out as much as you can, as soon as you can. We've had a request to go on television for a live national interview. I want you to do it. Do the best you can. I'll try to cope with all the other problems. We must get our side of the story over rapidly, before we're crucified." Roger pleaded that he was new in the job, had not had sufficient time to organise things properly, had never spoken to a journalist and had not been trained. "Nonsense. Any fool can cope with some ill-informed inexperienced jumped-up journalist. Make sure that you've the latest information and for God's sake, say sorry and, above all, be honest." Roger had no choice. He was to appear on television.

CHAPTER 1

BACKGROUND

This chapter discusses society's stance towards emergencies and why organisations, large and small, international and local, should co-operate with the media. The press and broadcasters can disseminate company messages economically and speedily, to increase their prospects of survival. The advantages of communication and the penalties of failing to tell the world what is happening, are considered here as are organisations' "reasons" for not dealing with the media. Although the book is based on emergencies, defined later, companies may be confronted by issues, such as their stance on climate change, and parts of this book are relevant to this kind of challenge.

Recent years are littered with major accidents that caused severe loss of life, tragic injuries and significant damage to the environment. Aircraft have fallen out of the sky, vessels have sunk, trains have collided, industrial plants have blown up, major pollution has occurred and some products have proved unsafe. Man's inhumanity to man, manifested in wars and acts of terrorism, has added to the grim list. Nature, too, has wreaked havoc with potentially disastrous diseases, earthquakes, hurricanes, the tsunami, severe and regular flooding and unexpectedly sharp extremes of temperature in ill-prepared regions as the world faces the prospect of climate change. Many communities have been devastated by disasters and few countries have escaped totally unscathed. At a different level, organisations, confronted by an emergency have been driven out of business, partly by adverse media comment.

The impact of these crises has frequently been exacerbated by a lack of planning and, in the case of business-related emergencies, by corporate arrogance, ignorance or incompetence. In the past, the need for basic planning, which could have prevented some consequences of accidents, was often overlooked by society. Now, the public accepts that some accidents will occur, but demands that organisations involved in emergencies act promptly and effectively, to say what has happened, where, when, to whom and why, to explain what they are doing to minimise the repercussions and to say what action they are taking to avoid a repetition. They cannot meet this demand unless they plan.

Even the largest organisations cannot convey their emergency-related messages speedily to their numerous global publics without the media, which offer a multiplier effect and help to keep people informed. Whilst a large organisation can survive an emergency, a smaller company might not remain in business, but it, too, must try to answer basic questions via the media. Some of the commercial groups involved in emergencies remain in business but are scarred, morally and financially, and will be associated with these catastrophes for many years. Others, perhaps less resilient because of their size, or blamed for the incident and an inadequate response, have long since gone.

The media, which have a profound influence on public opinion, and thus on legislation, are now more experienced, intrusive, demanding and influential and seeks to ensure that incompetence is exposed and that the guilty pay the price. Consequently, a company must convince the media that it had plans on how to cope with an emergency and that it handled the incident efficiently. Unless it succeeds, and this will only be achieved by communicating, it will be deemed guilty, however good the performance on the ground. Customers, influenced by media coverage and urged on by pressure groups, may boycott the company's products and services, jeopardising its future. Even if a company survives, despite the perception of an inadequate performance, it could have difficulty in maintaining sales, raising capital for new ventures and retaining and recruiting staff. Other groups within the industry might be reluctant to link with the "guilty" company in alliances.

All this may be unjust but this book confronts perception. Communicating effectively and promptly with the media does not make an accident and its repercussions disappear but it does minimise the prospects of becoming involved in a second crisis in which the public lose confidence in the organisation with potentially disastrous consequences.

Many well-publicised calamities such as Piper, Bhopal, Exxon's Alaskan oil spill, *Braer, Sea Empress, Herald of Free Enterprise* and the *Concorde* crash have become enshrined in history. Headlines have also been devoted to many railway accidents and appalling shipping disasters, involving the loss of thousands of lives, not least the Egyptian accident in 2006 which prompted riots from those who vainly sought information about friends thought to be on the hapless ferry. All these have had major implications for the companies involved. History will also remember the January 2006 mine disaster in West Virginia, in the US, where men confirmed as survivors were later reported to be dead and Europe's biggest peacetime fire, in December 2005, at the Buncefield oil terminal in the UK.

That said, many emergencies involve smaller organisations which can easily be undermined. A butcher's shop, selling contaminated meat, a small company with a computer-related problem unable to pay its staff promptly, a local council that has not repaired a wall properly which fell on a pedestrian or a small coach company, depending on the immediate area for its business, and involved in a serious road accident, can all face sudden problems and the interest of the local media.

Many organisations are increasingly at risk as business becomes more complex and dependent on technology. When that technology fails, disaster can follow, as the potential for chaos increases in inter-dependent communities. The media constitute an important group: they can convey a company's messages and they themselves are a potent force in influencing public opinion. No company, wanting to communicate effectively, should be portrayed as a villain solely because it does not understand the media or performs poorly in front of a live television camera. Equally, companies must learn how to make the best use of the information that they have and become aware of what is demanded by the outside world.

Piper Alpha and *Brent Spar:* promoting change

Some years ago, two significant events promoted major changes. In 1988, 167 men were killed when Occidental's UK North Sea *Piper Alpha* platform caught fire. The calamity, of such intensity and devastation, compelled executives to accept that the unthinkable could happen. The belief that the systems in place could prevent an accident becoming a major catastrophe was cruelly exposed as unjustified optimism. Equally, the opinion that a good safety record effectively ensured a safe future, collapsed. Industry thinking was changed irreversibly and all sensible contingency planning now confronts the worst scenario. Plans make greater provision for reducing the impact of disasters, as well as seeking to ensure that they never occur. Realistic training and exercises, including media response, are becoming obligatory in some sectors.

Some industries, such as shipping, attract significant media coverage and political attention, but they are not unique. All manufacturing industry, especially petrochemicals, the nuclear industry and the transport sector, face intense public scrutiny at times of disaster. The media's insatiable appetite for informed comment means that if companies fail to respond, others will speak on what has happened. They will seldom be as keen to defend the organisation as the company itself.

Some sectors are also at risk if an issue is perceived to have been badly handled. After pressure from Greenpeace, aided by a frequently gullible and lazy media, Shell cancelled a decision to dump the UK North Sea's *Brent Spar* loading buoy in the Atlantic. Despite having secured all the appropriate approvals, Shell under-estimated the need to explain the complexity of numerous issues to many non-governmental and industry audiences. The *Brent Spar* saga changed the relationship between big companies and society. The key word now is transparency and this puts additional emphasis on all organisations, whatever their size, on communicating through the media. More executives now accept that they must explain actions to a wide audience because society has a right to know and pressure groups can exploit their complacency.

The public no longer invests automatic trust and respect in commercial organisations and comments from government and big industrial groups often provoke instant cynicism. Authority and respect have to be earned. Frequently, society now feels that, in a confrontation between large commercial groups and seemingly dispassionate pressure groups, the former are guilty until they are proved innocent.

Communicating what has happened, what the organisation is doing about it and how it feels, will not eliminate all the problems nor will carefully-chosen words eradicate significant difficulties in the time taken to devise and mutter a soundbite or quote. Without effective communications, companies involved in an emergency may fail to win public support so will be penalised more severely. Indeed, an initial potentially serious incident can then become a crisis if any of the "publics" sense that the company has conducted itself badly. In a sense, therefore, there is a two-fold reward for successful communication. An organisation is not condemned to a second crisis and may even mitigate some of the effects of the operational problem. Indeed, occasionally, companies perceived to have handled an emergency effectively, enjoy a better reputation because management has been seen to be competent in dealing with the problem.

COMMUNICATING WITH THE MEDIA

The main objective of crisis or emergency management is to minimise the damage to people, environment, property and the company's reputation, an important corporate asset. Benjamin Franklin allegedly remarked that "it takes many good deeds to build a good reputation and only one bad one to lose it". It also assumes that communicating is essential but some business people doubt the wisdom of meeting the media. A poor communications performance, or, indeed, silence, which might be seen as a "cover-up", can reinforce an initial impression of serious incompetence, at worst, or lack of preparedness, at best. Even if an excellent operational performance is minimising the repercussions, the company must explain what is happening otherwise the perception may well be unfavourable. However, unjustly, the organisation will attract negative publicity until it proves that, whatever the cause of the accident, it is working hard to minimise the impact. Journalists believe that large companies, in particular, should be sufficiently organised to minimise the possibility of accidents and then, if something goes wrong, to communicate effectively.

The media will ask whether an accident was caused by human error or the failure of a piece of equipment. All disasters, except those caused by an act of God, are ultimately caused by human error which may mean a failure of management. The enquiry into the North Sea *Piper Alpha* disaster noted that senior management was too easily satisfied that safety was being maintained. Even for acts of God, questions will be asked why the authorities failed to take proper precautionary measures in advance, of, say, a flood in New Orleans.

One organisation told its staff that, as a responsible company, it believed that "members of the public and the press have a right to know of events or factors affecting the company, its personnel or the environment in which we operate. The company will therefore try to provide the facilities required to keep those seeking information properly informed. The best way the company can show its appreciation of its responsibilities and maintain its reputation, even in difficult circumstances, is to be as co-operative as possible." Another argued that "it is important to appreciate that the press, radio and television have a legitimate interest in obtaining prompt and accurate information on behalf of the public and should be seen as the principal links between the company and the public. No company gains by locking its gates to journalists: barred entry, they may use rumours and speculation, instead of facts, in what they write". They may also approach other sources which may attack the company involved in the incident. Unfortunately, many organisations, literally or effectively, still say "no comment", presumably thinking that they will then escape scrutiny: such a negative stance can stimulate the media to investigate more deeply.

Communicating, effectively now a commercial requirement, given consumers' growing influence, is not a favour to the outside world: it is a basic demand. Comment is essential; there is no real choice. Even the largest corporations need the media in an emergency to convey information to the various publics, globally, if the damage to their reputation, a major asset, is to be minimised. The media, especially radio and television, increasingly broadcasting news 24 hours a day, should be regarded as a resource: the price for using this valuable service is the effort in understanding how it works, what it wants and how the company's message can be conveyed, whilst simultaneously assisting the media.

Sectors to be reached

The media provide the opportunity for that immediate "multiplier". In an emergency, the company must influence most or all of the following groups and if the overall perception of these "publics' is one of a lack of planning, relative indifference to the emergency or inept handling, the company will become embroiled in a second crisis, superimposed on the "operational" one.

- Government, at local, national, regional or global level, through the United Nations or a similar international grouping
- Political parties, national and local politicians, regulatory bodies and other official groups
- Financial organisations, shareholders, existing and potential
- Next of kin, friends, relatives, academics and "experts"
- Former, existing and potential employees
- Pressure groups, especially those involved in health, safety and environment, and the local community in which the incident occurred
- Actual and potential customers
- Other companies, including suppliers, contractors, distributors, existing and potential partners and trade associations
- The media itself and its audiences and the general public

Objectives of communicating in an emergency

The ultimate commercial intention is to minimise the damage to the company's reputation, which is an asset built up, possibly expensively, over the years and which can be destroyed speedily. This important objective can be secured via telephone response, press releases, press conferences and broadcast and press interviews. All these tools are discussed in this book. The main advantages of communicating are to:

- Show that the organisation is controlling the incident and doing all that can be done to minimise death, injury and damage to the environment and to property
- Allow the company to express regret, to refute unfounded rumours and incorrect "facts", to minimise their spread and to explain what it is doing to mitigate the impact of the incident and minimise damage to its reputation
- Defuse the anger that might otherwise have been directed towards the company, especially towards large groups that are often regarded with suspicion

- Establish the company as a responsible group, competent, keen to communicate with the media and as a prime source of information
- Control the flow of information about the incident and be seen as a single authoritative source of information and to deter journalists, believing that the company is "covering up", from "digging"
- Ensure that standardised, consistent and authorised information is provided
- Reduce the prospects of others taking space or air time, which could damage the company, by communicating sensibly
- Collect information from the media, especially in relation to rumour and allegations
- Provide as much information as possible, to deter journalists from visiting the company's operational centre or the incident site, and from seeking more information from others less likely to defend the company
- Enable the organisation to shed its anonymous façade and show a human face
- Ease some of the pressures on the personnel manning the telephones and dealing with the media's questions, in part by holding a press conference at which journalists can question senior executives who can demonstrate that they are well organised and can cope with the problem
- Avoid all the penalties listed in the next section, and, particularly, to deny the prospect of creating a second crisis through bad communications

Penalties for not communicating with the media

The penalties for failing to communicate effectively range from a fall in profitability to being driven out of business, especially if the company was not doing well before the accident. Here are some possible consequences of failing to convince an audience that an emergency is being handled competently:

- Government, at local and national levels, may be less inclined to grant the organisation new permits and may take adverse action against not just the company but also the industry. This could hamper or even end the "victim" company in its efforts to seek new partners.

- Shareholders, unhappy with the bad publicity and management's apparent failure to react adequately, will sell shares, thus undermining the group's ability to raise cash and to attract future shareholders. Companies can then become liable to take-overs and shareholders may succumb to the better prospects offered by a new management team.

- Customers, especially at the local level, may spurn a company's products or services.

- In diversified groups and in large fully-integrated companies, an incident in one business can adversely affect another: for example, an oil company causing pollution offshore might have its gasoline stations boycotted.

- Similarly, international companies may effectively be penalised by customers, or governments, in many different countries, for an incident in another region.

- Employees, reluctant to work for a company that, seemingly, is unprepared to cope with an emergency and slack on safety or the environment, may leave.

- All companies need to discuss routine matters inside the sector. When an emergency is handled badly, the entire national industry is castigated and may face more demanding legislation and higher taxation.

- No company wants to be identified as having caused or having been involved in a major incident. Companies frequently form consortia, to spread risk, or to build a joint plant to secure the economies of scale that a solo stance would not yield. Those perceived to have acted badly will not attract partners.

- Pressure groups, anxious to talk to the media, unlike some big companies, will ensure that an emergency and its aftermath will remain in the public eye.

- Financial groups may withdraw their support.

- Suppliers may decide against dealing with a company that has a poor reputation in safety or environmental matters.

- Residents, who live close to a site involved in an emergency, can sustain a campaign, especially if backed by the local media which may have their own interest in prolonging the emergency. Residents may oppose applications for plant extensions and take up significant management time.

- Alienated regulatory bodies can severely disrupt local plans for expansion, or even a continuation of trade.
- Local and national politicians can wield significant and adverse influence.
- The local media will probe further and influence local opinion adversely over a period. Local media representatives also assist national media, so the crisis will not necessarily remain local.
- Environmental and other standards are rising: companies must adopt the most stringent regulations, worldwide, whatever the local demands, as they can be penalised in the home country as a result of the perception of its behaviour overseas.

The costs, direct and indirect, that will be incurred by a company, in dealing with an incident, can be horrendously high. No organisation will want to increase the bill by incurring "extra charges" following action from any of the groups listed above. "If you think that safety is expensive, try having an accident."

If the need to communicate is so clear and the penalties for failure so potentially dire, why do so many organisations not make even basic plans?

"Reasons" for not planning how to deal with the media in an emergency

Arrogance, ignorance, complacency and incompetence

An open approach to the media during an emergency is unlikely to be forth-coming from companies that shun transparency in routine activities. Some still believe that making profits for shareholders justifies disregarding others' "irrelevant" demands. Others think that their reputation and the occasional friendly but authoritative comment, perhaps reinforced by donations, should suffice to ensure continued goodwill. A few groups, divorced from reality and basking quietly in an imaginative but ill-conceived cocoon of their own making, indulge in massive self-deception: they believe that they could never be challenged by a crisis. Companies with any of these characteristics will have difficulty in responding positively to a persistent media during a crisis and could therefore pay a heavy price. "Be prepared or prepare to fail: an issue ignored is a crisis ensured" are trite but valid propositions.

Fear and distrust of the media

A reluctance to face the media may be based on fear. The familiar landscape has vanished, there are insufficient people to cope and everything is being challenged. The organisation must react positively to a pressure that few employees have experienced. Some managers distrust the media. They believe that it is malicious, manipulative, arrogant and superficial and trivialises, personalises and over-simplifies complex situations. Some parts of the media are guilty on some of these charges, sometimes, but the charges cannot be sustained against the entire press and broadcasting sectors and does not merit a complete boycott.

Sometimes, executives' lack of trust has been generated by a "misquote" following a previous interview, or it might just be sheer prejudice. Another factor might be the recollection of some very hostile interviews, often involving evasive politicians, and the fear that executives could be similarly treated. This is unlikely, unless the company is perceived as complacent and incompetent. These worries are based on the assumption that all journalists are hostile, rude and have scant regard for facts. This general condemnation is wrong. Nevertheless, the media do not often apologise for their errors with the same energy and prominence that characterised the initial story. Understandably, some executives see this as a major danger and decide that they cannot "win" so prefer not to participate.

Senior executives are uncomfortable unless they are fully informed and feel able to deal with any relevant topics. They equate ignorance with incompetence, so, especially early in an incident, when information is scanty, appearing on television, for example, seems dangerous but the media and the public may feel that silence implies that the company has something to hide. Within reason, a lack of information, at an early stage, does not matter. It is important to express regret and to indicate what happened and what will be done. Later, the company can plan answers to easily anticipated questions. Training can overcome an executive's prejudice and increase confidence.

Lack of commitment from senior management

Without senior management commitment, a company's plans will be non-existent or inadequate. Corporate culture can prompt this negative stance.

A regime that discourages internal debate and near-miss reporting, for example, is more likely to have an accident than a more open group. Some chief executives, who under-estimate the nature of an emergency, erroneously believe that they could cope with a crisis on the day, or, if history is any guide, on the night. Apart from handling the unexpected, for which they have received no training, under pressure seldom experienced, they must sustain routine business which can suffer if too many executives become involved in the incident. This is a good reason for hiring specialist crisis management media consultants who can assume much of the main burden and which can be very helpful, particularly, to smaller organisations. Otherwise, the company's inexperience and incompetence can be exposed, with predictable consequences.

Other reasons for failing to devise a plan include financial restraints and senior managers' fears of being shown up in front of junior staff during comprehensive exercises. The cost of failure to communicate could dwarf any costs of basic planning and training. Managers may be effective on routine matters, on which their careers and reputation have been based, but they are reluctant to see all that vanish because of a careless remark in an emergency. In exercises, telephone responders, having just been bombarded with questions on the phone, usually have great regard for their senior colleagues who face the same journalists in front of a camera or at a press conference. Managers who decide against media participation in "real life" can lose the respect of their workforce. The latter may well feel that there is a good case to answer and they become angry when they hear "we asked the company to appear in the programme but they declined, saying that they were not prepared to comment/had no one available/did not have sufficient time to prepare/ but they did offer a statement".

We are too small to bother, have nothing to gain by being proactive or we are not at risk

Even the smallest organisations should prepare and it is no defence to claim that low staff numbers preclude systematic training. It is even more important for smaller companies to prepare. Lacking substantial resources, they could disappear if unable or seemingly unwilling to communicate. If they have few staff, outside consultants should be retained, to allow them to take routine telephone calls during a crisis and to offer relevant advice.

Familiarity with the media, secured mainly to enable executives to cope with a crisis satisfactorily, can also give small companies a competitive advantage in "peacetime".

Frequently, companies which decide that they are not at risk, change their minds when some possible crises are suggested. Companies claiming that they are not exposed to serious risk should recall the collision between a dredger and a small pleasure vessel on the River Thames, in which 51 people were killed.

Our role would be limited and no two crises are the same, so why prepare?

Some groups believe that if a disaster did occur, other organisations, especially the emergency services, would effectively take over and thus they, the companies, would have no real role. That is misguided. Although the police and other services have key roles, the challenge of minimising damage to a company's reputation is its alone. Crises resemble kaleidoscopes in their constantly changing patterns and movements, but, although all emergencies are unique, there are many common elements. Companies of all sizes should consider their main potential risks and prepare for those. Even if a different emergency then occurs, the company will be less inclined to flounder.

Why should we have plans just to assist the media? We could only deal with a few media calls.

The plans are not for the benefit of the media. Some groups maintain that they could only deal with a fraction of the demands made upon them so it would be better to rely on external and official emergency services. Who, then, would defend the organisation and how would it look if broadcasters say that nobody was available from the company? No organisation, however large, can answer all the media's questions but that is no reason for not trying to deal with the majority or the more important ones that could determine a company's survival. "Merely" preventing serious allegations from appearing is a very great advantage.

We can only spare a limited amount of time for training.

Even large organisations often restrict training sessions, claiming that personnel cannot be spared for more than an hour. This is ill-advised.

Devising and testing plans and being prepared could make all the difference between survival and extinction. Even in normal times, there are advantages in having a trained company spokesman.

We could not deal adequately with media criticism.

Some companies, absurdly, maintain that as they could not physically refute all the adverse points that would be made by the media, there is no point in trying to deal with any. No organisation can deal with everything reported by the global media but an attempt must be made to rebut the more serious and false accusations.

We could not perform satisfactorily at a television interview or press conference or write a press release.

By studying this book and undertaking some training, most executives could perform very well.

CHAPTER 2

WHAT IS AN EMERGENCY?

"There has been an incident at our factory in Erehwon." What is an incident? From the media's viewpoint, an emergency occurs when it so decides but from a company perspective, a media-defined emergency might just be an unimportant incident.

Incidents, emergencies and crises

When does an incident become an emergency and an emergency become a crisis? From the media's perspective, none of this matters: it may cover the story in detail even if the company regards the incident as trivial. Factors influencing the media's interest will be determined by location, the industry involved and its reputation on safety, the availability of personnel and equipment and other stories competing for space or broadcasting time.

For small organisations, subtleties of definition do not matter: they must respond if the media respond. The only justification for large companies struggling to define incidents, emergencies and crises is that the extent of their response will be determined by the answer.

A small fire at a fish and chip shop could finish a local business but may interest only the local media. A fire of the same dimensions might be handled easily by the local staff at an industrial plant and ignored by the media. However, the media might be interested if it was one of many such incidents, had safety implications for the community or occurred on a slack news day.

So, seeking precise definitions, that fit all organisations, sectors and contexts neatly, is futile. That said, a broad definition of an incident could be an unplanned event that has, or could have, an impact on routine operations, affecting people or the environment, property or company reputation. Alternatively, it might be an occurrence that cannot be dealt with adequately by in-house emergency services. One international group defines a crisis as occurring when it is losing control: for another, a crisis occurs when problems affecting an individual company could have an impact on the group. Some large organisations identify potential incidents and list them by type to allow them to determine, as rapidly as possible, just how high up the global corporate ladder, individuals and teams should be alerted. Airlines, for example, have about 100 types of potential emergency for which they have planned responses.

Events that could prompt a meeting of a big company's crisis management team, concerned not with the incident *per se*, but with its overall strategic implications, could include many deaths, the possibility of a public enquiry, serious public/national/political concern, potentially serious damage to the group's reputation, a major strike threat, a big financial problem, a boardroom rumpus, the possibility of more-demanding legislation, a serious environmental problem and the possible long-term media interest.

Another consideration is the likely duration of an emergency. Coping with the operational factors can last for weeks but, apart from local journalists, media interest seldom lasts for more than a few days, unless there is little else to occupy print space or broadcasting time or the story is a big one, with many different characteristics.

Reaction

Potential disasters are not always obvious initially as minor incidents can become emergencies and that it why it is preferable for an organisation to over, rather than under, react.

The company involved and the media may have some initial difficulties in determining how to react, partly because the nature and potential of the incident are unclear. Many journalists have covered emergencies and are skilled in reacting swiftly. In contrast, most business people lack this background so have little understanding of what might be involved until they experience the frightening nature of an emergency with its alarming potential for total chaos. The company's relative position may be even more difficult if the public affairs function is not highly regarded by senior management and is excluded from routine business decisions. Smaller organisations will not have a public affairs function and this emphasises the desirability of appointing someone on a part-time basis, with major support from a specialist consultancy.

Staff conversant with routine activities must ensure that their familiarity does not blind them to the potential consequences of a problem. Minor incidents, if undetected, or if inadequately handled, can become creeping crises. Although many major emergencies apparently originate from a single cause, implying that they are readily discernible, most subsequent investigations reveal that numerous factors contributed. An equipment failure, a management omission, human error and a lack of judgement or a failure to heed warnings or advice can combine with devastating effect.

Furthermore, what is insignificant at an individual company, such as a minor problem with a particular kind of airliner, might be totally ignored by the media but, if it then becomes apparent that the same fault has occurred to aircraft in different fleets, a story is in the making and the main interest will fall on the airline involved in the latest incident.

An apparently minor event can suddenly erupt into a major crisis because the company either ignored it or decided that it did not merit immediate action. Ideally, organisations should be able to detect a potential emergency very early and prepare to cope with media interest so the first rule in determining reaction is to assume that an incident might develop seriously. Preparing for the worst and then standing down some parts of the emergency organisation if the incident proves to be minor is recommended. Reacting adequately only when the crisis is apparent will be difficult and the company will take longer to accumulate and organise its resources than the media, accustomed and structured to dealing with emergencies. Some years ago, within seven minutes of an aircraft crash-landing on a UK motorway, questions were received from the media in Australia.

All that said, there are some "non-emergency" occasions when a company can maintain a low profile, at least initially, especially when another group is perceived as the "villain". It is often a difficult decision on whether to stay silent and to see how the situation develops and the media react rather than be proactive. This decision must take account of the duty to shareholders and the staff not to exacerbate a situation unnecessarily but much depends, of course on the nature of the incident. The organisation, however, must be fully prepared to react energetically if the media become very interested or the situation develops in an adverse way, affecting people, environment or property.

Big groups must ensure that there is continual communication between local sites and head office, with its wider perspective. Individual locations or businesses seldom see the fuller implications for the group. The media, by contrast, looking through recent news stories, may discover that, for example, this is the sixth fire that a manufacturing group has had, worldwide, in the last year. What began as a minor and local incident suddenly becomes a potential crisis for a large group.

A company can easily assess how the media see the incident in terms of coverage: if the number of media calls is high and increasing, the organisation should call out its telephone media response team and set up a management group so that authorised information can be fed to the journalists. The company's view, that a minor incident does not merit such a reaction, is irrelevant. Ultimately, the media decide for how long it will cover an incident. During the *Braer* tanker disaster in 1993 more than 500 journalists, from around the world, were on the Shetlands anticipating the vessel's break up. Whilst waiting, they conjured up many different stories but the scope for new articles faded eventually and most journalists left the island at the end of the first week, a few days after the tanker went aground and before it succumbed to nature. Media interest usually tends to be relatively short-lived unless there is the whiff of incompetence or illegality or the incident is major, such as the Buncefield oil depot fire, or has major implications for the environment.

Physical accidents and other emergencies

Many major disasters, inevitably, are "physical" or caused by nature, such as earthquakes or the tsunami. What happened at Aberfan, Bhopal, Chernobyl, Lockerbie, Sveso, Kings Cross, Bradford, Sheffield, *Piper Alpha et al* were serious. By their very nature, some sectors, such as transport, are at risk but there are many other types of emergencies. As the quest for drugs to alleviate the problems of old age intensifies, companies in the health sector could be increasingly vulnerable and product recalls could become crises. Furthermore, an undetected issue can soon become a major challenge as was shown when the UK public's anger at gasoline prices resulted in the blockade of fuel depots.

Easy targets for the media are industries dominated by large companies which react slowly and have many critics, especially in the environmental lobbies. Equally, any apparent examples of incompetence, as in a hospital, or indifference to the environment, will attract media attention. As society becomes more complex, inter-dependent and global, relatively minor incidents or issues can cause massive and possibly international upheaval. Other types of emergency are indicated below.

Companies must also identify and plan for those apparently minor incidents that can suddenly develop into an emergency. Serious hotel fires can start on one cooker in a kitchen and rail crashes can occur if a signal is defective. Aircraft can crash because of a faulty door lock caused by a minor error or inadequate inspection. Emergencies can also develop rapidly where difficulties are never anticipated. The collapse of an improperly-constructed foot bridge, suddenly sending people to their deaths in the river below, is a timely reminder.

The list that follows, of course, is subjective and organisations, as part of their planning, should compile their own.

Human problems
- Loss of life, injury, missing personnel
- Allegations of serious incompetence
- An unexpected resignation
- Kidnapping of personnel
- Sudden death of senior executive
- Labour problems and a major strike
- A major health problem

Physical problems

- Fire, explosion, accidents, collisions
- Product contamination
- Storm, floods, earthquakes, snow, hurricanes

Illegal acts

- Sabotage
- Kidnapping of a company employee
- Allegation of lawlessness or rigging the market
- Widespread fraud
- Claims of corruption against executives
- Efforts to blackmail politicians and other officials
- Theft
- Spying on other commercial groups
- Bomb threat or terrorist activity

Environmental problems

- A spill of any chemical or product able to damage the environment or water course
- A fire from which the smoke is toxic
- Impact of an escape of radiation etc.

Miscellaneous

- A boycott by customers
- A product recall
- Equipment failure
- Loss of key facility
- Takeover bid
- Big decline in share price
- A legal threat
- Official reports into emergencies

- Stupid remarks by leading executives
- Anniversaries of previous problems

Anniversaries and reports

The media note the date of major crises, study the official results and then may return to the scene, sometimes literally, to determine if the damage has been made good and if the company has done all that it should have done. The *Exxon Valdez* oil spill in 1989 returned to the headlines later when some parts of the media alleged that the coast remained polluted and that compensation was still unpaid. The 1984 Bhopal tragedy, when 8,000 Indian people were killed after cyanide blanketed the city, returns regularly on anniversaries, and, in particular, in 2004, 20 years on from the horror. Reports into emergencies, usually produced after a long interval, may induce temporary media interest.

Characteristics of an emergency

"When a disaster occurs, those who are not in a state of panic are those who don't know about it." In an emergency, the overall picture alters abruptly. It will take many different and unexpected turns before it ends and its duration remains uncertain. Each facet, which can become a new and separate crisis, influences another. For example, a delay in ordering a rescue helicopter to an accident could become the main story.

Apart from erupting suddenly, most emergencies are characterised by an initial sense of panic, disbelief, denial and disorganisation and a rapid and energy-consuming flow of events. All this can cause disruption to people, operations and routine business. There are always insufficient people, time and information and, obviously, the commercial consequences could be serious. Severe delays in response, creating disproportionate difficulties, can result from minor procedural faults.

Each emergency is unique but rules, procedures, the overall plan and experience will be helpful as some familiar features, facilities and procedures vanish. A plan must be backed by experience, sense and flexibility. It is easy to develop a siege mentality or to enter a state of denial as critics of the US administration maintain happened when New Orleans was flooded.

Priorities, pressure and punishment

Everything will seem urgent but it will be impossible to deal with every issue so tasks must be prioritised. For example, after severe chemical spillage, many sea birds may die but an organisation, unable to revive them, must acknowledge that its first priority is to minimise damage to humans and the environment and only then to concentrate on more important matters that could directly influence its future. Even in the best-prepared companies, there will be disputes but these must be resolved speedily.

Companies must not be merely reactive nor must they just attempt to do the "easy" tasks. They must be seen to be trying to alleviate the situation and to anticipate what needs to be accomplished. They must communicate regret and their plans to the outside world to ensure that its perception is of a company that has a plan and which remains sufficiently flexible to cope with new developments.

Crucial decisions have to be taken urgently, in the full glare of unaccustomed publicity, without the detailed consideration that such a choice would normally be accorded. This increases the prospect of an error but a delayed decision implies incompetence to the outside world. These decisions are then scrutinised by the media and others, who lack fundamental knowledge of what is really required. Bad decisions or incompetence are punished immediately, compelling the company to confront and solve a new and unexpected crisis.

Rumours, allegations and problems

Rumours can occupy a vacuum caused by corporate silence. Speculation and allegations are assumed to be accurate unless rebutted promptly with substantial evidence, which might be hard to marshal at short notice. Every action is watched by the media which can take a rumour, speculate on it and create a new and unexpected problem. Exaggerated public opinion worsens a crisis. Many executives resent the media's alleged irresponsibility and its facility to exaggerate an aspect of the crisis deemed unimportant by the company, which then necessitates a new response. Senior personnel also know that any defects in the organisation can be exposed whilst the media expect fair treatment, even after condemning the company before it could mobilise. Many executives deplore the fact that journalists can write inaccurately about an incident, possibly causing significant damage, and then move on, leaving others to repair the damage. Perception can be worse than pollution.

In this febrile atmosphere, however carefully the various media responders have been chosen, someone may perform disappointingly. When this happens, some flexibility is essential to overcome the gap created in the team. Individuals, accustomed to reacting within a given set of rules, every day of their working lives, now find that they must operate differently: frequently, there are no rules and imagination and flexibility are required. Once again, here is a valid reason for small organisations to hire a specialist consultancy. The media will not be lenient towards a company just because it has few staff.

The "correct" number of company participants is seldom achieved. There is always too much work for the people involved but, after a point, dedicated rooms can become too noisy and diminishing returns set in. Complex information has to be disseminated briefly and simply but many technical personnel are unable to outline fundamentals to a lay audience and are deeply hostile to "semi-hypothetical" questions, especially those that demand an answer in just one short, easily-understood sentence. The media may try to describe the crisis in simple terms, thus riling personnel who resent over-simplification. Company personnel resent the "personalisation" of the crisis which is a favoured media ploy. Frequently, neither side really understands the other's problems and this can undermine relationships.

Most organisations have a strict division of labour and specialisation so few individuals can see the whole scene and, importantly, think ahead strategically. This imposes a big burden on relatively few people. Additionally, a company may lack certain skills, background knowledge and experience. Finally, many talented individuals, below the level of senior management, are reluctant to stray outside their specialist fields. This seems curious to many journalists, who are experienced generalists and fluent in everyday language. This lack of competent generalists in the company, capable of seeing the strategic aspects, can be minimised by hiring appropriate specialists who can work alongside the company during training and exercises.

Many organisations and groups will besiege the company, mainly seeking information, but several will try to persuade it that it can assist with equipment or skilled personnel. Former employees may claim that they predicted that this accident would occur and that their warnings were ignored. Some "experts", sharing their ignorance of the industry, the company and the facts, will pontificate freely and irresponsibly to the detriment of the organisation. Some politicians, too, may be looking to derive some benefits from the accident, busily arguing that this accident proves the validity of a case that they have been making for many years.

CHAPTER 3

BASIC INFORMATION ABOUT THE MEDIA

An understanding of who the media are and how they operate should help a company communicate more effectively.

The press, radio and television are treated very differently around the world and this is reflected in the structure of the media in different countries and how they cover an emergency. In some states, the media are subjected to stringent regulations and may be restricted in what they can ask business leaders or politicians. Even where relatively open coverage is allowed, the attitude towards business people can vary greatly. In some, they are treated with exaggerated respect: in others, journalists regard all people as equal, except, possibly, business leaders and politicians!

The UK has a well-informed specialist business press but, with cost pressures, fewer specialists are employed so companies involved in an incident must explain what has happened in simple non-technical language. The significance of specialist journalists is that when, for example, an airline emergency develops, writers who concentrate on this sector may contribute to reports and programmes across the media. They may also advise broadcast programme researchers so have the indirect potential to criticise the company which has no knowledge of the ultimate source of the story.

Although there are fewer specialist journalists, the number of media outlets has grown and the establishment of 24 hour global news channels has created more challenges for organisations in emergencies. This increasing proliferation of television stations means that demands for information will originate from more "media organisations" and competition between the stations will intensify, as journalists vie to be first with the news or with a different angle.

Many stations in different countries co-operate, exchanging video footage and stories, thus maximising coverage. Increasingly, major emergencies can have international repercussions. Thus, if the handling of an accident in France receives critical coverage locally, the "victim's" operations might suffer in countries where media restrictions would have prevented such direct reporting. The business world is shrinking and the speed of communications means that negative news about an organisation's reaction to an emergency can reach the other side of the world within seconds.

Some individuals, unskilled in the art of journalism, but armed with small high-quality video cameras or mobile phones with cameras, roam urban streets, "covering" stories as they happen and then try to sell their work. One London programme invited viewers with mobile phone cameras to "register with us, so we can contact you when a news story breaks in your area, because we want you, the viewer, to feel a part of the exciting world of newsgathering". The problem for a company is that a local accident may attract someone with a camera who takes a few shots and immediately sends them to a news organisation, long before the company is organised to cope with media enquiries. Worse still, these amateur "journalists" unskilled in seeking confirmation and unable to distinguish between facts and speculation, could easily cause panic unless their stories are carefully vetted by the professionals.

The internet not only allows journalists to discover background information about a company but can spread information globally in seconds. At the end of the first day after the London bombings of July 2005, BBC Online had received 20,000 emails, 3,000 text messages and 1,000 images. A recent survey for Yahoo showed that around 40 per cent of people in Germany, Spain and Italy now use the internet as their primary source of news. Overall, across Europe, apparently 85 per cent of people use the internet as a main source of news. This means that information is available to the public and the media. Already, some UK newspapers, challenged by rising costs, supplement information by seeking data on key websites. Additionally, of course, journalists can opt to receive breaking news from a company via an instant email. If the public can access press releases from company websites, this puts extra pressure on journalists to seek additional, but less widely-available information so the company involved in an incident should expect even more questions. No journalist will want to rely exclusively on a widely-available press release.

Increasingly, companies and, especially single-issue pressure groups, provide their own video "press release" which may be used virtually as it stands. Few companies have contemporary footage of installations or vessels and whilst this would not replace current film of, say, a wreck, it could prove valuable. After a minor fire at a US manufacturing plant, a local television station used some elderly footage. The company was then pilloried for operating such an old-fashioned site and lost the goodwill that would have occurred if the results of its intensive investment had been seen.

The declining cost of publishing modestly-produced newsletters is inspiring more specialist publications, devoted to meeting the needs of small niche markets and, although their circulations may be modest, some have significant influence with the broader media.

Most of the population in the UK and US now rely on television for their news: over half of US citizens never buy a newspaper. Consequently, newspapers are continuously reviewing their own roles and looking for what lies behind the story. The assumption is that television has covered the basics but often lacks the time or resources to mount a major enquiry. One advantage for the print medium is that many television news journalists cannot undertake much research as they have to fill another two-minute slot on air every hour.

The media industry is undergoing substantial changes. Organisations in an emergency must ensure that their response personnel and structures reflect the changing media demands which can be virtually insatiable in terms of the volume of information required and the speed with which it must be delivered.

What do the media want?

It is not suggested that all the journalists' questions and demands should be met, or that they will all want the same information. However, some questions will be common and each will want to be first with the news. Specifically, they will want:

- Accurate, intelligible, relevant, timely and truthful information provided promptly, especially about the people involved and the environment
- Responses that deal with the questions of who, what, where, when and why
- Background material on the incident, company, the site and employees
- Access to key company officials and to individuals involved in the incident, especially survivors, their next of kin, friends and colleagues
- Quotes from key people in the crisis and eye witness accounts
- Photographs, maps, footage, biographical details of personnel involved, a chronology of events

Who are the media?

Although the word "media" is often used as a label to describe a group, implying a certain homogeneity, there are fundamental differences between the different parts which are reflected in their various approaches to a story. Company personnel answering the media's questions on the telephone will perform more effectively if they are aware of both the distinctions and the similarities.

The structure, style and nature of the media will vary from country to country, as will restrictions on their activities. Typically, the media could comprise the following groupings:

- News agencies
- Radio and television, local, national, regional and international
- "International" newspapers
- National newspapers
- Local, free, evening and Sunday newspapers
- Specialist publications, teletext services and the internet

Although most of the media will concentrate on the human and environmental aspects of an emergency, the emphasis may differ from one part of the media to another: an incident at a local company will stress the impact of the event on local employment.

Media responders must be prepared to cope with questions on the financial implications of the emergency from international business newspapers or magazines and technical posers from specialist publications. The latter can assist the company if it is able to assure customers and investors, for example, that supplies will not be jeopardised. Although different journalists in different parts of the media will have varying knowledge, skills and contacts, one common feature is that they will all be anxious to secure as much accurate information as rapidly as possible.

News agencies

News agencies collect stories, filed by their own journalists, and despatch them, globally and within seconds, direct to their contracted clients, newspapers, broadcasters or magazines. Their journalists may have a greater understanding of specific industries or regions than many other scribes and broadcasters because the agency's size permits some specialisation but the trend against specialisation continues. The agencies use the most modern technology, because speedy dissemination of stories is fundamental to their success. Their reporters will want to unearth as much as possible, rapidly, and because their clients are in different parts of the media, around the world, some deadlines are always imminent. Direct links with thousands of newsrooms around the globe means that news of an emergency is soon known internationally. This could have an immediate global impact on a multinational company, which must advise all its overseas offices of any major emergency almost instantly. Finally, as "wholesalers" of news, the agencies cannot make many mistakes because they would lose customers. Stories are written in a straightforward fashion, without any colourful language and free of speculation.

Radio and television

Radio and television are effectively international, as many stations have agreements to exchange stories, interviews, film footage and photographs. Television is about pictures, so, in any major emergency, television will press for footage and/or interviews. Both radio and television have regular and frequent news bulletins, so will be keen to secure interviews and more than one journalist may be used on a story. Competition between the proliferating stations has predictable consequences for companies involved in emergencies. Radio and television journalists' determination, prompted by imminent deadlines, can lead to an apparently abrasive style but company media responders should consider it tenacious rather than pugnacious and not respond in kind.

There are major advantages for organisations to co-operate with these "instant" branches of the media because other journalists listen to the radio and watch relevant television coverage. Thus, with frequent broadcast bulletins, there is a virtually immediate opportunity to disseminate the latest company information and to correct any serious errors in media coverage etc.

One important trend that poses problems for the broadcasters is the advent of rolling news on a 24-hour basis. The concept began in the UK in 1989 and some maintain that journalistic standards have been eroded and deadlines are less relevant. The constant pressure to report new news means that seeking confirmation of a comment or development may be difficult, so journalists can become more involved in repeating speculation.

"International" newspapers

Some quality business papers, such as the *Financial Times* and *Wall Street Journal,* have an international circulation so any serious incident soon becomes known globally, having an impact on share-dealing, for example. These publications are also regarded as papers of record so are frequently quoted elsewhere in the media. The influential *Lloyd's List,* often regarded as the world's leading shipping daily newspaper, will be very interested in marine incidents. International papers now employ fewer specialist writers but, usually, they will have some understanding of industry and their reputation allows them to consult external specialists successfully. One problem for them is that with increasing costs and the defection of much advertising to the internet, their contents have to be diversified so some specialist outlets may become less specific.

National newspapers

In many countries, where there are genuinely national newspapers with widespread distribution, the publications can be divided into neat categories. "Quality" newspapers will probably be reasonably informed on the industry and possibly even on the company. They may supplement coverage with contributions from specialist writers. Their focus, like that of other publications, will be on the human aspects, but they may want significantly more. Like other parts of the media, they might put a team of journalists on to the story, with each reporter being given a specific area on which to concentrate. Approaching an incident in this way allows the outlet to produce a valuable and usually accurate report very quickly.

The paper, having dealt with the emergency's basics, may then be interested in the implications for the national economy. Because of their greater understanding of industry, and lacking a natural bias against it, unlike some other newspapers, quality papers may be more sympathetic in their coverage, if not in content, then in language. This is useful for the company involved because broadcasters scan the quality papers intensively for additional leads or a different angle. Indeed, journalists on quality newspapers, like specialist writers on the industry involved, may participate in broadcasts.

"Middle-ranking" newspapers will also be mainly interested in the "human" aspects of the story but they are likely to pay more attention than the red-top tabloids to the context in which the companies or organisations involved in an emergency operate. Some may have journalists who cover industry overall and who understand how different sectors operate. They will have reliable, well-informed contacts who understand the media's needs and the pressures of deadlines. Some newspapers in this group tend to editorialise in their treatment of stories and often wage campaigns.

Red-top tabloid or "popular" newspapers are the mass circulation papers and, in the United Kingdom, there is sustained and intense competition, so their pressure for information and photographs can be very demanding. Despite widespread criticism of their occasionally sensationalist approach, they employ some excellent journalists who can not only write a story accurately and speedily, but know where to find the information quickly. "Popular" newspapers will dwell almost exclusively on the human and environmental aspects of any emergency. They will concentrate on the number of casualties, the numbers and nationalities of those working at the site, rescue efforts, investment in safety and training, and the possibility that the emergency might have been caused by alcohol, drugs, terrorist action or gross negligence. They may even decide why an emergency occurred almost before the official enquiry has been convened. These papers may tell the tale through one or more survivors or a relative. Their stories are often accompanied by a chronology of events which, despite a cautious stance from the involved company, can be astonishingly accurate.

These papers are unlikely to employ specialist journalists who have a deep understanding of industry: coverage may concentrate on accidents, price rises, the impact on the environment and "excessive" profits. Stories about shipping almost always relate to accidents and tabloid journalists will be particularly interested in the nationality and experience of the crew and the age of the vessel and the flag under which country's safety regulations it operates. Many industrial sectors are probably perceived as guilty until they are proved innocent and whilst companies involved in accidents may justifiably resent this, in the context of meeting the media challenge in an emergency, the emphasis must be on reality.

Some "popular" papers may not allow facts to spoil a good story so some organisations assume that they will always twist the truth or invent some colourful fiction. This does not justify a company policy of silence towards such newspapers: they must be treated fairly, especially as silence will be construed as, at worst, guilt or, at best, incompetence. Their journalists will seek other sources that will be less persuasive in the "defence" of the company.

Local, free, evening and Sunday newspapers

Local and free newspapers will tend to cover a "local" emergency in more detail and for longer than the national media. For them it is a big story and they should be well informed on the company if it is a major employer in the area. This, *ceteris paribus,* suggests that they might be more favourably inclined to the company involved in the emergency, but that cannot be assumed automatically. Because of their potential influence, apart from sensibly assisting the local journalists on a day-to-day basis, companies should know the local reporters and editors. This should help during emergencies, not in suppressing facts, but in providing material to outlets that already have some understanding of what has happened.

Local members of the media might also work for national papers and will file the initial reports on an emergency. The nature of these can easily have a disproportionate influence on subsequent coverage. Additionally, journalists covering a local emergency often request help from the local media for background information on the company involved.

Free papers are probably of less influence than those which are for sale, but they should not be forgotten, especially if the emergency is essentially local.

Evening and Sunday newspapers have different approaches. The evening papers will be printed at different times during the day, depending on the number of editions. The production of most daily papers, for example, begins around 18.00 hours onwards, with some as early as 16.00 hours. Sunday newspapers will be more interested in finding out what lies behind the story, and, unless the emergency obligingly develops on the Saturday, any coverage will be more inclined towards investigation of the causes and of the personnel involved.

Specialist publications, teletext services and the internet

Some UK business sectors are well served by an experienced specialist press. Many general publications, including magazines and newsletters, have been appearing for decades and the specialist ones, who are unlikely to savage "their" industries, may still be very critical. Some popular publications can make trenchant and objective comments but these will be tempered by their knowledge of the industry and the implications of an emergency. Thus their journalists' questions are usually better informed and more technical and they will reflect more interest in the non-human, economic aspects. Because of their experience, their questions can be difficult and may reveal a knowledge of some previous incident that the company has genuinely forgotten so the latter must be well prepared.

Companies must ensure that teletext outlets are provided with up to date information although the extent of their coverage is very limited.

More importantly, website users will want the latest information and this is a fast-growing sector. The internet offers significant information about individuals and organisations and this may or may not be accurate. Because users may take the information at face value, it behoves companies to ensure that all references are correct and that any "errors" are eliminated before they can cause damage. An organisation's monitoring of coverage must include checking teletext and internet sources. Finally, consumers and journalists alike can be alerted to breaking news via their mobile phones.

How the media work

The media, like multinational companies, co-operate and compete within their own ranks, depending on circumstances. Competition is most evident within each section of the media so the company responder will feel the extra pressure as journalists press hard for basic information or a different angle. Few outsiders understand the demands on a journalist in this situation. He may know little about the company or the industry and this frustration will be exacerbated if no details about the emergency are forthcoming. Information, gleaned from many sources, has to be understood, evaluated, checked, ideally confirmed by two sources, and written, very swiftly, in a comprehensible form.

Different parts of the media operate in different ways, but the pressure of deadlines, and the availability of manpower and equipment, may help to determine whether a story is covered. Initially, a story might be broken by stringers, often freelance journalists, who cover a geographic area for a national paper. Thereafter, the story, probably, will be covered by a staff journalist.

This book concentrates on how to cope with the pressures dealing with journalists as they use "conventional" methods to secure information. Their efforts are usually justified, legitimate and transparent. Some may go further to reveal a different angle to the story. As newsgathering becomes more competitive, unorthodox methods will become more widely used. Recently, for example, journalists have secured jobs inside organisations, allowing them to report on security lapses.

Securing information "unconventionally"

- Journalists may pretend to be officials or next of kin, either in person or on the telephone. In the latter case, if there is any doubt, the company representative should offer to take the telephone number, check it and then ring back if it is authentic. Rigorous security must be enforced.

- Some journalists may assume "knowledge" that may not be accurate which induces a premature comment from the company. *I hear that 45 people have been killed. No, it's only five.* That should not happen, as only confirmed information must be allowed to reach the telephone media response team room and, in this instance, it is assumed that the responder has not been given a figure that can be released.

- Sometimes, rather than appearing ignorant, company spokespeople can be trapped into discussing an unheard comment, accurate or false, an unseen film clip or study. For example, an interviewee might be asked to comment on the remarks made by someone who has a vested interest in supporting a particular point of view. It is a useful method of provoking a company involved in an incident to become embroiled with another group or individual.

- Journalists may gain "unjustified" access to, for example, a hospital, pretending to be medical staff, just to speak to survivors, who may already have asked the police to ensure that they were not pestered by the media.

- A common ploy is to discover the identity of some of the leading personnel involved in an accident and, especially when the incident occurs overseas, then visiting or ringing the next of kin, or neighbour, to find out the views of the person at the centre of the emergency. The media may also speak to children whose parents might be involved, asking them how they feel and what the parents had said.

- One popular method of finding out more about a company is to gain access to its office or installation and then to start filming. Some groups may rely on their security but ruses can triumph.

- Staff not allowed to speak to the media may be cornered.

- It can be fruitful interviewing a former and disaffected member of staff: some will contact the media themselves.

- One tactic is to play off one company against another, often with distorted views of what the other might have said.
- Junior staff may be doorstepped as they come to work.
- Telephone operators and security personnel may be asked "innocent" questions and invited to respond to certain leading comments. Surprisingly, undaunted by ignorance, many oblige.

The extent and duration of coverage

Interest, and thus coverage of an emergency, will depend on myriad factors. Editorial bias will help determine whether a story is covered as will the geography and competition from other stories. Sometimes, after one topic has dominated the front page for some time, editors want something new. If an incident occurs in a hospital, for example, it may not be covered, but if it is the third such instance, journalists will detect a story.

Here are some factors that determine the extent and duration of the media coverage:

- The availability of other stories and therefore competition for space and airtime
- Availability of journalists and equipment, the location of the emergency and overall editorial policy
- Different interpretations of an emergency, which will be determined, in part, by considerations of its magnitude, numbers of people involved, etc, and, especially, the perceived interest of readers or viewers and their ability to identify with the story
- The relative strength of the human, environmental, technical, financial, political, economic and commercial factors, in relation to the main interests of that part of the media
- The attitude to industry, the environment, safety and health. Some parts of the media consider large groups to be guilty until proved innocent
- The frequency of editions and the deadlines in relation to the emergency
- The local, national or international aspects of the emergency and its location

- Any hint of a scandal, or a cover-up
- Whether the story reinforces a campaign, fits in with earlier relatively minor incidents, which together, make a good story
- Involves a large company and the popularity of the industry in difficulties
- Likely duration of emergency

Coverage of a story is not determined by a committee, meeting regularly to evaluate these factors and charged with taking decisions. Meetings do take place, but initially, the likely significance of an emergency cannot be assessed by the company or the media. The former, arguably slower to organise and less experienced in handling an emergency, should "over-react" rather than "under-react", lest its failure becomes the real story. The media may divert relatively modest resources to the story until it is clear how serious it is. At that point, massive resources can be directed to the location very promptly.

Sources of information

The company, of course, is only one source and corporate silence will encourage media probing, not an abandonment of the story. Any list must be a generalisation but the following merit mention:

Libraries, company publications and "press cuttings"

All journalists have systems for storing and accessing press cuttings. Equally, they have easy access to information via websites or databases. Items that dominate the "press cuttings" are often of earlier accidents, which explains why so many stories about current emergencies make reference to previous problems. Such information is relevant and readily available so company media responders must be well informed.

Recent company literature will be scanned for any comments from senior executives on the environmental or safety record of the group. The media also use company publications and relish articles, signed by the chief executive, saying that every department must cut costs immediately! After an environmental accident, journalists like to find boastful company quotes on such matters and then to read them back to the media responders, asking how this stance can be reconciled with the incident. After the bullish comments made in advance about the opening of the new Terminal 5 at London Airport in March 2008, the subsequent chaos gave the media even more grounds for critical coverage. Some commentators have suggested that British Airways lost thousands of customers because of what happened at the new terminal.

Emergency services, hospitals and contractors

These valuable contacts may have a "separate agenda". An emergency service may exaggerate its role if it needs more political support and money. Companies must agree a common "media" policy with their contractors or other organisations involved in any kind of alliance or consortium. This is not to silence others, especially the emergency services, but a common approach and swift, accurate information, disseminated to all involved parties, is essential to avoid an impression of disunity or chaos. As injured are brought into the hospitals, media can discuss the emergency with survivors, who will doubtless be shocked and emotional, with all that can imply for their reactions, and with hospital staff. Companies need representatives at the hospital, primarily to assist the injured. In the UK, the police have a role in this and they, too, can help in handling media enquiries.

Eye witnesses, friends, next of kin, relatives and academics

All these sources can be useful to the media, even if they know little about the company or the sector. Friends, next of kin and relatives may even contact the media directly and academics often relish the publicity.

Offshore accidents can be witnessed by others on a vessel and helicopter pilots and sometimes even crew on nearby ships be useful to the media. Onshore, of course, witnesses are even more plentiful, especially in the era of mobile phones with cameras. The less the information coming from main sources, the more likely are the journalists to seek assistance from this group. Colourful yet often ill-informed comments from either eye witnesses or survivors may be used. Although it may be difficult, and the company risks being charged with suppression of free speech, it is advisable to hide survivors, who are employees, from the media. They have just undergone a truly traumatic experience and anything that they say might be influenced by what they have suffered. *It felt like a lifetime, lying there and wondering if you'd get out alive.*

A crew member, in the early stages of a shipping incident, may phone the media to pass on information about the incident and why he thought it happened. In such instances, all that the beleaguered company can do is to say that it has heard such reports but must await a full and official investigation before commenting.

Disaffected staff, ex-employees, consultants, experts, company contacts and its competitors

Many journalists have "unofficial" contacts within organisations and former staff, especially those unhappy with their treatment by the company. These people often provide the media with informed comment as do "whistle-blowers". The media will also seek other sources including contacts in rival companies, consultants and crisis management experts.

Industry bodies, including trade associations, learned societies and trade unions

These groups can help the media although learned societies will usually confine themselves to explanations of technical matters. Trade associations will obviously defend the industry against any charges, if possible, whilst simultaneously explaining any technical aspects. Trade unions will have a different view and, if the issue is on safety, they will invariably be vociferous and, probably, critical. A shipping accident might be seen as an opportunity to suggest that a cause might have been the working conditions on board the vessel. Consequently, companies may find that "their" airtime has been stolen by an astute trade union which also poses the company with the difficulty of commenting on the new charge, as well as dealing with the incident itself. Unlike most other groupings, unions are keen to speak to the media.

Environmental and other specialist pressure groups and others dedicated to single issues

Environmental and other pressure groups may claim that an emergency substantiates their views so are keen to help the media. Single-issue pressure groups may not be as assiduous in checking facts as commercial organisations and may allow an inaccuracy to remain uncorrected if it furthers its cause. Their understanding of the media is often excellent and companies must work hard if they are to secure a reasonable hearing. Pressure groups, frequently perceived as objective, are often more pro-active than companies.

Companies that claim they could have avoided the accident

Some organisations, with technology that they believe could either assist in the rescue or have prevented the accident, will contact the media. Sometimes those groups may have already approached and been spurned by the company. The media do not know this and may not have time to ask the victim company for comments. In such instances, the organisation involved in the crisis can look callous, complacent or mean.

Politicians and other journalists, the internet and teletext services

Politicians and others often have opinions on emergencies and the media know how to contact those who have a reputation for instant comment and who are not deterred by their ignorance. These people, whose ready availability is confused with knowledge of the topic under discussion, need to be cultivated. Journalists often exchange information and, of course, the internet is a massive potential source of information, some of which is unreliable.

CHAPTER 4

THE PRESS REVIEWED

Many company personnel who respond to the media are subsequently disappointed with their performance. Usually, self-criticism is unwarranted because it is impossible to answer every question perfectly and responders cannot influence headlines. No communication would guarantee many more-severe problems. Performance can be valuable also for what is not reported. No spokesperson can make a bad incident disappear and responders can only influence a part of the media's output.

Headlines

Unfortunate errors

Some headlines are conjured out of a responder's answer to a question. After one serious shipping accident, the ship owner, responding as a shipping man, and not a public relations person, was challenged on whether his ship was off course. He replied that thousands of vessels had followed that route before. He implied that there was no reason to change but he might have said *naturally, we shall investigate all aspects of this accident but thousands of vessels have gone this way before safely.* The following day, one newspaper produced a front page photograph of an oil-coated seal with the words *As this baby seal fights for life, disaster tanker boss says we'd let our ship do THIS again.*

A stupid comment can haunt a company. The master of a passenger vessel left his sinking vessel before the passengers. Challenged, he responded *I said 'abandon ship'. What more do they want? If they decide to stay, that's up to them!* Subsequently, one UK paper shouted *CAPTAIN COWARD: Shipwrecked Greek admits he quit liner.* Suddenly, the company was confronted with two crises and an urgent need to prevent mass cancellations of forward bookings.

Speculation, emotive language, factual, positive and unusual headlines

Unlike companies, newspapers can speculate in a headline which is strengthened by emotive language, to the detriment of the company. *Cancer fears as oil slick gives off toxic vapour.* Some headlines, however unpalatable, may be factual. *Disaster in the Aegean: 82 feared dead as ferry runs into rocks.* Some headlines can be positive but these tend to be confined to the "quality" or specialist press which is more interested in conveying the reality than finding an odd angle. They offer a more balanced picture than might appear in other parts of the media. *Tanker was no rust bucket say shipping experts.* Some headlines may reflect editors' efforts to find a new angle or some way to attract interest. *Staff at Japan N-plant played golf during fire.*

Headlines using the paper's own interpretation or another disaster

Some newspapers link an incident to a well-known previous emergency. After the film *Titanic*, many shipping accidents were related to that disaster. Once it was even used by a liner passenger when not a single injury was sustained and was repeated in the press. When 51 people drowned after a Thames riverboat overturned in 1989, the headline was: *Marchioness was a disaster waiting to happen.* Another headline in this category was *Bhopal-style disaster averted.*

Media errors, words and culture

Of course, newspapers can make mistakes themselves. Examples include *General McArthur flies back to front* and *42 INJURED IN CANARIES STAMPEDE.* More modern examples include *Cemetery could be death trap* and *Man who killed best friend warned to behave.*

Company personnel, annoyed by the press's language, can challenge "conflagration" in relation to a minor fire, during a telephone call with a journalist but they cannot insist that this emotive and often inaccurate word is ignored. The company communicator can only ensure that the true story is conveyed to the press: after that the treatment is beyond their influence.

Newspapers are also fond of such words as "time bomb", "nightmare", "doom", "fury" and "flee", as dramatic language sells papers. Journalists can also convert a regular and well-accepted practice into something that sounds much less safe. For example, a partially-rebuilt ship might become a "patched-up vessel". Different cultures will also influence media coverage.

Units, what matters to the company and a pleasant surprise

The media like small units which make a spill, for example, seem more impressive in litres than tonnes. Journalists often overlook what may be crucial to the company which can only stress its key points as often as possible. The fact that nobody was killed or injured received little coverage during one shipping disaster in 1993. The sustained emphasis was always on the pollution.

Occasionally, companies involved in an accident may find that they are not the focus of attention if the media perceive that, for example, the rescue attempt is being conducted badly or an unusual fact is revealed. Questions on why the accident occurred in the first place fade away. The possibility of an explosion on a stricken chemicals tanker, just off the coast, prompted the Scottish police to impose a three-mile exclusion zone which included a home of the former Queen Mother. When a container vessel was deliberately grounded, to avoid more severe problems, the media focused on thefts from the containers stranded on the beach and ignored the cause of the accident to the vessel. If the media can find a hero, that, too may take over from the accident itself as the main story. *Hero tug skipper ready to tackle risky tow.*

Miscellaneous coverage and who is to blame?

Companies are often surprised at the speed with which the media can devise maps and detailed drawings of what is involved in an incident. One danger for them is that if they provide a detailed timetable of events, the information may be used to suggest a sluggish and inadequate response. Captions might include: *Here is where the highly toxic chemicals are stored* and *Questions over lost time.*

Journalists will soon demand to know who is responsible for the incident and newspapers will list what they perceive to be the key questions.

Frequently, having consulted many different sources, some of whom might be genuinely knowledgeable, they produce these challenges that, in the main, the company cannot meet because of the imminent official enquiry. What follows became a classic. *Who pays the price? Built in Spain; owned by a Norwegian; registered in Cyprus; managed from Glasgow; chartered by the French; crewed by Russians; flying a Liberian flag; carrying an American cargo; and pouring oil on to the Welsh coast BUT who takes the blame?*

CHAPTER 5

THE MEDIA RESPONSE PLAN

Company planning must ensure that documents are up to date and that relevant personnel are selected and trained for their responsibilities. These include answering journalists' questions on the telephone, writing and distributing press releases and participating in press conferences and broadcast and print interviews. These topics are dealt with in later chapters. A valuable document to aid emergency responders is the Media Response Plan, part of the overall emergency plan, which is concerned with internal procedures and organisation.

Devising and implementing an overall emergency plan is essential if a company, large or small, wants to meet certain objectives. These include safeguarding personnel, minimising damage to the environment and property, containing and controlling an emergency and increasing its prospects of surviving by defending corporate reputation. Without a plan, devised in relation to perceived issues and risks, and then tested, a company may fail, not least because it must maintain routine business whilst simultaneously confronting the emergency. However, the plan must be sufficiently flexible to allow personnel to apply their skills and judgement to the myriad unexpected incidents that can occur. A plan alone will not save the company.

The overall plan stipulates who does what, where, when, under what circumstances, how and with whom or what. It is concerned solely with procedures and the section devoted to the media, for example, should not discuss how to write a press release but it will detail who is responsible for its composition and the approval procedures. It will also contain checklists to ensure that certain necessary actions are taken. The media response plan, like the overall emergency plan, of which it is a part, must be reviewed, updated and tested regularly. Revisions must incorporate experience from exercises, real incidents and other factors, such as changes in call-out procedures and any changes in either staffing or company organisation. Plans in isolation are worthless: all procedures must be adequately documented, preferably in a modest-sized, well-designed and easy-to-read handbook.

The contents of a media response plan and the relevant procedures will reflect the type and size of the company, its exposure to risk, the industry in which it operates, its location and the number of sites where an incident could occur. Some imagination is required to devise a list of possible emergencies and their location so inventing a fictional incident and then working through the implications, detailing each novel problem and devising a solution, may assist.

Where will the media response centre be located?

The plan must list possible crisis centre venues for its crisis management team and media responders. A small organisation may be unable or unwilling to operate from its normal location. So, lacking alternatives, it may select a local hotel, near its offices or the site in trouble, for a temporary base. In such instances, the company must ensure, in advance, that the accommodation and facilities are adequate. Ideally, the centre for the journalists covering the incident should be away from the company office, so a hotel might serve two purposes, providing the company personnel can have some privacy in a secure area to which access is denied to those lacking a security pass. Sometimes, the scale or nature of an incident requires an external authority to assume overall control so the venue for media response will be chosen by officials. Authorities in areas dominated by ports or offshore terminals often have dedicated centres available to organisations involved in a serious emergency.

Who goes on site?

A big group should send some of its media experts to help local personnel, at home or overseas, and this should be noted in the plan. However, the local people may have to cope with the initial pressure before support arrives. Consequently, some companies, realising that the media will arrive before their own experts or those hired from a consultancy, train local management on how to meet journalists' early challenges. This is important because the tone of media coverage during the emergency is determined very early. Small enterprises use specialist consultants who travel to the site as soon as possible.

Media co-ordination in a big group

Large groups must detail the links and procedures between local offices and the centre. Can local staff, in the UK or overseas, implement their own plans? Must they rely on Head Office to approve all aspects of media response? Can decentralised companies respond professionally, if the groups' overall reputation is at stake? A large company must also consider the longer-term implications for the whole organisation in the different countries in which it operates and ensure that its local media specialists are properly informed on the emergency. Details must be included in the plan to avoid misunderstanding. Communicating promptly with relevant colleagues is essential and the identity of the appropriate individuals should appear in the plan. However, the plan must not become cumbersome by involving too many layers of management.

For smaller companies, the plan should be devised in conjunction with their specialist external advisers and one key feature must list who does what and when. Rather than anticipating every possibility, it might be easier for the small organisation to list what it will do. The remaining tasks, by definition, will be the responsibility of the hired help. Regular exercises will be valuable in testing the agreed arrangements.

When devising a media response plan, a new, streamlined organisation, distinct from that in organigrams, and characterised by its ability to move quickly, must be created and details of its responsibilities, organisation and objectives published in the media plan.

Auditing

In some industries, especially where an accident in one company could have repercussions for others in the sector, organisations may audit each other's plans. Some companies use external consultants who offer extensive experience, based on different companies and industries and who are more candid than insiders. Whatever the details, the objective is to ensure a speedy provision and flow of accurate information. Plans place more reliance on systems and procedures than on personalities. The factors listed in the next section are only indicative: it is impossible to construct the outlines of a media plan that encompass all industries and businesses.

More elements of the media response plan

The plan must be distributed to all personnel involved in media response including telephone media responders and executives who would represent the company in broadcast interviews and press conferences. As a minimum, the plan should contain details of the following:

Introduction

- The purpose and scope of the media response plan
- The company's objectives and the basic rules determining the release of information
- A list of some of the more obvious types of potential emergency and the likely reaction to each of them. For example, a very minor incident might require telephone response team members to be put on standby only, at least initially
- Checklists on the different actions required for the crisis management and telephone response team members, to ensure that nothing is omitted

Call out and travel

- A complete list of all personnel involved, showing office, home and mobile telephone numbers, email and home addresses and role in the emergency teams. The telephone team must include the responders, the co-ordinator, board writer, at least two individuals familiar with computers and their software, and runners. *(See chapter 8)* The duties of each team member must be laid down.
- Call-out procedures, indicating who is responsible for calling out specified personnel, and in what sequence. Likely travelling times to the scene should be taken into account when summoning individuals

if the emergency is out of office hours. Some companies call out staff, as far as possible, in relation to the time taken to travel to the office. Responders must be told of the venue to which they must report.

- Reporting relationships and details of who goes where, when and how, including a senior person to the site
- Regularly updated information on the means of travel available for those required to go to the site or overseas, especially at night

Security

- The method of alerting security at the office or venue where media response facilities will be set up, so that if the emergency occurs out of office hours, incoming personnel can gain immediate access
- How to organise security arrangements at all locations, including sheltering the survivors or those involved, from the media
- Procedures on advising the security officer or telephone operator where to divert media calls, for how long and what to say. For out-of-hours emergencies, some companies keep one media representative at home, to receive media calls, diverted to him by the security person, until the team is in place at the selected venue.
- The name and telephone number of the company official who can call out security in the middle of the night, if all else fails

When in the office or the hotel

- Whoever arrives first should know how emergency response rooms should be arranged and should check all telephone lines and other equipment as listed in the plan
- All staff must know the location and layout of the media response room, press conference centre and other rooms allocated to media response teams and to journalists if applicable, as well as facilities for press conferences and interviews, especially for television
- Then staff must check the availability of all support material, including information packs, white boards, blackboards/flip charts, signs for directing media, if necessary, videos and supporting footage, television and radio sets and recorders, fact sheets, photographs, brochures and group material etc.

- The plan should indicate how to send staff and a fully equipped unit, containing communications equipment, including mobile phones, fax machines, laptop computers etc. to emergencies at distant locations.

- Staff must know who:

  prepares, approves and despatches press release one, the holding statement

  arranges film coverage

  maintains the log of activities and action taken

  updates the website

- Staff must know how to:

  inform others, especially employees, and media teams in other affiliated companies around the world, via regular and updated checklists

  organise additional secretarial support and information technology aid if necessary; book and or organise rooms for a press conference

  organise food, drink, accommodation and other essentials for team members; warn reliefs if the emergency lasts for more than a few hours

  arrange coverage and recording of broadcast comments and a press cuttings service; distribute data, press releases etc.

  maintain communications with other groups, involved in the emergency, specifically in relation to media response and how to establish links with other offices and organisations

Information to be included in the plan

- Checklists of necessary action
- Details of who writes, approves and disseminates press releases
- Press release distribution lists and method of dissemination
- List of names, telephone numbers and possibly email addresses of spokesmen in emergency organisations, other companies in the industry, trade associations, regional authorities, local and national media, including news agencies, hospitals, coastguard, police etc. This information may be needed by the telephone response team co-ordinator, not his teams.
- Arrangements for maintaining routine activities

- Dealing with media at the site
- Specific advice on how to handle media aspects of terrorist actions or a criminal act

Miscellaneous

- In most industrialised countries, other organisations, official and unofficial, are significant in media response, so relevant details should be included in the media plan. For example, some police forces set up their own press bureaux, which can absorb some of the pressure. If requested, they will protect personnel, especially survivors, from the media.
- Procedures if journalists or next of kin arrive at the site, head office or a local office. It is difficult to offer a universally relevant generalisation but it is preferable to try to keep journalists away from offices and, if possible the site, if it is dangerous, or renders control of the overall situation more difficult for the company.

CHAPTER 6

THE FACT FILE

The Fact File is an important tool which enables telephone media respon-ders to provide background information to the media, especially when an incident has only just occurred. This chapter concludes with a comment on media or press kits.

An early and positive response, based partly on the Fact File, in an emergency, when details are sparse, shows that the company can provide background infor-mation and has anticipated journalists' needs. This encourages the media who are more inclined to return to the company for news and comment, because they have been helped to write the initial story. Furthermore, the telephone media response team, *(See chapter 13),* many of whom, unlike the journalists, are probably dealing with their first genuine emergency, gain confidence at a difficult time when they are experiencing unique pressure. Conversely, a poor initial impression will encourage journalists to seek other, potentially critical, contacts and to pay less heed to routine company statements later. Puzzled that the company cannot provide basic information even about itself, they may perceive the group to be badly organised and unprepared and may even speculate that the accident could have been caused by similar incompetence.

Early in an incident, it is important that the organisation:

- Demonstrates that each member of the telephone media response team can deal with "routine" questions that put the company and its activities into a context
- Can take the initiative in offering information that assists the jour-nalist to file a story with appropriate background, before the facts of the emergency can be disseminated

- Ensures that all members of the response team have the same, basic information. Consistency of information, especially in the early stages, is important, as differences can easily be exploited, possibly causing the company to lose control of the information flow for the duration of the emergency.

A copy of the Fact File, also known in some companies as Fast Facts, must be given to each member of the telephone media response team. This publication should contain details about the company and the industry and the second part discusses the media and how it works. The next section can include details of sites, locations, offices, vessels, aircraft, vehicles or any other perceived potential centre of an emergency and may include a draft holding statement: the relevant details will be filled in on the day. The final section contains advice on how to deal with media questions. *(See also chapter 17)*

Each team member must be familiar with the layout and contents of the Fact File which should not be bulky and which offers swift access to major sections. Later, as the incident evolves, the questions will move from the background to the incident itself but a well-written Fact File can be valuable throughout an incident.

The Fact File is, simply, a book or file, printed on one side of paper, divided into clear sections. The contents can be disseminated to the media, verbally and verbatim if required, with the exception of the section relating to any previous accidents and their outcomes, which can only be used if requested. Copies are not for external distribution.

Some companies put the information on computer but this is not necessarily wise and, of course, some information may be required before the machines are active or from a member of staff who is "holding the fort" from home before his colleagues reach the office.

If the data is in a book, participants can study it when they lack access to a computer. Many media response team members feel happier with a familiar book and are loath to trust a computer exclusively. Some companies provide responders with a Fact File and with access to more information via a computer but this can be confusing. Finally, of course, computers sometimes refuse to function so printouts of the data on the machine, or the Fact File must be available. Whatever system is used, some companies include everything they can, to ensure that responders can answer almost every question. This is self-defeating, because responders will soon suffer from information indigestion and there will be unacceptably long delays whilst the correct page is being found. One key aspect to the "correct" length of the Fact File is whether its contents can be reasonably assimilated by a hard-pressed media responder.

The contents and style of the Fact File should be reviewed and updated regularly, especially ahead of any major event in the company and after each training exercise. Fully updated additional copies must be kept in the telephone media response room because some team members may arrive without their own personal copy.

Contents

The precise contents will be determined by the nature of the industry, the company and the type of possible emergencies. Some brief general suggestions are offered below.

Part one: Company, group and industry information

Here are some ideas on what could be included and these are geared to the larger and thus more complex company. Smaller organisations will have less difficulty in considering and including relevant information.

- Background details of the company, its personnel, procedures and facilities, especially in relation to safety, health and the environment
- Globally, a brief history, founding date, number of countries in which operations are carried out, outline of activities, total number of employees, overall safety, health and environmental record, including any accidents and their details, (but only to be used if asked), awards won, investments in safety and environmental matters, relevant financial details, key executives and any other important points, including technical innovations
- Nationally, history, especially start-up date, number of employees, range of activities in the country, environmental record, number of offices in

the country, finance, including investment to date, names of key executives, relative significance of the country to overall group activities and any other important points, including technical innovations

- An indication of the organisation's involvement in the industry in the country where the incident has occurred

- Details of previous accidents and the results of the enquiries and the overall safety record. These results should be included because there may have been some incidents in which the company was cleared of wrongdoing. Unless this is pointed out to the media, journalists will automatically assume that the company was at fault. That said, the **responders must not offer details of previous accidents: this information is to be used only if asked, as stressed above.**

- The highlights of the company's activities in the previous year

- As the media will have looked at recent press "cuttings", whether on paper or stored on computers, organisations must ensure, on a continuing basis, that members of the telephone media response team have copies of potentially damaging stories and, if necessary, the company response. They should also know about good stories that could be used to advantage in a crisis. Team members should not be caught out by the journalist who might otherwise sound better-informed on the company than its own staff. The more-serious stories, and the company response, as well as the items of good news, should be included in the Fact File. **Naturally, information on negative matters should only be used if raised by the journalist.**

- Some sectors are complex and technical and most journalists will have little or no relevant knowledge so the company must explain what has happened, in simple, non-technical terms and in the context of the particular industry. This cannot be done satisfactorily unless the media response team understand some of the basics themselves. Consequently telephone responders should have some information, either in the Fact File or from the co-ordinator, on the fundamental features and procedures of the sector. This can be daunting but the company must respond to these types of questions during an emergency.

- Responders must also be familiar with the emergency plan. It is humiliating to have to admit ignorance to a journalist on the meaning of "all necessary steps will be taken, in line with the emergency procedures laid down".

All this may seem demanding but, by studying the Fact File regularly and participating in exercises and presentations, team members will soon learn enough to represent the company satisfactorily.

Part two: the media and how it works

This section permits members of the telephone media response team to acquaint themselves afresh with what they were taught during training sessions and exercises. Typically, there would be sections devoted to the following topics:

- Objectives of a positive stance during an emergency and sectors to be reached *(See chapter 3)*
- Who the media are, what they want and how they work, including tricks that they might use
- Responding to media calls in an emergency: what to do and what not to do
- Possible questions and answers during an emergency
- Lists of what to do and what not to do in relation to interviews, doorstepping and press conferences but these three topics will not be relevant to telephone responders

A section in which to file press releases, to ensure that the latest is used when talking to the media is useful. Some responders underline bad news on releases in red and good points in green. Another useful section, especially for personnel charged with distributing company material, including emails, is a comprehensive and accurate list of those journalists, divided into sections by their interests, who should be informed about the emergency. The details should include name, address, affiliation, and telephone and email addresses.

Part three: specific site and incident information

Determining the most useful data, and its skilful presentation, is fundamentally important but it is difficult to generalise over many different sectors of business and industry. A manufacturing company might be asked about the background to a site:

- Its location, the nearest town and how far away it is?
- How many people worked there, when was it built, what did it produce?
- How close is the site to either a residential area, office or storage facilities?
- How many exits and entrances there are to the site?
- How much has been spent recently on maintenance?
- What proportion of company profits comes from this plant?
- Frequency of emergency drills, fire-fighting and medical facilities available on site?
- Any regular emergency training sessions with the local authorities?
- Safety record and any pollution-related incidents?
- Plans for evacuating staff in an emergency
- Extent of insurance cover and which company provides it
- Relations with the local community

Part four: advice on how to deal with the media's questions. (See chapter 17)

The Fact File should also include a map and a holding statement. A holding statement is, effectively, an initial press release. It can be compiled in advance and lacks only the raw details of the incident. *(See chapter 11)* When an incident is confirmed, the telephone media response team co-ordinator should obtain the details that are available, such as the location of the incident, however approximate, and then, once authorised, should dictate the details to his team, for insertion in the proforma in their Fact File. Thereafter, of course, the holding statement can be dictated to enquiring journalists. For an example of a holding statement, see chapter 11.

Layout and presentation

The ideal Fact File is characterised by its contents, its layout and the style of writing. Hand-written, photocopied pages compiled unimaginatively and presented as tedious chunks of undivided text, are inadequate. "Shopping lists" under clear and unambiguous headings are desirable.

Some companies, wrongly, opt for a simple leaflet-style approach, merely stapling a few pages together. Company brochures are no substitute for media emergency response Fact Files. They will be written differently, for a different audience and for a different occasion. They, and the stapled leaflets, often lack a detailed contents page and prove inadequate in an emergency. There is no real substitute for a properly-produced robust Fact File which allows the pages to remain open without human intervention.

Book style or flip chart style

- The majority of Fact Files are usually of A4 size, and have the index tabs on the right, with pages being turned in the same fashion as a book. Some companies have opted for a version in which the pages are turned vertically, as for a flip-chart, but the conventional book style, in which pages are laid out horizontally, is preferable for practical reasons.

Indexing the different sections and the use of colour

- The book will often be used by mainly inexperienced personnel, working under considerable pressure. Consequently, the contents must be divided into distinct sections, separated by tabbed dividing pages. On the tab, the name, or the number of the section must be printed clearly. Different sections should be printed on different coloured paper, to facilitate identification.

The text: introduction and contents page

The first page should consist of a note, signed by the chief executive. He should explain the purpose of the Fact File and thank the team members who have volunteered for such an important role which could have a real impact on the company's reputation. *By reacting well to telephone calls, we shall be seen as proactive and efficient, and any damage to our reputation, inflicted by the emergency itself, will be minimised.* He should ask all team members to read the Fact File and to ensure that they understand what it contains: if not, they should seek advice. Finally, some words might be included along the lines of *The Board/management is grateful to all of you who undertake this important role. Let's hope that the emergency never happens!*

To maximise the benefits of the Fact File, assuming that it resembles a conventional book, the contents page should be on the left hand side, and printed on a gatefold concept, so that it can be opened out whilst the responder is looking at two open pages of the Fact File itself at the same time. In this way, pages can be turned whilst the contents page can remain permanently on display, which also facilitates improved knowledge of what is available in the file. Another advantage of the gatefold principle is that if the journalist then asks another question, on a different topic, the responder can glance at the contents page, already open, to determine whether the information is available, and, if so, where. This saves time and makes the company seem more professional. The concept of a gatefold is also invaluable if media responders are using an "old-fashioned" telephone rather than wearing headsets. The usual temptation is to ask the caller to hold on whilst pages are turned. Callers may then overhear background comments if the mute button is not activated. A swift response not only helps the journalist, for whom time is precious, but suggests that the company representative is well-informed or efficient.

The contents should be indented, because, if the Fact File becomes a fat file, it is difficult to see the opening letters or words, if the text starts too close to the left hand margin. After the entry, it is desirable to show the section in which the information appears, and then the actual page numbers. Some companies print the section numbers on the contents page, but omit any general headings, so each section has to be scanned for the headings.

Style of writing, spacing, pagination and emphasis

The Fact File must be written so inexperienced staff can read or paraphrase key information convincingly. Consequently, the text should be written so that it can be read, precisely as written, without sounding stilted or formal, and free of jargon, which would pose further questions. Solid blocks of text should be avoided. Preferably, individual points, under each heading, should be laid out, indented, under the appropriate title. In some instances, such as the availability of medical facilities available on a passenger vessel, it might be desirable to list them, like a "shopping list" which can be more easily read out to the journalist rather than solid text. A brief, clear summary of a key piece of information should be given at the top of a page, followed by the main sub-points, indented.

- The first page of each section should show a list of the contents, within that section, and page numbers
- All text should be double-spaced, and headings to new sub-sections should be in bold, to allow instant location of desired information
- The material should be well spaced to facilitate easy detection and a consistent system of headings and sub-headings permits familiarity.
- Page numbers should be printed in the bottom right corner of each page. Numbering pages in the centre, or even worse, on the left, means turning the whole page to determine its number.
- Each section should be identified separately, by page number, so that revised or additional pages may be added without having to renumber the entire work.
- Key sections should be enclosed in boxes, or distinguished in some fashion and important points should be emphasised in bold or in colour.

Fact Files should not be written in block capitals as this makes reading more difficult and eliminates the possibility of emphasising key points in upper case letters. Using italics can also help to distinguish points or to emphasise headings. Finally, it is easier for the reader if all headings are centred, especially if the Fact File becomes big.

A media kit

Some journalists will ask for a media or press kit. This is merely a folder in which the company inserts key information which could include some background information about the site of the incident, the company and its personnel, some relevant photographs and the latest press release.

CHAPTER | 7

THE ONSITE MEDIA REPRESENTATIVE AT EMERGENCIES

The company must be represented on site, or as close as possible, by its own employees, agents or consultants. Prompt action will ensure that the necessary services are provided for the "victims", by competent experts, authorised to deal operationally with the incident and its repercussions. It is crucial that a media relations expert represents the company on site.

Company or external consultancy media relations personnel must go to the scene, or as near to it as possible, promptly, because opinion against the company will soon harden. Included in the equipment taken to the scene should be a camcorder, a digital stills camera to record the scene, not least for the assessment of insurance claims, and, of course, a laptop computer and modern mobile phones. In the absence of a media expert, "local representatives", employees or outsiders will be perceived as representing the company on all matters, including media, but they must deal only with technical and operational aspects, unhindered by the media. Being inexperienced in media matters, their efforts to help journalists could end disastrously.

The on-site media person has many responsibilities:

- Prioritising tasks
- Liaising with all involved, including company lawyers and relevant individuals
- Seeking up-to-date information and reporting back to the office
- Determining trends in media coverage, advising accordingly and devising sensible responses

- Providing colleagues with photographs and video footage
- Finding any positive news, such as a salvage operation, and reporting back
- Providing information that could be used in a press release
- Helping to write press releases
- Dealing locally with media questions
- Conveying details of local interviews, in advance, so a transcript can be secured
- Organising local broadcast interviews for visiting executives and preparing them
- Arranging relevant photographs and video to help deal with any insurance claims
- Attending and reporting on any local press conferences
- Being briefed by head office
- Finding out any serious allegations and reporting back to the office
- Rejecting any inaccurate "facts" instantly
- Visiting the specific site, if possible, to convey the latest details
- Monitoring newspapers, radio, television, press conferences and websites
- Briefing journalists on site and interviewing company personnel involved in the incident
- Ensuring that no employees, especially those involved in the incident, speak to the media
- Keeping a log of events and action taken
- Most of this is essential if the company is not to be embroiled in a second crisis.

Problems in sending a media representative to an accident location

Companies should have travel and accommodation plans outlined in advance for all journeys to "predictable" locations, such as factories, depots and main ports. However, serious accidents can occur offshore or at remote locations that are difficult to reach quickly. Travel and accommodation arrangements should be made immediately as there will be major competition for seats and beds. Ideally, local transport should also be secured and, as there will be few hire car companies in remote areas, finding a local resident and hiring him and his vehicle for the "duration" is prudent especially as the only available accommodation might be many miles away from the crisis centre.

A place to work

A major accident, especially if there are environmental implications, can attract hundreds of journalists and camera crew personnel. Problems for a lone onsite representative include locating a space from which to work and finding some people to take messages and to provide occasional food and drink. Ideally, mobile phones should be reserved for calls from key individuals. Routine press calls must be either taken at the company's office or by the onsite representative during agreed and specified hours, preferably on a landline. Because the onsite representative will be besieged, prioritising tasks is essential. Technology can ease the burden but time must be allocated to talking to key individuals, to determine any trends in media interests and to safeguard the company's interests.

Liaison with others

The media person must liaise regularly with other company representatives and officials to determine what is happening and what problems might occur. Media contact must be confined to the media person only: other company personnel must not give interviews without the prior agreement of the media person and this must be understood at an early stage. The media person will also pass on any relevant information to onsite colleagues. The company should have some support from other organisations. For example, a shipping incident will mean that the P&I club, effectively the insurers, will be on site. The media person should agree with their representative on who says what to the media on which topics.

As soon as practical, the media person should seek out the key figures involved in the crisis to develop constructive working relationships. These individuals might work for the numerous authorities involved, any other company involved in the accident or those associated with "rescuing" the group, environmental experts and the police. It is also important to establish a pattern of working with the company's crisis management team. If practical, it is wise to agree specific times at which calls are made.

The media representative may be perceived as the company representative, irrespective of who else is at the site. This can prompt time-consuming problems so he should be as anonymous as possible. Any indication of affiliation should be avoided but retained for security purposes.

Stress and workload

The media person will experience severe stress and working effectively requires determination and a strong will to prioritise tasks. Initially, there will be a sense of deep hopelessness, confronted by so many challenges and lacking local support. In a major emergency, a company should despatch at least three media representatives because the tasks are numerous and unearthing even basic information can take a long time. Indeed, sometimes, the sheer size of a crisis control centre can mean walking miles a day, just to cover meetings and to attend press conferences. The onsite individual must have background information about the company readily available, preferably via a laptop, and be able to take decisions on matters such as local interviews. He must also be empowered to decide on the extent of co-operation with television companies who want to make documentaries about the accident but such "instant invitations" should be rejected.

Some thoughts from the crisis media consultant at the site of a major shipping accident

Alone at an often barren and boring location, life becomes uniquely difficult. The individual feels as if he has been transported to a foreign land where the scenery is unusual, the language incomprehensible, days consist of but a few hours and the amount of work outstanding increases whatever efforts are made. The familiar has vanished, the cast of characters is unknown and there is pressure of an unusually ferocious and sustained intensity. He must shun everything that he cannot influence and concentrate only on the most important topics. Where is there space to write press releases and emails? If he is alone, can someone provide the occasional sandwich and answer a phone whilst he is active elsewhere? Having the necessary basic and backup equipment is essential as is knowing someone who can assist, when, inevitably, it goes wrong at a crucial stage. The individual on site will be too busy, too tired or ignorant to fix it himself. The sense of inadequacy breeds frustration: there will be insufficient time, assistance, information, energy and opportunities to eat and sleep.

CHAPTER 8

ORGANISING THE TELEPHONE MEDIA RESPONSE TEAM

An important part of an organisation's media communications, without which companies can help neither themselves nor journalists, is the telephone response team. This may consist of employees or specialists from a consultancy. The organisation and training of the employee-based team, often comprising relatively junior or inexperienced members of staff, is discussed here. Dealing with media phone calls is considered in chapter 13.

No one individual could cope with the volume of enquiries, so it is wise to create a telephone media response team, of at least three individuals, which answers calls on a dedicated telephone number. The frustrations of delay and responder ignorance, often encountered when ringing a call centre, in day-to-day life, must not be experienced by journalists phoning an organisation during an emergency. The overall company response to the media is provided by personnel trained and tested to ensure the efficient and speedy dissemination of accurate information to the outside world. This is achieved by individuals who can give successful television, radio and press interviews, mount effective press conferences and, importantly, deal with journalists' questions on the telephone.

The telephone media response team and the media

Because of this team's importance, some organisations are reluctant to field relatively junior personnel but, providing that they are trained and tested regularly and are accompanied by an experienced co-ordinator, the concept can work well. Apart from allowing the company to disseminate information and its messages speedily, contact with the media enables the organisation to determine the outside world's reaction to the emergency and thus to devise a suitable strategy, especially if serious allegations are being made. Being in touch with the media also enables a company to determine how its own output is being used and to make changes if necessary. Additionally, the media can be used for the dissemination of any warnings or advice: a water utility might recommend that all drinking water be boiled and a help line telephone number for next of kin can be publicised.

Management support, the role of professional PR staff and consultancies

The importance of providing a competent telephone media response team should be acknowledged by senior management which must provide the necessary resources and be seen to support the concept and the personnel. Sometimes, in large organisations, experienced in-house public affairs personnel, admitting to being bored by training sessions, try to opt out of exercises. Such behaviour should not be tolerated. Those who work in different functions must have the practice and to deny them assistance from the professionals is dangerous. It may suggest to the telephone team members that the system, and their participation, is unimportant or that they would lack experienced help should a real emergency develop. Because many telephone media response teams consist of volunteers, this is an important issue.

In a crisis, even a big company's in-house media relations team can seldom cope unaided because of the scale, intensity and duration of media demands. There could be thousands of phone calls from around the world, 24 hours a day, and dozens of requests for television interviews, as well as press conferences to be organised. The professionals will be frantically busy, involved, *inter alia*, in briefing television spokespersons, writing press releases and formulating strategy to minimise damage to the corporate reputation. Consequently, diverting any "routine" work to other trained personnel, which allows the professionals to do what only they can do, is advantageous.

Irrespective of an organisation's size, in almost all emergencies, more personnel will be needed to respond to the media. Consequently, when the problem arises, some companies, even large groups, immediately hire a local or a non-specialist public relations consultancy. This is unwise, especially if the advisers have not been involved with the company before. Additionally, the outsiders may have been engaged only because there is no alternative. Many years ago, after a pollution incident, the hastily-engaged consultants suggested that the company should make a film, showing how it coped with the emergency (which was not very well) and that it should have a wide circulation. However, the film would only be available months after the incident had been forgotten by the public!

An inexperienced and newly-appointed consultancy will lack the detailed knowledge that exists within the company, be ignorant of what is in the Fact File and have no feel for its culture so may offer irrelevant advice. It may also only have a very rudimentary understanding of the industry involved so could easily make a major mistake. Senior executives, about to undertake radio and television interviews, need to know the details of difficult questions being asked on the phone by journalists and how to respond. An inexperienced consultant might offer poor advice.

The lack of skilled personnel can be overcome by engaging a specialist consultancy with wide experience of different emergencies and which knows something about the industry afflicted by the emergency. Such an appointment, to be successful, should be made before, and not during any emergency. The advisers can then learn about the company and the sector in which it operates and can develop trust with the executives and others with whom it would operate in a real emergency. Meeting a senior executive, for the first time, at 3.00 in the morning, just as an emergency is developing, but having little knowledge of the individual, his company or industry, does not create the essential mutual trust. Consequently, astute companies, large and small, have a regular training schedule, especially for all their responders and put experienced and competent advisers on a retainer system. As indicated above, some specialised consultancies can provide a telephone media response team which is particularly useful for smaller companies.

Some organisations, rather than "gamble" their reputation on the abilities of temporary "press officers", use multiple emailing or faxing of statements, sent to pre-determined lists of journalists, to support a limited telephone response facility. Alternatively, they merely put information on their website and take no further action. This denies journalists the opportunity of obtaining significant background information which may be particularly relevant to that specific publication or outlet. The company also loses a chance to emphasise some additional positive points, and, of course, having relatively few responders, in relation to the demand, encourages the media to look elsewhere for information and comment.

Even those journalists who do call may tire of waiting to speak to a limited number of press officers, who seem permanently engaged, about an emailed or faxed statement. This policy also erroneously assumes that all parts of the media have similar interests. Finally, the company cannot guarantee that all the journalists interested in the incident are on the pre-determined circulation lists. In a major crisis, such companies, in these circumstances, might collapse under media pressure and hostility after journalists have decided that it cannot be regarded as the prime source of information.

Other companies have an "outer ring" of telephone responders, inaccurately called an information centre. The unfortunate people seconded to such a unit are only given the latest press release to read after which they can only bleat *I'm not in a position to answer that.* Journalists must then queue again, to speak to the telephone media response team. The system merely antagonises journalists, all of whom will have questions many of which a well-prepared company should be able to answer.

Volunteers and selection of the team

The beguilingly simple concept is that a team, usually of volunteers, who, in their normal jobs, have no contact with the media, will respond to the torrent of media telephone calls. This permits any in-house professional media relations personnel and outside consultants to do other, specialised work. The creation of a telephone media response team also removes some of the pressure that might otherwise fall on operations personnel dealing with the incident. Those who maintain that the media are without scruple, will invent quotes, have no right to ask questions and pester the company when it is pre-occupied with the emergency must be excluded. Exercises are very useful in refining the composition of a team.

Ironically, some of the scribes may be similarly hostile to large organisations, which, they may feel, are damaging the environment whilst making excessive profits. Others, covering a marine accident, for example, may believe that shipping companies jeopardise safety by registering vessels in states that are supposedly less demanding in terms of safety and then crew their vessels with ill-trained nationals from developing nations to save money. Such serious charges should be met by the responders calmly, objectively and with relevant information. Any responder who loses his temper may give the media a very useful and damaging quote. Hopefully, corporate hostility towards the media may be fading as executives see the consequences of ignoring journalists and realise that the media can assist by disseminating positive information to a wide variety of audiences swiftly.

Who, then, should be in the team? The basic choice is to select a team of inexperienced personnel, because, knowing little, little can be revealed, or, alternatively, to choose more mature personnel, who should be discerning, even under sustained fire. Exercises can demonstrate the dangers of knowing too much as easily as knowing too little but neither problem is insuperable. The main fear is that more experienced personnel will stray from authorised information and offer the media details from their own background. In practice, however, the experience of the more mature individuals usually enables them to avoid these pitfalls, and, after media training, they can perform well. Their experience can be valuable and at least one such person should be included in a team. That said, even inexperienced personnel, especially those who hold posts that demand an understanding of confidentiality and, perhaps, are accustomed to working on the phone, can do a difficult job well, provided they are trained and tested regularly. Those adjudged inadequate, usually a very small proportion, should be moved to other associated work if they wish to be involved in the company's overall response.

Should the company appeal for volunteers or make the initial selection itself? In both instances, the choice must be refined through training and exercises. Some companies give insufficient thought to the selection, training and motivation of teams, so attract relatively few genuine volunteers. Occasionally, this reflects the belief that an accident is very unlikely and that serious preparation would be a waste of time. Others maintain that the managing director, as well as managing the incident himself, will handle media enquiries!

Poor selection and inadequate training could jeopardise a company's reputation and thus its survival. An organisation, having invested heavily in creating a reputation for professionalism, should not gamble that commercial asset, by asking, for example, inadequately-trained and inexperienced receptionists, some not even employed directly by the company, to respond to media questions during an emergency, even with the aid of the sources of information that are discussed in chapter 6.

Frequently, the media response team is composed of female employees, possibly because it is thought that a female voice is more soothing. Whilst this may be relevant to the personnel response team, journalists want information and are seldom exercised by such factors. Why are so many responders young inexperienced females? Some companies claim that they employ so few experienced personnel that all will be involved in dealing with operational aspects of the emergency and that the only available personnel would thus be receptionists and secretaries, who, fortunately, deal with people on the phone.

Individuals need the assurance that their careers will not be jeopardised by one unfortunate remark to the media whilst doing a job for which they have volunteered. In some companies experienced personnel refuse to "volunteer", which is unfortunate and which should worry management. Their reluctance to help the company may reflect hostility to the press or a desire not to become involved in something outside the job description, where an error could not only cost the company money or reputation, but damage an individual's career. The relatively high status of such individuals, compared to receptionists and secretaries, for example, allows them to refuse to participate, which is a luxury usually denied to junior staff.

Nevertheless, teams of young, inexperienced personnel can perform adequately, particularly when supported by an experienced co-ordinator, but the dangers of having a youthful team, without adequate support or training, are clear. Some people break down during exercises, others resort to rudeness and some become over-bearing. Although a small minority, these individuals must be identified before facing the media during a real crisis.

Motivation and training

Whatever the composition of the team, and whether it consists of volunteers or volunteered, it must be treated as a significant unit. Team members are assuming extra responsibilities and they must be trained properly so that they are familiar with their own company and industry and media response techniques. The novelty of the work adds some interest to day-to-day routine. Whilst individuals can become familiar with media techniques they may be ignorant on their own company and industry unless background training is offered. Some companies take their teams to specific sites and this helps to put the printed word in the team's Fact File (*see chapter 6*) into perspective. However, they must not admit to journalists that they have visited a site involved in an emergency, or one similar, as that could create problems in answering specific questions. Employers should offer a retainer for the extra responsibility because individuals might have to come in to the office in the middle of the night, to safeguard the company's reputation. In the context of what is potentially at stake, such remuneration would be totally insignificant.

Individuals must be able to leave the team without any adverse comment on their staff records. If companies rely on volunteers, the supply will soon be exhausted if it is perceived that the organisation is ungrateful. This is important because at least 20 people, even in a modest-sized company, should be trained to cope with media enquiries. Whenever an emergency develops, some of those trained will be sick, on holiday, away from home or, for some other reason, unable to participate. Furthermore, if the emergency lasts for more than a few hours, teams must be rested and because a major incident can attract attention from the other side of the world, a 24 hours-a-day service is required. Ideally, each team should consist of a minimum of three and preferably six responders, whilst other trained individuals are ready to replace them. At least two runners, whose function is described below, a board writer, a deputy co-ordinator and co-ordinator will be required.

Time spent in training telephone media response teams is valuable and, apart from the knowledge that it could cope with the media in an emergency, the company derives extra benefits. Colleagues who do not know each other develop friendships and links that assist routine business and morale can be improved which may reduce staff turnover. Training ensures that individuals become more familiar with their company, thus improving performance, whilst making them better-informed ambassadors in their day-to-day contacts with the public. Finally, team members, through training and meeting journalists, develop a better appreciation of the work of the part-time public affairs person or, in larger companies, personnel. This fosters a greater understanding of what is involved in building up and sustaining the company reputation.

Background knowledge

A well-informed telephone media responder should know about his company, its personnel and the industry in which it operates. (*See chapter 6*) Team members should also know something about the safety procedures imposed by government and the other measures introduced by their own companies. Where relevant, they ought to be familiar with medical and safety procedures and methods of evacuation from an affected site. They should also be aware of what happens at different locations and arrangements made for the transportation of raw materials or finished products from the site. As indicated above, where necessary, visits to typical or even specific locations will prompt questions from the team, the answers to which might help to put the site into a context if an accident occurs. Another advantage of these visits is that it emphasises the importance with which the company regards the role undertaken by the volunteers. It is also an investment for the company because inadequate responses to the media will suggest that the company is incompetent in other functions.

Many industries are complex and technical and most journalists will have little or no relevant knowledge so this imposes an obligation on the company to explain what has happened, in simple, non-technical terms. This cannot be done satisfactorily unless the media response team understands some of the basics and are provided with some valuable information in their own manual. By studying the Media Response Plan, which deals with how the team is called out and functions, and the Fact File regularly and participating in training, most team members will soon have gleaned enough basic information to represent the organisation satisfactorily.

Organisation of the telephone media response team

Accommodation

Members of the telephone media response must all work in the same room. One large company decided that the team could work at different places in two large open-plan offices and then wondered why there were major inconsistencies in the disseminated information! The same applies to efforts to maintain two press centres. Occidental Oil, when the *Piper* North Sea disaster occurred, initially maintained press offices in Aberdeen and in London but it soon became impractical and the London centre was closed.

The room should be either dedicated or capable of being converted within minutes and must be sufficiently spacious to allow the team to operate efficiently. Some observers and relief members of the team, awaiting their turn to participate, may need to be accommodated in the room, so it should be big enough to allow a few chairs to be placed around the perimeter, without impeding movement. Many rooms are too small or have inadequate white boards, or space for flip charts. *(See chapter 13)* The room should be light and, because noise accelerates fatigue, it should be thickly carpeted and have noise-absorbing ceiling tiles. Ideally, it should be close to the crisis management room, to facilitate the flow of information, and there should only be one route between the two.

Another room should be fitted with banks of video and audio recorders, radios and televisions, so that all comment can be monitored. Many companies automatically record every telephone conversation, as it is important to have a detailed record of action taken. Ideally, a third small room should be set aside for the press statement writer.

Equipment

Material for the media response team, including telephones, should be stored in a cupboard, and all members of the team should be able to gain access and know how to set up the room. Whoever arrives first, and who has no other more-important duties, not necessarily a media response team member, should organise the room in line with details on a checklist pasted on the wall. These duties include putting material from the cupboard on to the desks, which are preferable to tables, if space allows, and plugging in and testing the phones. Sometimes, despite the early arrival of some staff, setting-up has been left to a team member, so valuable time has been lost, especially if the telephones then fail. The room must become operational as quickly as possible so that all media calls can be directed to the team with minimal delay.

A few companies favour the extensive use of new technology in the response room, especially in relation to the white boards which show the latest information, but this should be introduced only if it is more effective, reliable and easier to use than more conventional methods and, most importantly, is wanted and understood completely by those who will be using it. Mobile phones belonging to the team must not be taken in to the room.

The following basic equipment should be made available:

- A telephone for each team member plus at least two extra, additional internal phones and directories
- Sufficient places at desks or tables
- A clearly visible clock and, if the incident is overseas, one showing local time
- A pad of numbered log sheets for each individual, writing pads and pens
- A Fact File for each individual lest they have not brought their own copies
- Glasses, soft drinks and biscuits
- One filing box for each responder and one for the co-ordinator's desk for extra copies of press releases etc.
- A flip chart and white boards on which the latest information appears plus pens and a cloth
- A separate board for displaying press statements and completed sheets from the flip chart
- Brochures about the site/location involved in the emergency, the organisation, the latest annual report and recent press releases
- A map of the location, a photograph of the site or a cut-away drawing, if relevant, visible from all seats

- Waste paper bins, extra chairs and small tables for others involved, including runners
- Fax machines, photocopiers, scanners, computers, printers, televisions, video cassette/DVD recorders, radio and "audio cassette" player. To minimise noise, these should be located in a small anteroom.

Because the team's role is to provide accurate, confirmed, consistent information to the media swiftly, most of this is obvious and requires little elaboration. Nevertheless, sometimes the obvious can be overlooked: for example, all team members must face the white boards, on which the latest information appears.

Systems

Members of the response team will rarely be required to initiate internal or external calls, but extra phones may be required by the co-ordinator or the deputy. The team should be consulted, in advance, on the kinds of phones that are preferred. Many responders prefer telephone headsets which leave both hands free for writing, logging calls and searching through the Fact File or other sources for information with which to answer questions. To reduce noise levels, some companies favour phones that flash rather than ring. Whatever system is selected, it must allow responders to speak quietly, whilst being heard clearly by the caller, as noise creates problems. Most companies choose a hunting system by which incoming calls are automatically routed to any telephone that is not engaged.

Log sheets serve many useful functions. The company must know which journalists are covering the emergency and the nature of the questions. No attempt should be made to summarise a long telephone conversation, but, as a minimum, the name and affiliation of the caller should be logged, together with a few words indicating the main focus of interest. If the incoming questions are significant or the responder feels should be answered promptly but lacks an answer, they should be written in more detail. For example, any allegations relating to inadequate maintenance, possibly made by a former employee to the media, must be conveyed immediately to the crisis management team, via the co-ordinator, so that responses can be formulated. The vehicle for this would be a comment on the log sheet, which is collected by the co-ordinator, as soon as a hand is raised to indicate that something important has been noted.

One log sheet should relate to one call. This system is particularly useful if a company executive is about to be interviewed on radio or television or is scheduled to appear at a press conference. Knowing what is exercising the media most, or being aware of an erroneous view, can assist the company materially.

For the responder, having to fill in the basics at the beginning of each phone call, imposes some discipline and offers a few seconds to become adjusted to a new caller. A tabloid journalist will adopt a different style to one from the business press and a brief pause offers the opportunity to change mental gear. Completing the form means that the chances of forgetting to ask the caller's name are reduced. Information should not be given without first confirming that the caller comes from the media. Once a call is completed, the log sheet should be placed in the filing box and picked up by the co-ordinator, or a designated runner, for analysis and action if necessary.

The telephone media response team co-ordinator

The media response team must not feel isolated. A co-ordinator, preferably with some media-related and company experience and, ideally, also with some technical knowledge, must be based in the team's room. Although he has to visit the crisis management team occasionally, to seek answers to important questions or to report allegations, he must not spend too much time there. He should also have access to a technical adviser who can convey complex technical issues in simple language without undermining the concept. A deputy co-ordinator should take over when the co-ordinator visits the crisis management room.

If the co-ordinator feels that a response needs to be standardised, it must be written on the white board. All team members must see it: some companies use a bell to draw attention to new information, whilst others prefer more informal ways, such as drawing a green arrow against details to indicate that they are new. Other organisations, which use more electronic methods, favour new information highlighted by steady flashing.

The co-ordinator's task is demanding. He must be prepared to take over a phone call if a responder is in difficulties. Sometimes, receiving the same information from a different voice satisfies a journalist but this intervention must not be too frequent as it undermines the system and prevents the co-ordinator from fulfilling other roles. Apart from securing information from management he must watch team members carefully, to ensure that none are flagging or becoming over-stressed. When fatigue sets in, a new team member must be introduced, and several substitutes should always be waiting, during which time they are familiarising themselves with the details of what is happening, aided by the co-ordinator.

He must also watch or listen to any television or radio interviews, so that he can brief his team on what was said and how to react to any resulting questions from the media who may well have heard or seen the interview.

The co-ordinator usually liaises very carefully with the public affairs representative, either a company colleague or an external adviser, in the main crisis management room, who should be seated closest to the door, to minimise disruption. If there is no such person in the crisis room, one member of the management team must be named as the main contact for the co-ordinator. As the crisis unfolds, it will become apparent from journalists' questions that some information, possibly even on basic issues, must be provided. This may emerge from a quick analysis of the log sheets or from a particularly difficult telephone enquiry. Equally, the co-ordinator, familiar with the media, may feel that it is imperative that the company anticipates some questions and secures answers in advance of their being asked. He will then compile a list and, if busy himself, will give them to a runner for attention by the public affairs representative or the designated individual.

One big advantage of having a senior public affairs specialist in the main management team is that he can then press for information when the co-ordinator has returned to the telephone media response team room. If this task, of seeking more information, is left to the telephone media response team co-ordinator, as it is in many companies, the relatively lowly status of the person holding that temporary job can inhibit a demand for basic information. The co-ordinator must receive answers to fundamental questions, or, failing that, reasons for the inability to respond. This, of course, will not necessarily be passed to the media, but it might enable the co-ordinator to construct an alternative answer for the press, after discussions with the public affairs representative.

The co-ordinator is also responsible for ensuring that all team members understand each new statement, before offering to read it to journalists. Any technical phrases must be explained in simple language, although all press statements should be easily understood by laymen. Journalists' questions on the new statement should be anticipated, and answers prepared. In practice, this may be difficult, as the phones will always be ringing and it is unwise to stop all incoming calls for a meeting. That said, there are occasions when important new information has arrived and the co-ordinator wants to address his team. For a short period, ignoring the phones, for a few minutes, is the lesser of two evils. If possible, a supplementary sheet with written advice may be put alongside each responder. Team members find it helpful to underline good and bad points on statements in green or red, respectively.

The public affairs representative

This person, the most senior relevant expert involved in the emergency, based in the crisis management room during the emergency, should be supported by at least two experienced individuals to whom tasks can be delegated, one of which would be to brief security on any attempts by the media to enter the building. The public affairs representative is primarily responsible for liaising with the company's media representative at the site *(see chapter 7)* advising senior management on overall public affairs and media strategy, writing, securing approval and ensuring distribution of press releases, including the holding statement, briefing executives before radio and television interviews, organising monitoring of press, radio and television coverage and ensuring that press conferences are organised efficiently and briefing company personnel before them.

As already explained, he is the link between the media co-ordinator of the telephone media response team and the crisis management team and it is ultimately his responsibility to ensure that the telephone media response team receive accurate, confirmed information speedily and secure answers to difficult but essential media questions.

Runners

The telephone media response team room needs information and assistance from the crisis management team and, possibly, from other parts of the company or the building. Runners carry messages and copy and scan documents, send emails, operate photocopiers, fax machines and computers, find experts to repair broken phones etc. and undertake a variety of tasks requested by the co-ordinator. Apart from plentiful energy, patience and persistence, the main requirement for this under-rated task is a knowledge of the company's organisation, the lay-out of the building and an understanding of how the machines work, and, if they fail, who to contact.

Board writers

The white boards, stretching down a long wall, should be divided up by topic. The selection of information recorded, which can be given to the media, will be determined by the emergency, but typical main divisions will be headed incident details, including time, weather, people and environment. Another might be vessels/aircraft/helicopters/rescue vehicles/ in the area, progress to date and plans. Other headings might be devoted to *ad hoc* information that should be given out to each caller.

A few companies favour having another board on which there is information that should only be given out if a specific and relevant question is asked. That may make sense in some circumstances, but it can tempt responders to try to avoid giving out such information because the company would prefer that it was not publicised. Worse still, some unthinking organisations have a board labelled "unconfirmed information". This is effectively company speculation and the concept should never be used.

Some organisations favour detailing a chronological sequence of key events on a part of the white boards, which ensures consistency in the dissemination of such information. However, all times for incidents should be approximate as otherwise the company, unwittingly making an error, for example, might be pilloried for not calling the coastguard earlier. Any precise times in the chronological sequence on the white boards should be the time at which the information came in to the room and shown in brackets. This also reduces the prospect of a responder missing a key point or wasting time persistently double-checking. An individual with neat writing, who understands the need to post only approved information, received from the co-ordinator, records the information on these boards.

The receptionist/telephonist and security

These people should be briefed, in advance, on how to react if the company is involved in an emergency. If an incident takes place, they must be alerted and given a copy of the holding statement. They can then read it to enquirers before the telephone media response team is in position and able to receive calls.

How to deal with telephone calls is discussed in chapter 13.

CHAPTER 9

PARTICIPATING IN A BROADCAST: PLANNING

Many of the concerns that worry anyone undertaking a broadcast, especially during an emergency, are discussed here. Planning for radio and television interviews is similar so much of what follows relates to both types of outlet. However, some specific thoughts that relate just to radio appear at the end of the chapter.

Planning, especially on deciding how the company would react to an invitation, is essential. A request might appear at short notice and broadcasters need a prompt reply. The company's response will be determined, partly, by the prevailing circumstances but the "default" position should be affirmative as television is the most powerful of the different forms of media and can influence total media coverage.

In the past, organisations involved in an emergency would rectify a problem before considering whether to communicate with the media. "Investigative" journalism, mainly, lay in the future and the media were then much less intrusive and competitive. Few stations specialised in 24-hour news and society was less inclined to want early detailed information about an incident. Now, requests for television interviews will be made very early in the evolution of an incident, reflecting society's demands for instant information. On 7th July 2005, when terrorists bombed London, the organisation Transport for London received more than 200 requests for interviews from all parts of the media in about two hours.

Many managers, frightened or flattered, reject or accept invitations to broadcast virtually immediately. Such alacrity is wrong, even if the "default" position is to participate. Appearing could aid or damage the company. The decision must be based on whether, on balance, it is advantageous to appear and no decision should be made until the nature of the programme and relevant details have been determined from the researcher making the initial request. Leaving essential questions to later might be costly: a subsequent opportunity may not occur. The business person might meet the presenter seconds before the programme commences and then be confronted with an articulate and experienced critic.

Questions to ask the programme researcher

Organisations should devise their questions in advance so, when the request comes, it can be considered logically and calmly. All requests for media interviews or participation should be referred to the in-house media relations staff or the external consultant. Without such an agreement, laid down and publicised in advance to all staff, problems can arise.

The company contribution

- Do you want an interview, live or recorded, participation in a debate on air or a solo performance?
- Do you want a very brief clip or quote?
- How long will the final broadcast version of the company contribution be?
- When will the contribution be broadcast? The company must know this so it can record the programme.

The programme

- What is the name and nature of the programme, its usual audience and how serious is its approach? Some programmes seek conflict between participants or between the interviewer and the interviewee or are biased against business. A large organisation or an external consultant should have this information on file.
- What is the format and will the emergency be the sole topic?
- Will other people be appearing, and, if so, who? Will it be a debate or just two people being interviewed in succession, on the same topic?

- Will the interview be in a programme where critics can respond, either then or later?

- How long is the overall programme and will it be broadcast locally or nationally? If the programme is to be broadcast only to a small area where a company is not represented and where it has no intention of becoming involved, and there are no national implications, it might be wise to reject an interview which uses up valuable management time.

- Will there be a live audience? If the organisation is to participate in a debate, care is required as the company's contribution might be preceded by some snide comments about business.

- Who will be the interviewer or presenter? The company must not under-estimate a junior or little-known journalist. They can ask difficult questions and some young journalists have less respect for business people than their more mature colleagues. Unlike the company spokesperson, many journalists have direct experience of incidents and will understand the key issues. Conversely, the executive should not panic if the interviewer is a national figure although many in the audience will side with the famous broadcaster. Most interviewers are competent understanding people who will only be hostile if confronted with corporate arrogance, callousness, indifference or evasion. Inter-viewers are just trying to extract as much information as possible from the interviewee in a short time, to convey to the audience.

The interview

It is assumed here that the contribution will be in the form of an interview but much of the advice also appears to other forms of participation.

- What time must I be at the studio or the desired location?
  An early-morning call or a car to the venue may be required. If spokespersons have to be at the studio early in the morning, they may well arrive worried, flustered and tired. If the executive has not broadcast before, the prospects of having much sleep before an early morning interview are not good.

- Where shall I be interviewed? (This is discussed below.)

- How long will my contribution, assuming it to be live, last? (See below)

- What are the broad parameters for this interview?
  Any topics not for discussion should be made known to the broadcasters at this stage.

And finally...

The company must know the researcher's name and telephone number and the time by which a response from the company must be offered. Even if the answer to the request is negative, this should be conveyed to the broadcaster at the time agreed, so that they can make alternative plans.

All this may seem time-consuming but these are important questions and dealing with them will not take too long. If the company cannot secure an unambiguous answer on a key aspect, it should press hard and, if that fails, the broadcaster must be told to ring back with their reply. The company must not gamble: it could be damaged and an executive's career undermined: perhaps it might be more appropriate for a trade association or even an academic or an informed journalist to appear?

The case for participating

An early appearance means the company is seen as involved and ready to communicate. Participating will also help to discourage the media from approaching others who are unlikely, unable or unwilling to convey the company view as effectively as the company itself. Broadcasters will always approach other individuals or groups for an alternative view but a positive approach from the company diminishes their appetite to look for other sources, especially if time is short. Interviews on major topics are also broadcast internationally as many UK broadcasters have agreements with their overseas counterparts to exchange interesting material. Additionally, an interview may be replayed on another national or local programme and broadcasters who are pleased with a contribution often ask the business person to appear, almost immediately, on another programme.

Some companies prefer to wait for all the operational details of the emergency before participating in a broadcast but that is wrong because it is important to be seen, or heard, as soon as possible, partly because the media's overall reaction to a company in an accident is greatly influenced by the latter's performance in the first few hours. The opportunity to address all the relevant sectors, simultaneously and at minimum cost, should be spurned only under exceptional circumstances. The only "cost" is executive time and the challenge of having to answer questions, some of which may be difficult. However, with modest effort, even the most difficult question can be converted into an opportunity to stabilise or even enhance the company's reputation. After one airline accident, an executive's strong television interview actually prompted increased bookings. When deciding whether to participate in a broadcast, executives should note that few interviewers are hostile unless provoked by a negative or arrogant stance. Their direct approach, often prompted by the limited time available and the need to cover some basic points, should not be confused with aggression.

Declining an invitation can suggest indifference or incompetence and the withering comment on air *we invited XX to appear but they declined, opting instead to give us a statement.* Having accepted an invitation, it is dangerous to fail to appear. *We invited XX to appear and they agreed but we have just heard that they have changed their mind.*

The case against participating

The usual objections to co-operating with the media are discussed in chapter 1 and worries about the techniques necessary to secure the optimum benefit from being in front of the camera are considered in chapter 14. Many business people, fearing an interview, contend that television, in particular, dwells on disaster, failure and conflict. A broadcast interview is seldom an attack on the company or on the individual but, if a group harbours great doubts, the company should not be represented. It is not a contest between the professional interviewer and the amateur interviewee. The winner should be the audience who should be able to answer the simple question of *what did he say?*

Even although most people now rely mainly on television or the internet for news, there are circumstances when it may be wise to decline a request for participation. Despite the imperative need to communicate, a company might be sensible to reject a confrontation, for example, with a vigorous, experienced and articulate environmentalist on a programme notorious for its lack of balance. An interview with an experienced broadcaster, known for his aggressive stance towards industry, for example, could create problems unless the company fields a good communicator.

A decision to turn down one programme must not, automatically, be carried over to all invitations. If the opportunity offered by the broadcaster is unacceptable, the company should try to negotiate an alternative approach. The broadcasters may want a contribution from the company as much as the latter needs television or radio exposure and broadcasters are unlikely to reject reasonable alternative suggestions. If an invitation has been spurned, the reason should be explained, assuming that this is sensible, and then a statement, expressing regret that the incident has occurred, indicating what is being done to mitigate its impact and thanking the emergency services, should be offered but this is a poor substitute for an appearance.

The reply

In practice, there may be no choice so the group must prepare and train. No organisation should say that, for example, it is too busy dealing with the emergency to undertake any broadcast interviews. This suggests that the crisis was very serious, that the group could not cope, that it was trying to conceal some information or that the public should mind their own business. Puzzled that the company would not discuss the incident on air, the media might then decide to investigate the group in more detail. Critics soon detect corporate cowardice, arrogance or incompetence. Such negative interpretations of a rejection of the request to appear might be entirely wrong but throughout this book the emphasis is on perception.

Television, in particular, is about impressions and this is particularly important in relation to the type of person who represents the company. An early response allows the programme planners to determine how to cover the incident. The company, of course, should have already decided, as a matter of policy, how it would react to an invitation to appear, who would represent the group and other details. (It might even initiate the opportunity for an interview.) Once the individuals have been identified, they should be trained and regularly tested. It is wise to have several potential public speakers to allow for holidays, sickness and the different topics to which the company is exposed.

Planning

Companies should ensure that they are fully prepared because the number of television and radio stations, some of which are keen to include local news, proliferates. Without planning, given the inevitable chaos that characterises at least the initial phases of a crisis, the prospects of being successful are greatly reduced but a competent performance can have significant benefits for the company including, for example, overcoming an indifferent performance at a press conference.

Questions for the company to consider in advance

A live or recorded interview?

Effectively, there may not be a choice but the company should be aware of the advantages and disadvantages. When asked to give an instinctive answer to this question, most business people opt for recorded. They feel that if their brains cease to function or if they make a mistake, a recording will be halted and they will be given another chance. However, many recorded interviews are "virtually live", possibly undertaken minutes before going on air, so are tantamount to live interviews and permit no second chance. Furthermore, even if the recording takes place some time before the broadcast, it is unlikely that the broadcaster will agree to do the interview again or to make changes.

A recorded interview can be undermined by bad editing, caused either wilfully, which is rare, or through ignorance. Friendly editing can cloak a speaker with unjustified clarity and eloquence but an editor may see the key issues differently from the company and cut a recorded interview accordingly so one or more of the main points never reaches its intended audience.

How the recorded interview is broadcast is entirely within the remit of the broadcaster so requests to see the list of questions in advance and to hear or see the interview before it is broadcast will be rejected. Making such a request immediately reveals the company's inexperience. This may encourage the broadcaster to take a more difficult line of questioning during the interview.

There is more: spokespeople and, especially senior managers, must be prudent in what they say and how they say it. Much is at stake: the interests of shareholders, employees, government and local officials, trade union representatives, customers, industry partners and many others have to be considered. Charities, for example, if unable to refute allegations that a disproportionate amount of donations were allocated to head office expenditure, followed by a poor broadcast interview, might well cease to exist. A poor performance may also damage an individual's career. All this induces a degree of caution which may make very boring radio or television. Consequently, the programme planners might also invite a contribution from another organisation, such as a single-issue pressure group. In sharp contrast, they are less inhibited in what they say, and how they express it, so the very valuable three minutes, originally allocated to the company, may be reduced to a few seconds. Furthermore, if a part of the interview is used, for example, in a news bulletin, the more colourful single issue pressure group comment might be pulled out as the soundbite, or quote, and, once again, the company loses its opportunity. A recorded session may also mean that the adrenaline is not flowing which could weaken an interview.

What is said in a live programme will be broadcast. Knowing that there is only about three minutes for the live broadcast and not, say nine from which three, possibly, will be selected for the recorded interview, concentrates the mind on the key issues and induces valuable self-editing and prioritising. The problems feared by most of those who favour recorded interviews relate to forgetting what to say and making a mistake. These potential problems are discussed in chapter 14 but such difficulties are rare, especially for trained personnel, and most interviewers will help unless they have been provoked by some silly comments or corporate arrogance.

A live broadcast encourages the flow of adrenalin. Provided this is not excessive, which can make the speaker sound over-confident or arrogant, it helps to avoid the complacency which can occur if the interview takes place in familiar surroundings or is recorded. At times of stress, extra adrenalin enables people to cope with an unusual situation.

The firm recommendation, if the option is available, is to undertake a live interview because the spokesperson can stress what he wants to say. A skilled communicator can convey key points several times in a long interview and this repetition will assist the viewer or listener to identify and recall what is important.

Where should the interview take place?

There is usually no choice because the broadcaster will choose. That said, interviewees should be aware of some of the advantages and disadvantages of the potential locations. Radio interviews, of course, can be undertaken down the telephone line, or, because there is less equipment involved, almost anywhere.

Many executives like to be interviewed for television in their **offices**. This is not recommended. It means that a television crew is inside the company building and, given the ever-diminishing size of broadcast-quality video cameras, it is difficult to prevent their filming something that could be used to the detriment of the organisation. Careless comments in corridors might be overheard or the interviewer might see something interesting on a notice board. If the interview takes place in an executive's office, the viewer may wonder why a senior person is not at the scene of the accident. Even for executives who travel extensively, the office remains relatively familiar so it can be difficult, in these friendly surroundings, to show sufficient gravitas. From the viewers' perspective, the context is incongruous. The well-furnished office looks luxurious in comparison to the scene of the accident and the executive who enjoys these comforts is not at the emergency location but is talking about it in almost detached fashion. Finally, setting up and dismantling the equipment takes time during which the executive is unable to use his own office.

Foolishly, some companies even allow cameras into the **crisis management room** for an interview. The cameras could detect some confidential information and the interviewee has to compete for the viewer's attention, during the interview itself, with all the activity around him. After one serious shipping disaster, a group permitted the cameras into a near- empty crisis centre, populated by a few young people who were taking notes not on company forms but on the corners of an evening paper. This prompted the astute reporter to comment that *wherever the centre of the crisis response is, it's not here.*

If no obvious alternative to the office is readily available, a nearby **hotel room**, a neutral venue, is preferable. One close to the office minimises travelling time and allows the company representative to resume his involvement in the emergency as soon as possible.

Interviews **in the street** are not recommended. Concentration is difficult because of traffic noise and pedestrians can speculate noisily on the identity of the interviewee and the reason for the interview. The executive is surrounded by activity which distracts the viewer and minimises the prospects of the audience recalling much of what was said.

Sometimes, there may be no choice but to undertake an interview from a **remote location.** The interviewee might be close to the scene of the accident and is questioned by someone in a studio. Here the advice is to treat the camera, if it is for television, as a human face to avoid appearing wooden in demeanour and pompous in language. If possible, individuals should avoid being televised where the context is much more interesting than the words that are being offered. **Do it yourself studios** should be avoided wherever possible. Apart from trying to determine what to say and how to appear, there is the problem of deciding how to follow the operating instructions and the fear that such incompetence may even mean missing the opportunity to address the nation.

Many accident-based interviews take place at or as close as is safe to **the scene of the incident.** There is much to commend choosing this location as it demonstrates that the company has despatched a senior official to the site. However, care is required to ensure that the picture on television neither reinforces the impression of disaster nor diverts attention from the interviewee's words. If the background picture is of a blazing factory, with ambulances and fire tenders rushing past the interviewee every few seconds, it will be as difficult for the viewer to pay attention to the speaker as it will be for the company to sound convincing and to secure maximum advantage from the interview.

Companies should not allow television interviews where the company name or logo hangs over the spokesperson's head. Anything that distracts the viewer from listening to the spokesperson or a scene that reinforces the impression of disaster and its association with the organisation must be avoided. If the interview takes place near the scene of the accident, safety clothing should be worn if appropriate. Hardhats may be essential, but they must not bear the logo or name of the organisation, as that will reinforce the negative impression for the duration of the interview. Furthermore, the hardhats should not reveal the interviewee's name as that person will be associated with the problem for ever. The remaining option might, therefore, be the **television studio**. How to cope with that demanding location is discussed in chapter 14.

Who should represent the company?

Even after training, some chief executives lack the necessary charisma or skills so the person selected should be the best available communicator at as high a level as possible in the organisation. A competent general manager is better than an inarticulate chief executive.

What are the problems?

Training sessions may reveal some senior executives to be incapable of speaking succinctly or seeming sincere. Some appear pompous and others cannot make key points from their own agenda, by bridging *(see chapter 14)* and slavishly follow the interviewer's route, thus losing the opportunity to convey the company's views. Some, possibly resenting the direct nature of the questioning, intolerable in their own organisations, become sullen. Others construe direct questions, often put bluntly because of a lack of time, as a personal attack. A few are unhappy at performing without notes and seem daunted by having to react, on the record, without full information. Dislike or distrust of the media can easily be communicated to the interviewer and to the audience, especially, of course, on television and this undermines the potential benefits that can be derived from the discussion.

Some cannot speak simply, especially if an adequate explanation of the emergency requires understanding of a particular discipline. Technical people sometimes cannot translate their knowledge into day-to-day language and resent the simplification required when facing a lay audience. It is crucial that the company representative is genuinely knowledgeable because television, in particular, soon reveals incompetence or ignorance.

Many executives cannot understand the need for a "public relations" approach. Assume that a senior shipping executive, being interviewed about a chemical tanker that has exploded in an inland port is challenged with the suggestion that it is too dangerous to allow vessels carrying such cargoes into inland ports. He might point out that many hundreds of vessels have discharged such cargoes, essential for local industry, over the years and that this is the first time that such an accident has occurred, so, sad as it is, there is no real need to change. Ideally, he should say this but end instead more positively by saying *a very tragic accident has happened and all those involved must see what can be done to avoid such accidents in the future.*

Some senior executives cannot edit their answers and thus leave viewers to determine what, in the welter of words, is important. The audience will be reluctant to make the effort so communicating key messages is drowned out by the verbiage. Occasionally, very lengthy answers are offered to ensure that as few questions as possible are posed but this undermines the reason for the interview and a competent inter-viewer will intervene and may show the executive to be evasive. Some people are not designed for a visual medium: up to a third of a short interview can be over before the viewer listens to the words, after having digested the picture on the screen.

Fielding a non-national for an interview

Despite the increasingly global nature of business, many organisations worry about fielding a non-national individual, even if the command of the local language is excellent. Overall, given comparable levels of relevant knowledge and experience and competence in the local language, it is preferable to field a national of the country in which the interview takes place. Many foreigners, notwithstanding their excellent English, speak too quickly, in the manner of their native tongue, and can be virtually incom-prehensible. It is also possible that foreign interviewees, speaking on behalf of a potentially controversial cause in the UK, for example, may arouse hostility, however unjustified, simply because they are not British. *Why are they telling us what to do? What's it to do with them?*

A crisis manager?

It is unwise to use a senior manager who is closely involved with the handling of the emergency. Taking a senior person out of the crisis man-agement team, for a full briefing before the interview and then having to bring that person up-to-date on developments whilst he was performing on television or radio, is too demanding in both time and mental effort. An enquiry into a major shipping accident concluded that the management of the operation was jeopardised by the frequent absence of key individuals involved in television interviews. The ever-proliferating number of broadcast outlets means that interview requests will increase.

Allocating this responsibility amongst a number of senior personnel is unsatisfactory. Continuity and consistency are at risk and the public will fail to identify with the organisation closely if a number of different faces appear. This is particularly relevant during major industrial disputes. The more interviews that are undertaken, the more confident and skilled an official spokesperson will become and more aware of the nature of interviews and the type of questions that will be asked at different phases of the emergency.

Other company personnel

Only company-authorised spokespeople should be allowed to participate in broadcasts. Whoever is responsible for public affairs should circulate a carefully worded but tactful note, long before any incident, explaining why only named individuals can speak to the media or "appear" on television or radio. Care is required in the composition lest the note reaches journalists who might construe the decision as censorship.

A public relations person or an outside consultant?

Organisations should never field a public relations manager or an external adviser, despite their experience. The broadcasters and the audience expect that a major incident justifies the appearance of a senior person, with an important job title and having operations knowledge. However, small companies or organisations, lacking such experienced individuals, must select the most articulate and personable individual available. For them, job titles have little significance. Consultants should never represent a company at a press conference or on radio or television because this implies either that the company does not care about what happened sufficiently to send its own representative or that it lacks anyone sufficiently competent on the staff. In both instances, the organisation appears culpable or uncaring which, of course, may be totally wrong. Consultants should be used behind the scenes, where their experience can be crucially important.

So who does appear?

The public will expect to see a senior person. Selecting an articulate and experienced senior manager, rather than an obviously incoherent and nervous chief executive is recommended. So, whilst it is important that as senior a person as possible is selected, some judgement is required. In well-organised companies, a number of key personnel, from different locations, are trained on how to cope with television during an emergency and tested with a series of interviews. Those who emerge satisfactorily from the studios are put on a panel from which the selection is made during a crisis. Progressive companies arrange annual "refresher" courses for their senior level spokespeople as practice is essential for a competent performance in front of the cameras or microphone. Confidence, so important for a satisfactory interview, and an understanding of the techniques, are advanced during these regular sessions. In "real life" a poor interview undermines the public's confidence in the company and thus may imply that such incompetence contributed to or caused the accident. That may be nonsense, but the company's stance influences perception of its actions.

The final choice will depend on the location of the emergency, the availability of key executives, the extent to which each is familiar with the details of the incident and the composition of the management team handling the operational aspects. Above all, the spokesperson must be properly informed and rehearsed. Business people should never participate in broadcasts, especially on television, unless they know what they are talking about.

Preparation before the broadcast interview

Anticipating the questions

Having accepted the invitation, the executive and his advisers must prepare immediately. The specialist adviser should have anticipated the request so will be well advanced in deciding how to maximise the advantages of participating. One useful indication of the types of possible questions is provided by the telephone calls from the media. The specialist adviser, in-house or an outside expert, should discuss this with the telephone media response co-ordinator to determine what the media most want to know and, more importantly, any allegations being made against the company. The interview provides an opportunity for the company to express regret and to say what it is doing to rectify the problem as well as correcting any inaccuracies and rejecting any incorrect allegations.

Major incidents evolve, sometimes very swiftly, through three distinct phases and an understanding of this aids in anticipating the questions that might be asked in an interview.

Mayhem

During this period, little is known about what happened and the company can only express regret, provide background information and stress the precautionary action that is being taken to alleviate the situation, the details of which are not known. Questions during this phase will centre around:

- What has happened? Where? Who is involved? When did it happen?
- What is happening there now?

Murder

In this period, the emphasis switches to the personnel involved. Typically, questions could include:

- How many have been killed or injured? Have they all been accounted for?
- How many people were on site at the time of the emergency?
- How many were men and how many women?
- Where were they and what were they doing at the time of the accident?

Manhunt

In this final phase, the media tend to concentrate on determining who was responsible for the deaths, injuries or pollution.

- Why did it happen and who is responsible for this disaster?
- When will the official enquiry be completed and will its report be published?
- Will you accept any recommendations made by the enquiry?

- Will legal action be taken against the guilty parties?
- Has anyone been suspended?
- What will be the repercussions of this accident, in terms of new regulations?
- Will this site be rebuilt, as it is so close to the local community?

Defining the duration of each phase is impossible. Much will depend on the circumstances and the responses that the media are garnering from various sources. The story will move quickly to the manhunt phase if the accident is in a city rather than in the middle of the Atlantic. As the media's experience in covering emergencies develops apace, supported by new technology, phases merge more speedily and certainly long before some companies can deal with all the anticipated questions. Organisations must strive to be ahead of the media, in anticipating questions and working out adequate responses and some large organisations hire specialists to do this for them during an emergency.

Having an understanding of which phase is current, provides some indications of the likely questions. Interviewees and their advisers should ask themselves what questions they would want answered at that particular stage in the emergency if they were journalists.

The response to the first question in the interview, whatever it is, must be preceded by an expression of regret and, if appropriate, condolences to the next of kin of those who, sadly, lost their lives. It is important to weave this into the interview as soon as possible. Expressing regret that the incident happened is not a corporate confession. Consequently, it will not upset the lawyers or the insurance company that might have a contract with the "victim" company that allows it to ignore any claims if the company involved has already admitted liability, publicly, without prior agreement.

The plan of action, three key points, a quote, an analogy and some bridging phrases

Preparing for an interview and learning some of the basic rules is designed to achieve the best possible results and to reduce the number of factors that worry interviewees. The company must find a way of describing the plan of action succinctly and how to convey it on air. A broadcast interview is not like a conversation. Few normal people would draw up a list of three key points, in advance, for example, that should be mentioned in a chat over coffee but that is precisely what should happen before a broadcast interview.

These three key points must be made, even if the appropriate questions are not asked. This is difficult because the natural tendency is to respond just to the questions and the severe pressure does not help. However, even if an interview is recorded, repetition, hopefully, means that at least one of the basic points should be included in the broadcast version. Ideally, the interviewee should write down these three points, partly because noting them helps to fix them in the memory and partly because the pressure, particularly on a live programme, may induce temporary amnesia. These points, the key messages that the organisation wishes to convey, can also assist the spokesperson in his efforts to ensure that the interview is not dominated by the broadcaster's agenda.

The interview does not "belong" to either the broadcaster or the interviewee but to the audience which wants to hear a balanced comment on what has happened and what the organisation is doing to rectify the situation. Devising the three key points in advance helps to determine the priority of the remarks that have to be made and which should be made as soon as possible in the interview. Rehearsing them assists in ensuring that they are less likely to be forgotten but there is another reason for constructing these crucial comments. Occasionally, in a tense interview on a difficult topic, brains can suddenly cease functioning. Unless the company spokesperson has been very negative, critical of the media or callous, the interviewer will probably help with a timely comment as there is no interest in a non-talking head. This allows the interviewee to revive but that may not always occur and, then, reverting to one of the key points is valuable.

Sometimes, it is helpful to devise, in advance, a "quotable quote", often called a soundbite, which will be used subsequently in news bulletins or by the print media.

The audience will not pay attention if a response is too long, too technical or difficult to understand. For example, if OPEC has reduced crude oil production an obvious question might be *will this increase petrol prices in the immediate future?* A comprehensive response would include comments on supply and demand, economic growth, the weather, stock levels and much else that cannot be speedily discussed in an interview. Consequently, an answer might be on the lines of *it's like watching a speeding car that has braked and is heading for a brick wall. At this stage, it's too soon to decide what will happen.* All answers should be full sentences so that, if it is important, the comment can be pulled out and used on news bulletins.

It must be assumed that some questions will be negative. Consequently, it is prudent to devise a few bridging phrases, possibly to allow the interviewee to move from the negative and even to include a positive point. *No, at this stage, I cannot say what caused the accident but what I can say is that we are now...*

New news

One very important part of any interview should be a new piece of information. Using this in a broadcast interview may ensure additional coverage on a subsequent news bulletin. Furthermore, other parts of the media, including the print sector, will use the news extensively and, as it is widely realised that broadcast interviews often do contain some new information, the media audience is larger. However, interviewees should be very careful not to introduce two equally newsworthy items but on different topics in one interview as only one may be covered. The key message must not be diluted nor must the media be encouraged to ignore it in favour of another piece of news.

The worst question, self-inflicted injuries and the need for rehearsals

The interviewee should decide, in advance, the worst question that could be asked and how he would respond. Who becomes involved in the quest for dreaming up the worst possible question, the three key points and other approaches will be determined by the immediate availability of relevant company personnel in the time available but sycophants should not be consulted. The possible answer should be tested by company personnel.

• What skeletons are there in the corporate cupboard?

- What might happen if a disaffected former employee reveals something to the media that reflected ill on the company, such as a warning that, if some expenditure were not made, an accident could follow and now it has?
- Questions on the safety record may arise so it is wise to determine whether, in any previous incidents, the company was adjudged guilty.

Interviewees must never provide the interviewer with extra ammunition! *Do you think that, on balance, even at this early stage, it was human error or a mechanical fault that caused the disaster?* The lawyer responded *It could have been criminal activity.* Some organisations are unprepared for the dangerous but obvious question. A water company, suffering high rates of leakage, said that many countries faced droughts! Pressed, the individual claimed that his company exported much water-saving technology. Asked again to address the UK problem, the response was that it would mean digging up the roads. The interviewer, predictably, noted that that happened anyway. A more appropriate answer would have included an apology, details of difficulties, costs, action taken and plans.

If time allows, the interviewee should be subjected to an in-house rehearsal, providing that this neither undermines confidence nor induces a lack of subsequent spontaneity. The practice interview should be undertaken by a well-informed colleague or consultant who has shed the respect which would normally be due to a "superior". Such a rehearsal may take place en route to a studio but, ideally, it should be undertaken in front of more colleagues, thus widening the range of likely answers. The potential pitfalls are more likely to be detected by a larger rehearsal group than a well-informed individual in a car en route to the interview location. That said, the exercise cannot be excessively democratic, especially as time is restricted. Usually, before a broadcast interview, the hapless executive is bombarded with advice and the task of silencing some of the colleagues and taking the final decisions on what is to be said must rest with the spokesman and his adviser.

Even if the spokesman is not part of the crisis management team, colleagues will be pestering the experienced individual for operational advice which must be rebuffed. Performing satisfactorily on air is demanding and requires concentration. Being diverted on to other matters, however briefly, could undermine the undoubted advantages that can be won by a good interview. Arriving early at the studio may create the opportunity to meet the interviewer before the programme and that might assist the company in the choice of questions but, given the pressure on scheduling, that is becoming increasingly unlikely.

Drinks and clothes

Interviewees should reach the interview venue in good time to avoid last minute worry and they should spurn tea or coffee as they tend to dry the throat. Naturally, alcohol should be similarly avoided, as, mixed with adrenalin, the consequences might be unhelpful! A soft drink is recommended.

Although public attitudes to fashion are changing, business executives should look like executives and not like refugees from the golf course. A general manager wearing one ear-ring, a tee-shirt and jeans, however eloquent, will not secure the audience's attention for the first few seconds of an interview because he does not look "right". Viewers, unconvinced that the caption was correct, will not listen for some seconds so the value of what is being said will be lost. For television, grey, brown or some shades of blue look good, unlike black, and white makes faces look dark. Checks, tweeds, a dogtooth design or stripes should be avoided as the lines can look lively on the screen, once again diverting attention away from the words being uttered. Shiny clothing, bow ties and excessive jewellery should be eschewed. A long jacket can become hunched up, creating the impression that the interviewee lacks a neck, so, as this could divert attention from the words being spoken, it is wise to anchor the jacket by sitting on it.

Take an audio recorder but don't use notes

It is helpful to take a small audio recorder to the venue for the interview. The broadcasters should see it, so that they know that the executive will have a complete recording so that if editing is required, the company will know what has been omitted and this action can deter injudicious editing. However, the recorder should be placed out of view before the interview starts. Interviewees seldom recall what was said during the interview. After leaving the studio, listening to an instant sound recording can be very comforting, especially because the sudden loss of tension can make the interviewee very deflated. The interviewee can take notes into the studio but must not use them or display them prominently unless the interview is on radio. It ruins spontaneity and gives the impression that he lacks confidence and even competence. Furthermore, studio staff will probably ask for them to be discarded before a television interview begins.

The role of an assistant

The interviewee should be able to concentrate on what is to be said in the broadcast so a colleague or an external adviser with knowledge of the organisation and media relations, should take responsibility for all aspects of the interview, apart from sitting in the studio and dealing with the questions. This leaves the senior executive free to concentrate on what he wants to say and how the three key points can be woven into the interview. Without such support, the interviewee's concentration can be deflected from communicating the company's main messages.

It may be impossible for the assistant to implement all these suggestions, especially those relating to the studio, but, ideally, he should ensure that:

- He knows all the details of the interview, the time, place, parameters etc.

- Transport is readily available to take the two to the studio in sufficient time

- The spokesperson is briefed on the latest situation and has prepared three key points and knows how to include the new news. The assistant, en route to the studio, should discuss the interview with the senior executive but must not swamp him with advice, thus undermining confidence. Efforts should instead be concentrated on the new news, three key points and how to deal with the worst question that could be posed.

- Video or DVD recording of the interview, if live, has been organised in the office. This permits the company to produce a transcript, which, in turn, allows the telephone media responders *(see chapter 13)* to deal with enquiries from print journalists who may have seen or heard the interview themselves.

- If the interview is recorded, an audio recording is made in the studio by the assistant

- If it is possible to alter the organisation, the assistant should ensure that lights are not shining in the interviewee's eyes and that the spokesman's chair is not one that could spin round or sideways as any movement could detract from the words

- The studio personnel know the agreed parameters of the interview. Often this will be irrelevant but, for example, if a manufacturing company, about to be taken over, suffers a major fire at its main factory, it would not wish to speculate on the accident's impact on the impending deal

- Wherever the interview takes place, the assistant should ensure that the physical context or background does not detract from the words and that the company's name does not appear on a colleague's hard hat or on a background gate or sign or on any protective clothing.

Types of interviewer

Many executives are convinced that all interviewers are aggressive, interrupt frequently, are ignorant and determined to ridicule industry personnel. That is wrong: the vast majority of presenters and interviewers are reasonable people who have to find out as many answers as they can, in a very limited time, to meet the demands of their audience. Whatever the provocation, company executives should not become angry and the calmer they remain, especially under intense questioning, the more favourable will be the audience reaction.

A competent interviewer will decide, in advance, an overall approach focusing on the key points from his perspective. He will listen to responses carefully and pose questions that he feels relevant, whilst simultaneously ensuring that, if necessary, his original approach is sustained. He must also ensure that his questions are put with minimal delay as it is important to use the limited time to maximum advantage. It is a task that requires no little skill if done well.

Hostile interviewers

If confronted by a hostile interviewer, the company person should be very calm and, if possible, say something like.. *I understand why some people may think that, but the reality is that...* The interviewee must not retaliate.

Sometimes, interviewers are aggressive just to push an interviewee into saying something that he might regret. Equally, if a spokesperson is too flat, a blunt question might be designed to put some life into the presentation. If interviewees become angry it implies that they have lost control.

Interrupting interviewers

Sometimes, the interruptions are initiated because the time allotted to the interview is nearly over and the presenter wants to discuss another topic. An interruption may also be made because the interviewee is merely repeating something said earlier or, in the presenter's view, being irrelevant. Some interruptions may be acceptable to the interviewee but, if interrupted whilst making a very important point, it is legitimate to continue speaking and to say, *please allow me to complete my answer. You have raised an important issue and it deserves a full response.*

The prosecuting interviewer

Some interviewers list many charges against an organisation. The company spokesman must stop the recitation of the catalogue as soon as possible as his employers will not want the audience to hear all these allegations. Furthermore, it is unlikely that there will be sufficient time to refute them all so it is sensible to stop the interviewer as soon as practical and deal with the allegation that is easiest to refute. At the very least, the interviewee should shake his head in negative fashion to emphasise that he does not agree, which is effective on television.

The calm interviewer

This kind of interview can be the most destructive. Relying on a gentle and disarming approach, followed by a serious and incisive question can destabilise the interviewee. One (mainly) non-political interviewer shook Prime Minister John Major by asking him if he felt that he could ever regain credibility.

Radio and down the line interviews

This section only covers points relevant to radio broadcasts. Some radio interviews are undertaken on the phone, or down the line as it is known, and may be very short, even during an emergency, so the pressure to include three key points is intense. Unfortunately, senior executives are seldom experienced in editing what they want to say and then offering a brief summary in a minute or less. Time is particularly crucial to radio reporters who must prepare almost immediately for the next story, or update, which may be only 30 minutes away. Some radio journalists may seem ill-mannered to novice interviewees who fail to understand what can be said in a very short time and become irritated at what they perceive to be rude and unnecessary interruptions.

Interviewees should devise a suitable soundbite as that may assist in ensuring that the quote is then used in a radio news bulletin. The company person should always listen attentively to the question and remember that the interviewer is listening to them. Answers should be relatively brief as listeners will lose the point if they are too long and, in any case, the interviewer is likely to interrupt. The interviewee should focus on the most important point as soon as possible to overcome any editing problems or lest the interview ends suddenly.

Pauses can be effective on television but create a very poor impression on radio, as do instances of two or more people trying to talk at once. Enthusiasm is important on radio as otherwise a voice can sound bored and there is no chance of overcoming this with body language. The pace and tone of the replies is important.

As an interview is about to end, it may be legitimate to raise a finger, indicating that the opportunity for one more sentence would be appreciated. Some interviewers may indicate that the last question is coming, either by "sign language" or by prefacing the question with a phrase such as "finally and briefly". Oddly, this clear warning is disregarded by some executives who then grumble because they were cut off prematurely.

Many company personnel prefer radio interviews as notes can be used which would look poor on television. However, excessive reliance on notes can destroy spontaneity and even a few seconds delay on radio, whilst looking for a note, creates a bad impression. Notes must be used with discretion as reading out facts and figures is unconvincing and implies that the interviewee is not fully conversant with the subject. If using papers, business people must ensure that the sheets are loose as turning pages creates an unwelcome noise and an impression of ignorance and a lack of confidence. Individual sheets should be used and moved quietly to a pile on the left, thus exposing the next required sheet on the right.

Radio interviews should always be "taped" by the participating organisation so that a full record can be created swiftly.

An interview down the line, undertaken in an office, can be difficult: the surroundings are familiar so there is a tendency for the interviewee to forget that the interview is both formal and on the record. Additionally, the call may be shorter than a face-to-face interview and shorn of some of the pleasantries that may characterise meeting in the studio or other location. As the journalist cannot be seen, there is no indication of whether what is being said by the company is of any interest and whether the interview is about to end. Consequently, it is important that the interviewee is aware of how much time remains during the interview. Many spokespeople forget the time as they are in their offices or even a distant one-person studio and then find that their key point has not been made and that the interview is virtually over.

CHAPTER 10

PRINT INTERVIEWS AND DOORSTEPPING

Most press interviews require as much planning as broadcast interviews so this section discusses the distinctions. The chapter also includes a section on how to react when the media arrive at a venue to find out what is happening before an individual or an organisation is prepared to meet journalists.

In an emergency, despite many requests for interviews, the involved organisation will have little time to devote to detailed one-on-one sessions. However, press interviews offer the opportunity of greater depth than that which can be secured by a broadcast interview so it is important to spend time on preparation once the outlet and the interviewee has been chosen. When confronted by a problem, it is unlikely that there will be time to give long individual interviews to many print journalists but there may be a case for granting interviews to respected writers from serious journals which reach the "right" audiences.

Apart from carefully selecting the journalists and outlets, the company must establish when the article will appear. If it comes out only after a long delay it may be out of date but, crucially, it will remind readers of an incident they had forgotten. The company should also know whether the interviewer has covered this kind of story before and the type of article that emerged. Is the journalist interviewing anyone else on this topic?

Most journalists will secure the bulk of their company information from press releases, the organisation's website, press conferences, watching television interviews and discussions with the telephone media response team or advisers. If they visit the scene, they may have brief conversations with senior executives. Additionally, of course, like their broadcasting colleagues, print journalists will also be seeking information from many other sources. The majority of print journalists can seldom spare travelling time and 50 minutes for a long interview during a serious incident, especially at the outset, when they are trying to establish what happened. Most scribes have to gather information on the emergency as rapidly as possible and then write a story, of possibly 1,000 words or more.

That said, the longer an incident lasts, the greater will be the demand for press interviews and, in particular, specialist publications and Sunday papers, for example, will look for different angles. If there are many requests for interviews, as there may be after a press conference, the organisation should suggest a pooled interview in which one or two journalists, ideally from very different outlets, "share" the interview, which is then made available to all parts of the print media.

Basic issues for the company

If the decision has been taken to speak to the press, the first objective is to decide what is required and who is best suited to undertake the interview. Obviously, anyone hostile to the press should not be allowed to participate in interviews, even if that person is best qualified to speak on a particular topic. Subsequently, the venue, timing, duration and parameters of the interview must be agreed. The duration of the interview should be repeated just before the interview begins because the journalist will want to cover a number of topics and will pace himself accordingly. Press interviews, usually, offer more scope for an intensive review of a topic and spokespersons should be aware that 30 minutes, for example, can be a long time. Company representatives must not terminate an interview prematurely and interviews often last longer than agreed.

Exceptionally, an interview might be granted on condition that the company can check the technical content of the proposed article but, generally, the organisation should not ask to see the piece before publication nor, indeed, the questions in advance.

The spokesman should spend some time with the public affairs representative or external consultant, deciding on the overall strategy and the key points that must be made, irrespective of the questions. Additionally, interviewees must understand the rules and parameters of the interview and a rehearsal with a well-informed but difficult colleague can be helpful. A third person, probably the public relations representative, should take notes during the dummy interview. The interviewee, although familiar with the company's relevant objectives may be ignorant on some significant matters. If asked about the impact of the emergency on trade in a particular region, he must apologise and say that the topic is outside his area of responsibility. However, such matters should have been excluded in advance, when agreeing the interview parameters.

Journalists also plan for a print interview and will have consulted recent media coverage and relevant websites so interviewees must be aware of recent adverse comments and be able to offer a reply. Notwithstanding the desire to adhere to the parameters of the interview, it may be sensible for an experienced executive to respond to any serious charges made, even if they do fall outside the limits but this must be agreed within the company in advance. If detrimental comments have been made, the organisation can refute them in an interview and should therefore find a way, if necessary, of responding. However, it is not a good idea to raise such an important issue until near the end of the allocated time lest the topic dominate the session, thus denying the company the chance to air other matters.

As with all forms of communication with the media, the company must anticipate the more obvious questions and plan responses and decide how to react to the most difficult question. The planning should include consideration of three key points that will be made during the interview, irrespective of the questions, and one or more particularly newsworthy comment that can be made. It is also helpful to devise a soundbite or quotation, providing that it is delivered with some spontaneity.

During the face-to-face print interview

These interviews can be difficult because they are face-to-face and, often, in the company's own offices, which can encourage informality and, possibly, a careless remark. Interviewees should be cautious. Although no two interviews are identical, the most successful are those for which the interviewee has been rehearsed and thus, hopefully, recalls most of the points that have been planned in advance. Interviews given instantly without preparation can fail to take full advantage of the opportunities for good publicity and can even damage the company.

Before the interview begins, the company representative should confirm the parameters of the interview and its duration. The journalist may ask permission to record the interview: this should be allowed. It is also wise for the interviewee to use an audio recorder so that the conversation can be heard again and any inaccurate factual points corrected before the article is printed. It must be stressed that this is usually the only area in which a journalist will permit such a change. Companies trying to alter the tone of an article will damage their reputation with the entire media. If it is relevant and true, the company representative could compliment the journalist for something that he has written recently, but this must not sound sycophantic. Company literature should be made available before the interview starts.

The interviewee must assume that everything said will be printed so jokes must be eschewed and the concept of "off the record" must be forgotten: that should be left to the media specialists in their routine dealings with journalists whom they trust. However difficult, the interviewee must offer the agreed quote and, more importantly, make the three key points. It helps the journalist if the interviewee moderates his tone or even pauses to endow the points with some significance. Body language can contradict what the interviewee is saying so the spokesperson should always look only at the interviewer.

Naturally, the company representative must never speculate or tell lies. If a question cannot be answered, as the truth would be dangerous, for example, in a legal case, the interviewee must explain why an answer cannot be offered. If ignorance prevents a reply to a reasonable question, the company representative should offer to respond later. Interviewees must never say "no comment" but should explain why they cannot answer and, if it is a reasonable question, offer to ensure that the company sends an answer after the interview. If the interviewee makes a mistake and notices it, it should be corrected and it is wise to ensure that the journalist has noted the correction.

The interviewee must not assume that the journalist automatically understands what is being said or its significance. Experienced journalists will immediately ask for an explanation, possibly in "plain English" but the company representative must not be condescending in his approach. Company personnel must avoid current clichés, the excessive use of statistics, technical language and jargon. They must answer to their satisfaction and always complete a reply even if it means interrupting the journalist's next question. Questions that commence with "why?" may be seeking an opinion and those that need a "yes" or "no" answer may be looking for confirmation. To secure information, questions may begin with "who", "what", "where" or "how". Interviewees must refute any misleading analogy or inaccurate descriptions immediately. Waiting for the end of the question or statement may mean that the company person forgets the adverse comment. As it has not been denied, it could become fact.

Time should not be wasted defending the whole industry and company personnel should avoid corporate boasting but give good examples of concepts they are discussing. Journalist will not necessarily print what is offered: they need evidence and justification for the points that are being made.

Answers should be relatively brief. If they are long, the main point will be hidden by the verbiage and the journalist might lose interest. Interviewees must be prepared for interruption from the journalist who may want to move on more briskly and they may challenge executives more abruptly than their colleagues would dare. This is neither necessarily rude nor disrespectful but is designed to elicit more information in the remaining time. Even if the journalist's style or questions are irritating, the interviewee must always keep calm.

If the journalist is neither writing nor recording the session, the response may not be interesting so a new approach might be desirable. Company people must be careful with brief but pregnant pauses from the journalist and should refrain from rushing in to eliminate the silence. If the interviewee has responded to the question to his satisfaction and has taken advantage of the lull to bridge to a key point, he should just await the next question. Interviewees must bear in mind, too, that the journalist's time is precious.

DOORSTEPPING IN AN EMERGENCY

In an emergency, some journalists will visit the scene of an accident, an office of the company involved or even a leading executive's home, hoping to talk to senior officials. A careless remark from any senior figure can lead to major problems and can even set the public and media against the company. It is not a good idea to berate the media. They have a job to do and being aggressive could easily become counter-productive even if being doorstepped can be trying: the mayor of London was in trouble once for abusing a journalist who doorstepped him one evening as he left a social function.

One of the most important rules for a company relates to senior personnel arriving at a site or office. As the media are covering an emergency, in which lives might be lost or serious pollution caused, it is inadvisable to emerge from an expensive car, smiling broadly at the gathering, which will doubtless include television cameras, before giving a cheery salutation to the journalists and commenting favourably on the weather. Some executives, who did not even know that there had been an accident, have been caught on camera in this most unfortunate way. It is imperative, therefore, that all senior managers are made aware of an accident immediately: modern technology permits no excuses.

Executives on the point of being "doorstepped" outside the office must refrain from responding in any detail without first thinking out what needs to be said and what must be avoided. This, of course, is difficult, because, by definition, the executive has not been briefed on the emergency and, even if he had a phone call on his way to work, it will not be sufficiently informative for the assembled media. Furthermore, what the executive has been told, if anything, is not necessarily what can be conveyed to the media. Additionally, there may have been more developments since the executive took the call in his car, even assuming somebody thought to ring him.

Unless the individual facing the journalists at the office front door has some confirmed information that can be released, he should merely express regret that an accident has occurred, assuming that it has been confirmed, and then to say something along the lines of *I need to find out for myself the latest position and that means that I cannot say much to you now. I, or one of my colleagues, will speak to you as soon as possible although, as you will realise, we are very busy indeed with the incident itself, but I shall do what I can.* This "delay" allows the company to gather some information and to make sure that all facts are confirmed. Any other immediate comments must be avoided. Later, if an official representative does address the assembled journalists, albeit in an *ad hoc* way, assuming that a full press conference is still some hours away, the basic rules still apply and, broadly, are those that relate to press conferences.

CHAPTER 11

PRESS RELEASES

Press releases, sometimes called press statements, are official comments from an organisation, or issued on its behalf from its advisers, on official headed paper, sent to the media and some other interested parties, usually by email. They are also posted on websites. This chapter explains how to write a successful and balanced release that will be used by the media.

Releases during an emergency must be prompt, interesting and informative and should contain as much relevant, factual and confirmed information as possible. They should be written so that minimal changes need to be made by the media and must anticipate and, as far as practical, answer journalists' questions, to relieve pressure on the telephone media response team.

This chapter concentrates on press releases issued during an emergency, but they can be distributed on other occasions, especially at the local level, where the media need as much good quality relevant material as possible. (Subjects could include new appointments, employment opportunities, contracts and awards, technical innovations, anniversaries, re-organisation and financial and environmental progress.) Even if a specific release has not been used, a journalist, subsequently researching a particular topic, may find the release "on file" and the company might then be contacted for more information.

Holding and reactive releases in an emergency

Many companies favour two additional variations of the press release. The first is often called an interim or holding statement, or, to confuse matters further, press release number one. This is written in advance, in suitably vague terms, and such details as are available are filled in when the emergency occurs. Some companies also use a reactive release. Unlike the holding release and the press release, it is not issued widely to the media. It contains information that can only be released when telephone media responders are asked specific questions by journalists. This policy is not recommended because it means that teams must decide what is disseminated. Individuals might decide differently on whether a journalist's question merited being told the official response so inconsistent information is given out. This violates the basic rule that should be followed by the telephone media response team.

Advantages of issuing releases

The advantages of distributing informative press releases promptly are those that result from all forms of early communication with the media during an emergency. In July 2005, on the day of the London bombings, Transport for London saw online reading of their press releases increase from 3,775 on an average day to more than 32,000 then nearly 95,000 in the next 48 hours. Some incidents are so unimportant that a release could arouse suspicion but silence, triggered not by the trivial nature of an incident but by the hope that the media will remain ignorant of something important, is never justified. If there are many media calls, seeking information, a release ought to be issued. Important news items will reach the public domain: many incidents are witnessed by the public, often armed with mobile phones with built-in cameras, who know that the media want "instant" eye-witness stories backed by photographs or even video footage.

An early confirmation that an incident has occurred is preferable to silence until most questions can be answered by which time most of the media will have gone elsewhere for basic information and will wonder why the company said nothing. Executives must realise that, whilst they usually say nothing until they have all the information, this practice cannot be followed during an emergency. Well-written and speedily-issued press releases cannot turn a serious incident into a non-event but they can ensure that the company voice is heard and that one incident does not become a crisis. A failure to comment can easily add a new crisis to the existing "operational" one.

Press releases in emergencies are judged on their contents and the speed with which they emerge. Some are appallingly bland and late by which time journalists have acquired useful information elsewhere. Vague releases imply corporate caution, suggesting to the media that other sources could be more helpful: this perception will be hard to alter. Poor or late releases reduce the prospects of securing free air time or space in publications, and thus the opportunity to express regret, to explain what happened, to list action taken, to deny rumours, to minimise speculation and to re-assure, will vanish. The air time or newspaper space will be occupied by others, some of whom may be critical of the company.

A well-written, promptly-released press release, and what is included, can influence the nature of the media coverage but there are other advantages:

- It can assist the telephone media response team by marginally reducing the number of calls and ensuring that journalists have the latest information. It also provides responders with a useful summary of what has happened and this is important because a tired team, denied information, can side with media critics. Journalists detect such frustration and use it to their advantage.

- The Human Resources team can use the release, in edited form, to answer background questions from relatives and friends of those involved.

- It can assist in keeping staff informed. Company personnel mingle with the general public and if they have to confess that they only know what they see on television, the company's reputation will sink further.

- The release constitutes an official record of the incident: the North Sea *Piper* disaster was covered in some 150 releases over many weeks.

- Media hostility is reduced and critics are denied coverage that they might otherwise receive if the company remained silent.

PRESS RELEASES –WRITING, STYLE AND CONTENTS

Who writes the release?

Ideally, emergency-related releases should be written by an experienced press officer, with access to the latest information, working in a quiet room and isolated from "helpful" colleagues. If a company lacks such a professional, an external consultant should be used but, providing some basic rules are followed, any intelligent person can write a sensible release. Apart from including what the company wants to say, one useful ploy, applicable to so many facets of media response, is to reverse the roles. If the press release writer imagines that he is the journalist, determining likely questions becomes easier and the composition of the release can then reduce queries by offering relevant information. For example, telling the world that a doctor might arrive at a stricken ocean liner, close to the coast, seven hours after an incident occurred would provoke media questions on the reason for the apparent delay, so that should be incorporated in the release if possible.

Another corporate concern is that few people can write technical material under pressure. This is not a problem because most media enquiries in an emergency will come from the general media, so questions will relate more to the implications for people and the environment, rather than technology. What is required is simple, day-to-day language.

How long should the release be?

Usually, releases do not extend to two pages, although it is legitimate to attach a second page devoted to *Note to editors.* (See later in this chapter.) If a release does venture into a second page, the bottom of the first page should be annotated MORE and the end of the release should be indicated. Some releases are in double spacing: this allows a scribe to write notes, especially during a press conference, or change words around or to add some additional information. However, as press releases are easily available via websites, their length is less relevant than before.

Releases should be accurate, consistent and self-contained

Information in a release must be confirmed, accurate, authoritative, uncomplicated, expressed in non-technical language, relevant and consistent with what has gone before. Each release should make complete sense so that journalists do not have to look at other releases to determine the key points and they must never begin with comments like "as we have said before" or "as you will be aware". Any apparently contradictory information from one to another should be explained and a new release must follow up on important matters mentioned previously.

Priorities

As with all other forms of crisis communications, the focus must be on people and then the environment. In a major exercise, a press release revealed in the first paragraph that the chairman was on his way to the accident and news that 30 people had been killed appeared in paragraph seven! Some releases detail what has happened chronologically so information on the fate of personnel and the impact on the environment appears late in the release. Some even relegate news of casualties to the second or third paragraph, after remarks on the state of company property!

No jargon, no boasting and short sentences

The inclusion of jargon will increase pressure on the media response team when journalists ask what is meant by an expression in the statement, especially if the responder does not know! Embarrassment ensues and faith in the company is immediately undermined. Telephone media response team members must be familiar with the contents and meaning of releases before being confronted by journalists. Sentences should be short and easily understood. Listing points, as on a shopping list, is not recommended. Corporate boasting is unwise and the overall tone must be one of regret, even if the company was not responsible for the emergency. Any temptation to attack others must be resisted.

Language

The word "incident" is widely used in industry, but the media dislike its use as a synonym for "accident": it makes the company sound callous and uncaring. Nothing should be written that is unconfirmed or is speculation so words like "apparently" or phrases like "it is understood" must be avoided as they imply uncertainty. Some companies prefer to use the phrase "unaccounted for" rather than "missing". Little words can have big consequences. "Only" 17 people missing may be meant to indicate that only a minute proportion of those at risk have not been accounted for but what about the friends and relatives of the 17? Press release writers must shun verbal abominations such as "further to" and "at this moment in time". *(See chapter 13 for more phrases that should be avoided in all communications with the media.)*

Another danger is corporate-speak. It is preferable to write that *sadly, two men lost their lives,* rather than *Bloggs Manufacturing can confirm that two men were killed.* Releases that begin *the company regrets to have to confirm* sound like a grudging concession that earlier rumours are true. Few journalists, and even telephone media responders, know what "appropriate action" really means. This may prompt journalists to ask the responder to "paint a picture" of what is happening at the incident scene which is an excellent opportunity to convey some very positive points but some responders' brains tend to cease functioning at this stage.

Abbreviations and acronyms should be avoided and statistics should be put into a context. Few journalists have any idea of the significance of an accident to a factory that produces saloon cars, so it should be explained that this represents Y per cent of national output. Companies and the media differ on the use of units relating to an accident. For example, assume that 100 tonnes of a product had leaked into a river. The company will opt for tonnes, the media for litres as that implies a larger figure. Press releases must ensure that the outside world, for whom the release is written, will not misunderstand the message. A chemicals company described a fire that was extinguished in 12 hours as "small", so journalists wondered what a "large" fire was. An explanation that it was safer to allow the fire to burn itself out gradually, rather than to attack it, was omitted.

Any pretentious or exaggerated styles of writing will increase the prospects that the release will be ignored.

In the beginning

The press release, printed on company-headed paper, must show:
- Full details on how to contact the company by phone, fax and email
- The group's website address, the name and contact details of the press contact

• The date and time of issue plus the number of the release: this is useful to the company and the media, not least in ensuring that the latter is working from the most recent release.

The heading and the first paragraph are most important and the last paragraph is the most expendable. They enable a news organisation to determine whether the incident should be covered and, if so, by whom and what resources might be allocated to cover the story. Headings and the initial paragraph should be brief, uncomplicated, and free of jargon, relevant and a sufficient stimulus to the journalist to read more. So, for example, **Fire on UK North Sea oil platform** is better than **Emergency on Pluto on block 16.11-b.**

Press releases on emergencies must reveal the bad news as soon as is practical. The fictional release below might have been issued by the container vessel owners.

FOUR MEN DIE IN NORTH SEA COLLISION

Four men were killed earlier today on a fully-laden modern container vessel, the *, when it collided with a ferry in thick fog in the English Channel. The managing director of the container vessel company, * of *, said that the company was shocked and saddened by the tragedy and that the families of those involved were in their thoughts. The next of kin have been informed.

After that, it is prudent to include some good news.

All other personnel on both vessels have been accounted for and are awaiting rescue. A lifeboat from * is on its way to rescue the 45 men and six women involved and is due to reach them within the next two hours. No oil pollution has been reported.

Now for some more bad news.

The five-year-old container vessel, now drifting towards the coast of *, was carrying * and some of its cargo has leaked into the sea.

So what is being done about it?

Specialists, experienced in the handling of such cargoes, are due to reach the stricken vessel shortly and local tugs are already en route to the vessel and are expected to reach it soon.

The most important point is to express regret as soon as possible. Some companies rationalise an omission of regret because it could imply a confession of liability. This is wrong and merely antagonises the media, which see a company that apparently lacks regard for people.

Content of press releases

Releases must use confirmed information only and be sober in tone. Some information to be included is fixed, such as the basic outlines of what happened and when, whilst other data is more ephemeral and changing, such as the impact on the people involved. As illustrated above, bad news about people and the environment, should come first, followed by any good news. The worst situation is to allow bad news to trickle out gradually, thus prolonging the agony and allowing the media to concentrate on this aspect, rather than on the remedial work that the company, presumably, is undertaking.

Rumours, allegations, lost production and alternative supplies

The press release gives the company the chance to address some pernicious rumours but caution is required. In refuting any allegations, the company may be drawing attention to gossip that has not reached parts of the media. Laments about the cost of the damage etc. should be omitted, but if there are any media questions on the phone, about the likely impact on supplies, as happened during the great Buncefield UK oil depot fire in 2005, the organisation should comment on this in the press release and say what action it is taking to avoid any difficulties. This will pre-empt media questions and indicate that the organisation is looking positively at the implications and is seeking a solution, if one is needed.

A quote from a senior executive and dealing with deaths or injuries

When people are killed or seriously injured or there is major pollution, a comment from a named senior executive must be included, which shows that the company has a human face and is sorry for what has happened. Secondly, the authorised quote can be used by journalists direct and this reduces the demands for interviews, mainly to secure a quote, and it implies that the media outlet has been able to talk to the senior person quoted!

In the UK, next of kin must be informed of fatalities before details are passed to the media, and of course, deaths must be confirmed. In some circumstances, it is possible to use phrases like "it is feared that" which is preferred by the police. This is one occasion when the company can use such nebulous words. If a journalist presses the obvious question hard, he may, in some circumstances, be told that one man has lost his life but that details cannot be released because the next of kin have not yet been advised. The company must be careful not to release any information prematurely that could identify the deceased. *I understand that the accident involved the crane currently working in the depot. How many cranes do you have on site? Just the one.* In many countries, detailing injuries in a press release is regarded as highly offensive.

Nothing that could have legal or insurance implications should be contained in a release. This can be difficult to detect and this is one reason why some police forces like to see releases before they are issued, so they can warn the company. For example, a specific reference to the weather could, conceivably, be used in a subsequent court case. Companies dismiss such interventions, opting to merely show the police the release, and contending that any legal repercussions are their own responsibility.

Withholding information

Bad news should be conveyed as soon as possible but sometimes it may be the lesser of two evils to delay its release. Many decisions in emergencies require the choice of the less undesirable option. For example, a company might decide to omit some details in a release, albeit briefly, whilst it works out responses to questions that will, inevitably, pour in once the information is released. Assume that a vessel, carrying several different types of potentially toxic chemicals, is severely damaged in a collision, which causes product to leak into the water. The company might know the identity of the product when writing the release but could decide to postpone revealing this information until it had more detailed information on its impact on marine life. However, this is a tactic that can only be employed briefly as otherwise the company could be accused of not knowing what its vessels are carrying which, in turn, could argue that is improperly prepared or has something to hide. It is important that the company understands the implications of including or excluding some information and is properly prepared.

Why did it happen? Don't pre-empt the official enquiry and don't blame others

However tempting, comments on the possible causes of an emergency must be shunned, as the results of any official enquiry cannot be anticipated. Similarly, releases must not criticise other organisations nor must they even imply that an equipment failure was responsible for the accident. The composition of releases should take into account, but not necessarily refer to, any comments made by company personnel on radio or television.

Later releases, information to be included and monitoring performance

As the incident evolves, the latest news should come first, as this saves journalists valuable time, trying to determine what has happened since the last release. However, the details of the emergency must be included because each company release must be self-contained. Some of the more obvious comments and questions are listed below, but it is not suggested that any press release seeks to address all these questions. Indeed, some of them, such as "why" must not be answered and, in some instances, other, apparently innocent questions must be ignored if possible responses could create difficulties. Telephone media response team members, in such situations, must be advised on how to deal with the difficult questions.

Some of the points that should be considered for inclusion in the release are listed below. This list can be adapted to assist in monitoring performance.

- *What happened, where and when?*

  There is a difference between what happened and why it happened and precise times should be avoided as the media may then be able to accuse a company of being dilatory in a rescue operation. If the emergency has occurred offshore, how close is it to the coast and what is the flying time to the site? If it is onshore, how close is the nearest town or centre of population?

- *Are there any injuries or fatalities?*

  If yes, who are they, what are their job titles, how old are they, where do they live, what is the extent of their injuries, how are they being treated and where, who employs the killed/injured personnel and for how long have they worked for the company? Not all this information should be given unless fully confirmed and, of course, details of personnel involved must not be given until next of kin have been informed.

- *If personnel are missing, or there is a fire, say what action is being taken to look for the people and who is fighting the fire?*
- *The organisation's regret and its sympathy for those involved should be indicated.*

Expressing sorrow is not tantamount to admitting liability.

- *Is there any pollution and, if there is, what steps have been taken to minimise it?*
- *If smoke follows from an onshore accident, and can be seen over a wide area, the release should try to re-assure the local community that it is not serious, assuming that is true.*
- *What is the company doing to control the emergency?*

Explain this in day-to-say language. Do not use phrases like "all emergency procedures have been activated". Give examples of what has happened and what is planned.

- *What was happening at the time at the scene of the emergency and how many people would have been on site at the time of the incident?*
- *What is the safety record at the location where the accident occurred?*

Obviously, if it is poor, this should not be highlighted in the release.

- *How old is the chemical plant/factory/ distribution centre/vessel/plane?*

Many journalists automatically assume that plant or vessels of more than a few years of age are old and that might have contributed to the accident. In this case, stress that maintenance has been carried out regularly. Similarly, new plant may be considered untried or experimental!

- *When did production start at the plant/factory etc and how much did the installation cost?*
- *If relevant, what is the weather like and what is the forecast?*
- *What is the significance of this accident to the country in terms of lost production? Will there be shortages and if so, how will these be circumvented?*

This is particularly important if the domestic sector is involved, such as a gas explosion in the winter.

- *If the accident involves the domestic sector, and is related to, for example, water contamination, what are customers supposed to do and what might be the impact on health of those who have drunk it?*

  People should not be frightened but a positive comment should be made if possible.

- *Are any other companies involved at the location etc. as part owners?*

  Partners may be reluctant to see their names used in a release, so agreement should be sought.

- *What is the impact on the company?*

  Some comment is only recommended if there is serious speculation on whether the company will survive.

- *Assuming that the accident is deemed sufficiently serious to prompt a very senior executive to go to the scene of the accident, this should be mentioned in the release.*

- *For land-based incidents, in particular, it is appropriate to pay tribute to the work of the emergency services, unless they were spectacularly tardy or incompetent!*

- *A telephone number for next of kin should be included.*

- *Finally, if the venue and timing of a press conference has been decided, the details should be included in the press release.*

Do not:

- *Say precisely how many individuals are involved until confirmation has been received.*

  Occasionally, some survivors have been counted twice.

- *Use phrases like "there are unconfirmed reports of casualties" or "at least three people have lost their lives".*

  Even if it involves some delay, it is crucial to ensure that the numbers of people killed, injured, missing and accounted for, equals the correct total. This is a frequent embarrassment for companies.

- *Speculate on why it happened.*

  If telephone responders are asked, the answer could be "It's too soon to tell; we don't know but the accident will be investigated by the..., and we must await their report".

- *Comment on a shipping company's policy on drugs and alcohol unless a serious and widely- publicised erroneous allegation is being made.*
- *Use unconfirmed information or anything that is tantamount to speculation.*
- *Imply that safety standards, or whatever is at issue, have fallen.*
- *Discuss compensation.*
- *Quote anybody within the company without permission.*
- *Write anything "unnecessary" that will make the task of media response more difficult.*
- *Give names of personnel involved prematurely as the families will then be subjected to media pressure.*
- *Comment on issues that are the rightful province of other companies or organisations.*
- *Attack any individual or organisation.*

   This will ensure that coverage of the incident lasts longer and encourages greater media investigation.
- *Write anything that could have adverse legal repercussions.*

APPROVAL, FREQUENCY AND DISTRIBUTION OF PRESS RELEASES

Approval

A desire to include the very latest information and the wish of many senior personnel to have their ideas included in a release will delay dissemination. Such efforts are doomed because new information comes in regularly, so an internal deadline must be imposed, after which no new information will be considered for inclusion in the release then being composed. The issue of emergency releases is often characterised by complicated and time-consuming approval procedures: the resulting delay denies the company the advantages of prompt dissemination and prompts the media to spend less time trying to contact the company and more time with its critics.

Some organisations stipulate that a director, a lawyer, a human resources expert and representatives of public relations or crisis consultants must confirm their press releases. If such a procedure were followed, which might work in normal times, the company would soon become involved in a new crisis because the involvement of so many individuals, all subjected to substantial but different pressures, and with so many different perspectives, would lead to grand procrastination. Approval systems for the clearance of press releases during an emergency must be simple and involve as few people as possible. Normal approval systems should be forgotten: the situation is abnormal.

Company personnel, confronted with sustained pressure in an emergency, understandably want the security of obtaining approval for draft press releases from as many individuals as possible. The draft should be confirmed just by the emergency controller or crisis manager. Copies should be passed to Human Resources and Legal representatives as well as partners, as laid down in the overall manual, if necessary, for comment, within a specified and imminent deadline, but they cannot have the power of veto unless there is a very serious objection. The media specialist knows that the company reputation is best served by telling the truth, or as much of it as possible, as fully and swiftly as possible: lawyers may not share this view.

The information in the release must be consistent with what is being given out by the Human Resources response team but when casualty details are included, regulations may require outside authorities, such as the police, to approve releases. In any event, it is prudent to allow them, and other involved officials, if required, to see releases before they are issued. However, as the company's reputation is at stake, outsiders' influence and ability to delay release must be minimal. Potential delay can be avoided by inviting officials into the response room although that can cause difficulties. The presence of a policeman in the crisis management control centre, able to take notes on who is doing what and when, could, under some circumstances, lead to major difficulties if the company were prosecuted for an inadequate response or negligence.

Press releases are written under significant pressure and it is wise for someone other than the author, and, ideally, someone not deeply involved in the incident, to check the release carefully, for sense, consistency, accuracy, statistics, typos and bad grammar.

Distribution, method and recipients

The preferred method of distribution is by email or via the company's website. However, there are examples of websites failing when under acute pressure and, in such an instance, a company will then have an additional problem.

Some groups may still use in-house fast multiple faxing whilst others entrust the task to an external bureau or their own email system. Whatever the method chosen, companies must ensure that all major recipients receive the release at about the same time. Modern communications also demands that when relevant, the media on the other side of the world have full information as soon as possible which is important to international companies. One problem for those relying entirely on email is that any messages relating to an accident could be submerged by the sheer weight of internal emails that many journalists already receive. Furthermore, in many large media organisations, the "copy taster" is invaluable in assessing what is important and what is irrelevant: that valuable function can vanish if email is used so it might be desirable to ring key contacts telling them of the accident.

Companies must place the press release, details about the incident and relevant background information on their websites. Because the purpose of writing and distributing press releases is to disseminate accurate, confirmed information and to publicise the company's views, whenever possible, they must be available in time for journalists to write the stories for the following day's papers or that evening's news bulletins.

Circulation lists for the receipt of press releases, must be drawn up in advance and, in some cases, different journalists, such as industrial and environmental correspondents on the same newspaper, should be sent copies. Lists must be updated regularly. Incorrectly addressed releases not only are a waste of time but show the issuing company or agency in such a bad light that their "work" will be ignored in the future. Apart from the media, business partners, government departments, trade associations, emergency services, semi-official groups and company personnel at different locations should not be forgotten.

Frequency

During an emergency, press releases should be issued as often as possible, but only if there is something new to convey. Companies must not promise regular releases on the hour, for example, as that may be impossible in practice, not least when there are no new developments. Furthermore, if a press conference is imminent, it is preferable to delay the issue of the latest release until then.

THE HOLDING STATEMENT OR PRESS RELEASE ONE

The holding statement or press release number one must be written in advance, so that, when an incident occurs, all that has to be inserted are the basic details, however limited, of what has happened. Speed is of the essence: the Occidental public relations manager was told of the *Piper Alpha* disaster at 10.30 pm and the holding statement was issued 23 minutes later.

The early issue of such a brief document indicates that the company is prepared and able to communicate. That is a very big advantage and will ensure that the media's first point of contact is with the company involved and not with potential critics. The composition of the short holding release, although written in advance, must take account of some of the points already discussed but it merely tells the media that something has happened and that the company is prepared to assist with more information as it becomes available.

Assuming that the relevant response teams are in place and able to deal with phone calls, the holding statement, which can appear "immediately" on the organisation's website, should include the appropriate telephone numbers for media and next of kin calls. News agencies will disseminate this message. Including these numbers in the press release will relieve pressure on the switchboard, caused by journalists and others who were unaware of them. The numbers and all press releases should be put on the group's website as soon as possible.

This first release will confirm that an incident has occurred, and, ideally, will reveal the approximate time and location and details of the immediate action taken. Wherever the incident has happened, it is desirable, where possible, to include reference to the number of people on site at the time of the accident. When this is difficult, a sensible range should be offered. Nothing undermines a company's credibility so much so fast as an inability to say, even approximately, how many people were on site at the crucial time.

The "where" question relating to an offshore location may be dealt with by indicating the number of miles from the site to the shore and the flying time. For onshore accidents at remote sites, companies should say how far it is to the nearest town. Some organisations maintain that this is offering the "opposition" too much ammunition but it saves the journalists time and avoids unnecessary antagonism.

Some indication that the company, knowing, for example, that the manufacturing sector in which it operates, is potentially dangerous, had taken precautions, is sensible. For example, the extent of safety training and drills and a reference to joint training with the local emergency services might be included. It is tempting to include much other information, for example, on what is produced at a manufacturing plant but anything that is added to the basic information will take time and delay the distribution of the holding release. Indeed, some companies have tried to include so much information that the release is delayed and the advantages of an early release squandered.

The holding release, which should be called "Press Release no. 1", like all releases, must contain the following essential information:

- Number and time of issue, together with the date
- Contact telephone, fax numbers, email addresses, website details, company name and address
- A relevant, jargon-free heading: the subject matter must be easily and promptly identified
- The basic facts, as then known.

It is impossible to devise a holding release that is suitable for all industries but what follows indicates an approach: the basic information recommended above should be added.

An example of a holding statement or release

Incident at...

An incident has occurred at...situated ... miles from... The chemicals plant/ depot/plant/ factory/... is owned/operated by... No details are available yet, but the company is doing its utmost to ensure that the incident is brought under control rapidly. The emergency services/other authorities/ have been alerted/ are at the site/en route to the site. The precise number of personnel on the site at the time of the incident is not yet known, but, at that time of day, the usual number would have been about... There are medical facilities on site and personnel are trained in first aid and fire-fighting and take part in regular emergency exercises in conjunction with the emergency services. Company experts are en route/are already on site, to assist in co-ordinating the response to the incident.

More information will be released as soon as possible.

Media contact number: (If the next of kin response team has been set up, their number should also be printed.)

Here is how these details might appear in a typical holding release for an exploration and production company that experiences an incident in the UK sector of the North Sea.

Incident in UK North Sea

Energy Oil Limited, the operators of the rig, **, currently drilling on block BB, in the UK sector of the North Sea, some ** miles off the north east coast of Scotland, confirms that an incident, which occurred at about ** today, has disrupted normal operations. No details are known yet but the company is doing its utmost to ensure that the incident is brought under control rapidly. Support services have been alerted and every action is being taken to assist those on the rig. The precise number on board at the time of the incident is currently unknown, but there is accommodation for 85 people. The weather is fine, visibility is expected to remain excellent and the sea is calm.

Offshore personnel are trained in safety, first aid and fire-fighting and all participate in regular drills and emergency exercises. Some medical facilities are available on the rig and on the standby vessel which is close to the rig. Both have helidecks. The rig is well-equipped with modern lifeboats and the standby vessel has fast life-rafts and, like the rig, has fire-fighting capability. Drilling stops automatically if an incident could threaten safety, but it is not yet known what was happening on the rig at the time of the incident.

A telephone line has been set up for next of kin and the number is:
The telephone number for media enquiries is:

End

Notes for editors

Additionally, most companies compile *Notes for editors*, which provide more information about the company. Such notes are very useful in emergencies and they can supplement basic information found in the Fact File. Here is an example of what might be found for the company involved in the North Sea incident described above.

Energy Oil Limited is an experienced exploration and production company, founded in 19** and based in **. It operates in ** countries and has been involved in the North Sea since 19**. The company's safety record is **: it has not had any previous serious incidents. Currently, ** is producing some ** barrels a day of oil equivalent, which includes oil and gas, from sources around the world but mainly from **. The group has offices in ** and at several locations overseas. It employs about *** people, of whom about ** work overseas.

Monitoring performance

Here are some questions that can be used to assess the performance of those involved in writing and distributing press releases. What should or should not be included appeared earlier in this chapter.

• Was a holding statement issued and after what delay?
• After how long was the first full press release issued?

- Were statements informative, timely and issued only when there was a new development?
- Did they contain information on contacts, addresses, website and email and were they timed and headed sensibly?
- Were they self-contained, contain a quote and express regret and say what the company was doing to mitigate the impact of the accident?
- Did they answer, as far as possible, the questions of who, what, where and when?
- Did they discuss people and then environment first, include any speculation or unconfirmed information, touch on compensation, include any relevant telephone numbers and use jargon?
- Did they occupy one page, include any precise times and did they contain long sentences and were they in double-spacing?
- Did the release offer bad news, followed by good, as far as that was practical, was the language sober and was there any reference to the impact on the company's finances shares etc.?
- Was there any corporate speak?
- Did the releases concentrate on people and what was being done to assist the injured etc.?
- Did the releases say what was happening at the site when the accident occurred and indicate whether any senior executives were going to the scene of the accident?
- Did the releases contain narrative, not just a list of key points?
- How many were produced over what period?
- Did the releases contain any names of those involved?
- Did the releases contain any boasting, any bad spelling, poor grammar or syntax or anything that could jeopardise the enquiry?
- Were the releases approved promptly by the necessary but small team?
- Did the releases take into account what the media had been asking about on the phone?
- Were the releases consistent with each other and within each statement and was the first paragraph sufficiently informative?
- If they ran to two pages did they contain "more" at the end of page one and did they include notes for the editor? How many were produced and were they posted to the website?

CHAPTER 12

PRESS CONFERENCES

This chapter explains what a press conference is and how to organise a successful one. A badly handled press conference can prove counter-productive so attempts to assist the media, and the organisation itself, may result in increased antagonism.

What is a press conference?

A press conference, sometimes called a press or media briefing, is a meeting, organised by the company involved in an emergency or an authority that is controlling an incident, usually held at a neutral venue, at which senior representatives from one or more of these groups, after being fully briefed, face the media. The latest information, some of which, ideally, is being revealed for the first time, is presented. Next, the chairman of the press conference, and possibly members of his team, answer questions for a specified but limited period.

Slick presentations will not persuade the media to ignore an inadequate response to the emergency or any strong evidence that the company was at least partly culpable. However, a successful press conference can reduce the damage that might otherwise have been sustained to a company's reputation, especially through rumours or speculation. An allegation not rebutted can become fact and press conferences enable a company to defend itself. Holding one also allows the organisation to address the key points that are exercising the media and to plan its future strategy in the light of comments and questions. Some of the basic rules and comments that follow also apply to routine business. (*See chapter 19*)

How does an organisation know whether to hold a press conference in an emergency?

Media interest, coverage and its tone, as reflected in calls to the telephone media response team, are relevant as is the availability of those who would represent the company at the conference. There may be an allegation that the company must refute: a press conference enables it to do this to a wide audience that can offer a multiplier effect. A new and potentially significant development may justify organising a conference. Managements without answers to every possible question, feeling exposed, may decide, wrongly, against holding a press conference. Ultimately, the company must decide on where the balance between advantages and disadvantages falls but in an emergency in which the media have already shown interest, the only real issue is when to hold a press conference.

Timing and frequency of press conferences

Timing

After a factory conflagration, a fire service organised a press conference before the company involved staged its own event and claimed that disaster was only narrowly averted solely by its efforts, casting doubts on the company's fire defences and putting the external service in a good light. Because involved parties may have different interests, companies must organise a press conference as soon as practical to allow them to say what they want to say.

If relevant information is scanty, it might be unwise to hold a briefing until some key facts are available, providing that does not involve an unacceptable delay which will antagonise the media. If a long delay seems likely, it may be wise to hold the conference and explain the reason for the delay or the absence of some key information.

Can journalists reach the destination, possibly remote, by a particular time? Even with modern technology, journalists still prefer the direct face-to-face opportunity allowed by conventional press conferences. Depending on the nature of the emergency, the first press conference should be convened within a few hours of the news breaking. What is the ideal time to hold a press conference? There is little point in organising one after the following day's papers are being published. Although parts of the news media now function for 24 hours a day, thus changing the concept of deadlines, companies must take into account deadlines for newspapers and significant radio and television programmes. There will be strong pressure from television and radio to have the sessions as early as possible, as the broadcast media's news appears more often and earlier than the daily newspapers. The frequency and significance of television news, which is closely monitored by the print media, thus offering an additional multiplier effect, must be considered.

However, the final decision on timing must be a compromise and, to accommodate the print media, the conference should be held not later than mid afternoon. If the incident is so serious that frequent press conferences seem inevitable, the precise timing is of less consequence. Organisations must not take too long to prepare to meet the media because by the time that every detail is available, it will be too late to brief journalists who will be looking for information elsewhere.

Frequency

Many companies believe that regular and frequent press conferences are obligatory. This is unwise. After the initial press conference, which allows the organisation to express its regret and to say what it is doing to mitigate the impact of the accident, press conferences should only be mounted when the company has new information or wishes to refute a damaging allegation. To confirm that a press conference will be held at, say, 10.00 hours and 15.00 hours every day, is inviting problems. Companies may have difficulty in finding something new or positive to say but journalists seldom experience difficulty in framing new questions, especially if there is nothing else to do at the location, apart from talking to each other and to outside "experts". Furthermore, the precise circumstances can never be guaranteed. Each crisis is different and events cannot be predicted nor can the availability of senior company personnel be accurately forecast so, if they fail to appear, for whatever reason, journalists, who also have very demanding schedules and who will have planned on the basis of the advertised time, will become irritated.

Because of the proliferation of news media in recent years, especially in radio and television, some analysts favour frequent briefings but the case against this is very strong, apart from the issue discussed above. As debated elsewhere, it is preferable to have just one main spokesperson, to avoid the possibility of confusing or even diluting key messages. Frequent briefings constitute too much of a strain on a single person and his advisers who may also be involved in writing press releases and deciding strategy. Equally, the time that a company spokesperson and his advisors require to determine the latest information, possibly from myriad sources and then to sort out the key factors and determine how they are to be presented to the media is demanding, stressful, difficult and time-consuming.

Where should the press conference be held?

Occasionally, companies wrongly favour holding two press conferences simultaneously, in different locations, so twice as many executives are involved in time-consuming preparation and presentations. Inconsistencies can occur as different spokespeople say different things, thus undermining the important concept of providing consistent and authoritative information. Ideally, only one senior individual should be identified with the company during a crisis. Having more than one confuses the public and prevents an individual from gaining valuable experience.

The press conference should be held at a location that is convenient to both the company and the media. Some groups favour using their own buildings, to prevent executives from having to spend valuable time travelling but this advantage is outweighed by the fact that the media gain access to the company's buildings. Small video cameras can film something in clandestine fashion, notwithstanding the presence of security guards who can easily provoke media hostility.

Occasionally, companies hold press conferences at the immediate scene of the accident. This is unwise. The media may see more than the company wants to show and may even be exposed to danger. In a crisis, when there is so much pressure on a company, it is sensible to reduce the number of problems requiring attention: organising a press conference away from an organisation's building or the immediate scene of the incident eliminates some worries. Whilst the venue must be convenient to the company, a remote site miles from transport links is inappropriate. Journalists who have travelled a long way to a press conference will expect to cover the story in some depth. Similarly, if television teams have moved expensive equipment and personnel to a distant location, they will want to transmit footage as often as possible.

In Alaska, after the *Exxon Valdez* ran aground, the journalists who had made such a difficult journey found themselves with few alternative activities, so pondered the story on a non-stop basis. The situation was made worse by the promise that press conferences would be held regularly so journalists, who outnumbered company and state officials, when not filing stories, were devising questions and their tactics for the next press conference. In this instance, the location for the press conference was dictated by the circumstances and the geography but for "more-typical" accidents, a local hotel is an ideal venue. This keeps the pressure off the accident site and the company offices and allows journalists who need accommodation to stay in the area. If the accident is serious and the control room at the site has been destroyed, a local hotel should be able to provide a substitute room.

Booking a local hotel when the accident occurs will probably be too late. Like so many aspects of crisis management, if something is left to the day of the accident, a new administrative crisis may occur, reinforcing the physical one. Companies should examine their physical operations and select hotels close to transport facilities and to their own sites that can offer adequate and suitable rooms suitable for press conferences and even for control of the overall incident. Some local authoritative provide suitable facilities.

Who should appear on the press conference panel?

Many organisations field too many personnel at a press conference probably because executives feel more comfortable if surrounded by as many colleagues as possible. Companies may believe fielding more specialists is a courtesy to the media as it shows that they are prepared to deal with different kinds of questions. There is no ideal number of personnel on a press conference panel. Each emergency may require people with different skills and experience but more than four could suggest that the chairman of the press conference team is relatively ill-informed and needs substantial support. Usually, the press conference chairman tends to take most questions himself, so, the more colleagues around him, the more obvious will be their silence.

Lawyers are unsuitable members of a press conference panel because they seldom seem able to think of a "public relations" type answer to questions. Other organisations involved in the incident may wish to participate on the panel and, of course, if a local authority is managing the emergency, the company can challenge neither the numbers nor identities of those who take part. When joint press conferences are organised, participants must agree a common view on some predictable topics to avoid the possibility that the media could exploit any inconsistencies. If a company representative is accompanied by several people from other organisations, the number of direct questions will be marginally less than if the panel consisted entirely of company personnel. That might be helpful but, ideally, companies should organise and run the main press conference.

Unless company personnel have undertaken training in handling press conferences, or are "natural" communicators who can absorb a brief but intensive preparatory session before the conference, novices should be omitted from the team. A careless phrase could have severe implications, not just in media terms, but in relation to legal and insurance matters. Pressure can induce odd answers and companies need to be aware of employees who might weaken in a crisis, make an inappropriate comment or attack the media. Representing the company adequately in such trying circumstances requires a range of skills, a suitable temperament and ability to think on the feet, under enormous pressure. Many chairmen and chief executives automatically assume that they should chair press conferences during an emergency but if they are relatively inarticulate or lacking in confidence, they should not participate. All this emphasises the importance of training and testing. Executives, especially the chairman of the press conference panel, must answer questions with the public relations aspect uppermost in their minds but many react as technical experts, and are thus incomprehensible, whilst others are too pompous to be exposed to the media.

Those who lack the facility to chair a press conference soon realise this during training sessions and then often engage in constructive discussions to determine who is best qualified to undertake this role and what contribution they themselves can make. The media expect to see a chairman or chief executive chairing the panel but if the incident is serious, and these individuals are deemed inadequate, their most senior colleague, charged with leading the company at the briefing, must explain why the boss is not present. Whatever the circumstances, it is important that the missing executive is perceived to be involved.

Some companies select the chairman from the senior management incident team which is co-ordinating the operational response to the incident. He is well informed and knows what is being done to contain the emergency but, disregarding the thought that so much knowledge could be a handicap, some organisations reject this approach. Such an individual has to surrender his responsibilities, whenever he has to be prepared to participate in a press conference. Continuity in the main management team is lost and more valuable time is expended bringing the senior person up-to-date again after the press conference. Consequently, especially as the media's demands for information and a talking head proliferate, partly because of 24 hour rolling news, some companies now favour the selection of an individual who will not be charged with the dual responsibilities of being an active member of the operational team as well as being the chairman of the press conference or chief media interviewee. Having a single, confident and articulate individual to carry out the senior media-related roles preserves continuity and consistency and allows the public to identify with one person.

Some organisations wrongly delegate their in-house public relations expert or external consultant to chair the press conference panel. The media and the outside world expect a senior company person to front the meeting. Journalists, who may have travelled a long way to the conference, want a direct quote from a very senior executive, preferably on the board and with operations experience, and the opportunity to question him.

Some journalists, on being told of the press conference, during a phone call, might ask who will be representing the company. A minority might say that their attendance will be determined by the rank of the company personnel on the panel. If this will not be known until later, the correct response is that, because many senior managers are involved in the incident, the company cannot say at that stage but it will be fielding senior and experienced personnel.

Depending on the nature of the emergency, the press conference team might also contain experts on Human Resources, Finance, Safety and Environment and the aspects of the business, operationally, involved in the accident. Companies may also like to include a representative from the emergency services at their own press conferences. In some rare instances, where a situation is very complex, companies might place a few more experts in the audience. Having too many specialists on the platform can intimidate the media, imply that the incident is more serious than claimed or that the main personnel lack confidence. However, the chairman of the press conference may want to call on extra expertise and those individuals can then contribute.

Who should be allowed to attend a press conference?

Press conferences can become chaotic and counter-productive if non-journalists are allowed to attend and even ask questions. One swift way to alienate journalists, who have frequently made long journeys to attend and who have to file stories promptly, is to allow others to take the time that has been specifically allocated to them. Furthermore, "outsiders", especially the public, may be able to talk to the media before during or after the meeting. Their comments might be sufficiently dramatic to encourage the journalist to ignore remarks from the platform as there is a better story coming from the audience. A conversation with such an individual before the meeting can result in a more difficult question from a journalist. Usually, only genuine journalists, preferably showing their press cards, should be allowed to attend a press conference. All other personnel should be denied access unless there are compelling reasons for their attendance and the public should be excluded

By allowing intruders, the company restricts its own opportunity to disseminate information on its position to as wide and varied as possible an audience via the media. Occasionally, it might be difficult to exclude some officials or representatives from pressure groups. They might be permitted access as observers but the press conference co-ordinator, *(see later)*, should be strict whilst handling the issue sensitively. A pressure group representative being ejected from a press conference makes good television.

Some organisations fear that, if the press conference goes badly, and they have allowed television cameras in, the repercussions could be serious. Given the influence of television, there is no choice and granting access shows that the company cares about what has happened, and hopefully discourages the producers from looking for another, less promising location, such as an area close to a company logo, over which to film a damaging piece to camera. Excluding the cameras from a press conference can lead to very negative coverage: on one occasion, a clip showing the cameras and reporter being ejected became the story. Television seldom uses much footage from a press conference. There might be an establishing shot of the audience and a few seconds of the panel of speakers. All broadcasters will also look for a key quote which companies must prepare in advance. This is important as it can be lifted from the presentation and used in subsequent television and radio news bulletins as well as by the press.

Television will be more interested in a one-to-one interview after the press conference. Such requests should be met as far as possible as they offer the company an opportunity to correct any mistakes or misunderstandings from the press conference and, more positively, enable key points to be made directly to a very large audience. If it is impossible, after a press conference, to give interviews to all the television companies represented at the event, the situation should be explained and the company might suggest that one or two of the journalists undertake an interview which would then be made available to other broadcasting groups.

All journalists who ring in with questions on the incident should be invited to the press conference and given appropriate details. The nature of the emergency will determine who else, from within the ranks of the media, should be invited. As part of the company's thorough planning, it should have media lists relating to different categories of journalists so that when the emergency occurs, those most interested, as well as the generalists, can be invited. The local press should not be overlooked. Some of them may also represent national papers so the damage for failing to invite them could be long-lasting. If they have been ignored in the past, and asked by "outside" journalists what kind of company is involved in the crisis, they might say that it is furtive and distrusts the media!

Possible media attendees should be sent text messages or emails giving details of the press conference and this information should also be disseminated by the news agencies, and, of course, on the company's website. Companies without adequate in-house facilities should use external agencies, suitably organised in advance.

Who, from the company, should attend the press conference? Experienced "reporters" from the company should be placed in the audience. If, for example, a press conference is held in Manchester, details must be passed to the London office swiftly, so that the journalists ringing there can be updated by the company on the telephone. Ideally, both offices should be able to see the press conference live, via modern technical links.

Representatives from Human Resources, dealing with enquiries from next of kin, friends and relatives, must have a realistic idea of how the emergency is developing, so one of their number should attend or see the video link, so that the personnel response team can be briefed. The same applies to the telephone response team because reports will soon be broadcast. The team will lose credibility if it is unaware of what was said. If a weakness in the company position was apparent at the press conference, media telephone responders must be given information that enables them to deal with subsequent questions on the phone from journalists who are aware of the broadcast comments. Similarly, the media and personnel response teams must be given copies of the latest statement that was presented to the conference and given to journalists as they left.

Preparing for a press conference

Content

Poor press conferences usually result from an inability to convey relevant and up-to-date information, a failure to anticipate and thus answer questions satisfactorily, or an inability to conduct the conference expertly. Presenting a poor press conference is inexcusable. Once again, the most important factor is preparation and, if time permits, a rehearsal. Most journalists attending any emergency-related press conference will not be experts in the relevant industry so companies must explain carefully, without being patronising, in language that is free of jargon and with relevant but simple statistics, where appropriate.

The opening statement and questions

Apart from presenting an up-to-date statement of what has happened and what plans it has, the opening statement gives the company an opportunity to refute any serious accusations. A company should be able to anticipate the majority of questions and devise answers in advance or explanations on why they cannot reply. It will be clear from the questions posed to the telephone media response team what is exercising the media and what stage has been reached in the evolution of the emergency. Input from the onsite media co-ordinator will also assist in determining likely questions. The press conference panel should consider whether corporate cupboards contain any skeletons and how any such difficult questions on potentially embarrassing questions will be dealt with if asked. Similarly, the company must plan how it is to cope with the most difficult questions, as well as how it will reveal any good news. As a general rule, in media relations, bad news must come first, in one piece, not as a series of "confessions". Most journalists will ask what they feel their readers, listeners or viewers would ask and that allows sensible planning of likely responses.

Organisation: the room

Obviously, the room, allowing good vision and offering loudspeaker facilities, must accommodate as many journalists as possible as comfortably as possible. If journalists can neither see nor hear, there are likely to be interruptions which jeopardise the coherence of the proceedings, as well as suggesting the company is unprofessional. No specific advice on numbers can be offered as some accidents attract hundreds of journalists and many television teams from around the world but rooms should be able to accommodate at least 100 media representatives. As many journalists might have travelled a long way, some refreshments should be available in an adjacent room before the press conference. After the briefing, they will be keen to file their stories. Company equipment, such as microphones, should be checked carefully before the press conference!

The company team should sit behind a table at which their first and last names and job titles are displayed prominently. This information should also be included in the media kits. The table, however, should not show company flags, nor should the company name, logo or a corporate boast be displayed behind the speakers. Having a security guard standing by the platform is a very poor idea: television may use such images to the detriment of the organisation.

Ideally, the media are some few feet away, so that the company team can leave the room without being trapped by more questions. *(See later.)* The television camera teams must remain at the back of the room because their equipment prevents the print journalists from seeing the company personnel and their attention may also be distracted if the television people are moving in front of them during the conference. Their journalistic colleagues, of course, can be in the main body of the room.

The room should have two doors. Once the proceedings are finished, the company team must be able to leave unimpeded. Television often captures memorable footage of executives trying to dodge additional and persistent questions, or flapping their hands around protesting that the press conference is over. There is another danger: once the press conference has finished, executives may relax mentally and then, if followed out of the room, say something that they will regret. At the end of the press conference, the company team should leave by a door at their end of the room, behind their table, whilst the journalists should be encouraged to depart via a door at the other end of the room, with a reminder that copies of the latest statement and visual aids are on the table close to "their" door.

Conduct of the press conference

Before the press conference panel moves to the room where the meeting is to be held, the chairman must tell his team how he will conduct the session. In most instances, the chairman will read out the latest release and then take questions. He will doubtless deal with the majority of the questions himself but may deal only briefly with some, before passing it on to a colleague. *I'll explain that as best as I can but after that, I'll ask my colleague X to tell you more.* In that way, X has notice that he is required to perform and that he has a few moments to compose a sensible response.

The first few minutes of a press conference can influence not just the tone of the session but of subsequent coverage. Despite a great clamour for instant information, especially at the commencement of the press conference, the company must keep control and adhere to its own agenda and communicate what is going to happen. The journalists will not necessarily know, for example, that they are about to be given the latest information, so they will bombard the company team with questions. To overcome this, it is necessary for a co-ordinator, preferably with media relations experience, to initiate the proceedings.

Once the journalists are in place, the company team, including the press conference co-ordinator, enters through "their" door. The panellists immediately sit down but the co-ordinator remains standing. He then introduces himself, gives his job title, thanks the media for coming and expresses regret at the circumstances that prompted the press conference, if appropriate. If necessary, he should also apologise for the late start of the conference.

The co-ordinator then introduces the team before announcing that the chairman will present a brief statement which incorporates some new information, which, doubtless, will answer some of the media's questions. He must explain that the panel will take questions for a limited and specified period. It is crucial that the reason for the time limit is made clear: *the press conference team must return to assist in managing the emergency*. A failure to indicate the duration of the press conference and the question session could have a negative impact on coverage. Finally, the co-ordinator requests politely that mobile phones are switched off and that each questioner gives his name and affiliation when the time for questions arrives. The questioners will then be handed a microphone and the proceedings should be recorded by the company. In an intense press conference, the system can break down but the co-ordinator must ensure that the practice is sustained because it will be important, later, to analyse questions and the resulting coverage by each media outlet.

Presenting the statement

The chairman now presents the statement: it is preferable to paraphrase the statement as reading it can seem wooden and imply a lack of familiarity with the details. It should not be presented too quickly nor too ponderously and any figures should be repeated carefully, but not patronisingly, to avoid misunderstandings. The statement must not be too long, nor must it be read slowly, as this will be seen by busy journalists as an attempt to reduce the time that would otherwise have been devoted to questions. Any attempts by the media to interrupt with questions must be resisted by the co-ordinator, who must appeal for quiet so that everyone can be updated by listening to the statement which *as I said earlier, does contain new information and which will probably answer some of your questions.* However, questions seeking brief clarification should be allowed.

Questions

When the chairman has finished, the co-ordinator invites questions and this is when chaos can ensue. Some consultants believe that it is preferable for the chairman of the press conference to appeal for quiet and to say that he intends to deal with as many questions as possible but he cannot respond to them all simultaneously. The argument is that if the comment does not come from the chairman, he appears weak. However, there could be some hostility because of the way in which the conference is handled and it is better for the co-ordinator to be perceived as the villain. After that, and assuming that some kind of order is imposed, the co-ordinator should subsequently indicate from whom each question should come, in turn. In busy press conferences, some companies put a second co-ordinator in the audience to ensure that his colleague on the platform does not inadvertently overlook any journalist. One way of achieving this is to use microphones, which are handed around, but that can slow proceedings and irritate the media most of whom are accustomed to making themselves heard.

The co-ordinator should reject more than one brief supplementary question from a journalist and this, too, is better coming from a media co-ordinator than a chairman, who can make such a comment sound like a magisterial rebuke. One advantage of this for the company is that it does not become ensnared in a difficult series of questions that are more like an interview, although, of course, other journalists might take up the same theme.

Although the chairman will take the majority of questions, his colleagues have a significant role, even if not called upon.

What happens if the chairman makes a mistake or omits crucial information? The other panellists should be listening carefully and, if they hear a serious error, they should correct it tactfully. A journalist might claim that what he just heard was different to what the company was saying previously. Which version should now be accepted and why was there a difference between company spokespersons? The "correction" from a fully-informed colleague might be on the following lines. *Perhaps it would be helpful if I were to try to clarify...* Alternatively, a colleague might say *perhaps I could just add a few words to what... has said.* Then, if the "correction" was significant, the chairman, whose error caused the clarification, and who must be listening carefully to his colleague, could say *thank you. That certainly is the position and I apologise if I unwittingly gave another impression.* That may sound bad, but it is less damaging than an incorrect statement and the impression that there is dissension in the company, which encourages a sense of incompetence.

During a press conference, a journalist may claim that he was previously told something by the telephone media responders and that this now seems at variance with what has been said at the press conference. In these circumstances, the journalist will want to know why something has changed so dramatically so fast. *I'm sorry if one of my colleagues did say that and I apologise if it has caused you any problems. However, as I have just said, the real position is that...* This response reduces the prospect that the journalist feels offended and will therefore compose a negative story.

Some questions, such as those relating to compensation and resignations are very predictable and are discussed in chapter 17.

Terminating a press conference

No press conference should last less than 45 minutes, as some journalists will have travelled many miles and might have had unsatisfactory answers to their questions on the telephone. The company team must concentrate on providing adequate responses and should not be diverted by watching the clock which is the responsibility of the co-ordinator. Even when the timing is indicated in advance, and the reasons correctly given, the co-ordinator must show some judgement when finishing the conference. It would be wrong to finish if the company is about to respond to allegations. This is the main reason that the timing must be given in advance: leaving suddenly, because the time is up but was not conveyed at the outset could look like cowardice. Equally, if some trenchant points were being made, it would be foolish to stop abruptly, merely because the time has been exhausted.

The way to indicate that the conference is about to end is for the co-ordinator to say that just two more questions can be taken *after which, as I said at the beginning of this press conference, my colleagues must return to dealing with the emergency.* This indicates to the chairman and the other panellists that, after they have dealt with two more questions, they must collect their papers together and leave the room through their door. As the team prepares to leave, the co-ordinator announces that copies of the latest statement and of the visual aids are in a media kit at the back of the room and, hopefully, that is where the majority of journalists will go, leaving the company representatives to avoid further questioning. Additionally, he should thank the journalists for attending and say when the next press conference will be held, but, as discussed above, this may be a dangerous tactic.

Monitoring performance

Here are some questions that can be used to assess the performance of those involved in a press conference. Others can be deduced from the text above.

- Was the decision on timing and venue of the press conference appropriate?
- Was the room adequate?
- Was the composition of the conference panel and chairmanship considered carefully?
- Was proper consideration given to the identity of invited attendees?
- Was preparation for the press conference team adequate?
- Did the co-ordinator welcome the journalists, introduce the panel, explain the procedures, indicate the duration of the conference and the reasons that it could not be any longer?
- Were the journalists asked to give their names and affiliation and did the panel members have their names and job titles in front of them?
- Was the chairman good in his role and did he express regret, retain control and use his colleagues sensibly? Did he complete the reading of his statement? Did it contain new information? Did he deal satisfactorily with any questions on compensation or *ex gratia* payments?

- Did the co-ordinator keep good control, watch the time and end the press conference sensibly?
- Was the press conference panel properly informed on key matters, such as the condition of those in hospital, or compensation levels, and was such information given out?
- Was the team fully involved?
- Was the end of the conference handled properly?
- Were copies available of photographs and/or illustrations, the latest statement and other material?

CHAPTER 13

HANDLING MEDIA TELEPHONE CALLS

The telephone rings. What happens next? How to handle calls successfully is discussed in this chapter. Occidental, operators of the Piper Alpha North Sea platform, handled over 10,000 calls in the first few days of the disaster but more-modestly sized companies, without help, could sink under a significantly smaller number.

Sources of information and fear of journalists

Telephone media responders worry about what can be conveyed to the media and fear that journalists will be aggressive and expect an answer to every question. The golden rule is that any information in the response room, but nothing else, especially based on their own knowledge or experience, can be given out. That avoids the problem of team members "editing" or selecting information, which can lead to significant inconsistencies and thus problems. What can be disseminated is:

- The contents of *press releases*. It may be helpful to underline good and bad points in green and red, respectively.
- Any information on the *white boards*. This will come from the crisis management team and will be conveyed to the responders, via the boards, by the telephone media response team co-ordinator. Similarly, answers to questions received by the team and passed on to the management team for a reply, by the co-ordinator, will be written on the white boards. These should be large enough to allow the board writer to include new information without obscuring the responders' views. Boards may have sections headed, for example, incident details, people, weather, plan of action, resources/on way/at site.

- Any data contained in the Fact File, **except anything that the co-ordinator says can only be given to the media if they ask for such information**

- Any other material given to the team by the co-ordinator: information available to any member of the team, through background knowledge or experience **MUST NOT** be divulged unless it has been authorised for release, in advance, by the co-ordinator and conveyed to the entire team either on the white boards or via a separate statement.

- Any company material, such as annual reports and brochures, can be used providing that their use has been authorised on an individual basis. The reason for this "reluctance", although the material is widely available, is that it might offer the media some more ammunition.

- Any information given out by senior personnel during radio and television interviews and at press conferences, providing that it has been cleared, in advance, for dissemination by the co-ordinator and passed to the team either via the white boards or a separate statement. Journalists will have seen or heard these broadcasts and the team members must be familiar with what was said. If any errors were made, the team must be advised on how to make corrections during their phone conversations.

The co-ordinator should see or hear any interviews, preferably when they are live. The company must monitor all coverage on the main channels and the co-ordinator must determine whether any part of the interviews will encourage additional media interest on the phone and then ponder how such pressure can be met. A careless remark, for example, should be met by a brief statement, explaining or apologising, which should be given to the telephone media response team for reading to the journalists, whether or not they raise the topic. If they do not ask, it does not necessarily mean that they will ignore what they heard.

The response team's room must not be "contaminated" by any news or speculation that cannot be revealed. The overheard comment that *this guy says that ten people have been killed, can I tell him that it's really 20?* is impossible in properly-organised companies because the responder will only know what can be released, whatever the figure is.

Only the telephone media response team co-ordinator can visit the main crisis control room from which confirmed information is made available for use by the telephone media response team. He might discuss news with the main public affairs expert or a senior executive if the company lacks a PR person or outside consultant. Together, they will decide what information can be released, and in what form, and then the co-ordinator will convey that to his team, either through a written comment or on the white boards.

The only exception to this rule on securing new information is that a runner may be despatched, but only by the co-ordinator, to another part of the building or crisis centre but that person is strictly a messenger and does only as bidden. Some companies allow response team members to drift into the main crisis management room, to find out a key fact, so that they can deal with a particular question. This leads to inconsistencies and the possibility that unauthorised information is released. It also means that telephones in the response room will not be answered whilst the team member is away. To achieve the relative peace that the responders must have, entry to their room should be strictly controlled as should access to the office occupied by the crisis management team.

Are the media rude and hostile to business on the phone?

Many telephone responders, never having spoken to journalists, are nervous and expect the journalist to be hostile, impatient and rude. Response team members do not experience such behaviour in day-to-day life so do not know how to react. This concern is misplaced. Many individuals' perception of journalists is probably based on their recollection of seeing loquacious politicians being questioned in persistent fashion by famous journalists determined to excavate answers to their legitimate questions. Such interviews are totally different to those that take place, over the phone, between less exalted journalists and a company's telephone responders.

Some journalists are naturally aggressive or rude and, because of an imminent deadline, they may be direct, especially if they feel that a company is being negative, evasive or patronising. However, during emergencies, the evidence suggests that they are understanding and, even in major disasters, the number of hostile calls is usually minimal. In an emergency, journalists will waste neither their time nor energy being angry with a company employee who, for whatever reason, cannot help: haunted by imminent deadlines, they will turn to other sources. Journalists are under enormous pressure to write stories speedily which induces a sense of urgency, persistence and, possibly, panic so they may be more direct and press harder than people in routine business. Some spokespersons, unaccustomed to journalists' deadlines, resent having to edit their own comments and tend to waffle, which irritates scribes who must write x hundred words in a few minutes.

Many journalists are thought to be hostile to business. Of course, a minority is and, in an accident, some will maintain that large companies should be able to cope with both the emergency and the media simultaneously. Unfortunately, a company's stance towards the media is often set by a senior executive who considers that, once before, he was badly treated. Industry often neglects to "educate" the media on what it does and how it does it but then condemns journalists for failing to understand complex points in a few minutes.

Some organisations foolishly try to manipulate the media who might then adopt a more aggressive approach to the company. Another cause of friction, and thus the perception that journalists are hostile, is prompted by irritated executives unaccustomed to direct but legitimate questions like "how do you justify that?" Some companies, reasonably, are angered by the media's early efforts to find out why an accident occurred. In particular, some Sunday or weekly papers, seeking a new angle, and reluctant to await the official enquiry, are prone to trumpeting premature conclusions.

Distrust of the media and sustained stress can provoke bizarre answers to routine questions. *Three people died, but let's put that into perspective. More than that are killed on the roads each day.* Sometimes a responder, irritated by persistent questioning, confuses this with rudeness and reacts aggressively. A trained and competent telephone media response team need not fear the media: the company wishes to disseminate key messages and information and the media, able to assist in this, needs help and answers to its questions. This is best achieved in a friendly but professional conversation, free of any preconceived views.

The need for consistency and logic

The telephone media response team, ideally helped by a co-ordinator and technical adviser, will have access to a limited number of sources of information. Only data from these sources can be used so consistency in the dissemination of information is achieved. There is also a problem of logic. A responder conceded that a helipad on an offshore installation was on fire, presumably because it was confirmed on the white boards, whilst the next responder speculated that the evacuation would be carried out via the same helipad! If inconsistencies are exposed, the media can portray the company as incompetent and it is then but a short step to suggesting that the group is so badly organised that it may have been responsible for the accident. That may be absurd but this book deals with reality and the media's perceptions, right or wrong.

Some team members may have detailed and personal knowledge that could be relevant. In the same way that team members must never reveal their "usual" job, see below, they must not draw on their specialised knowledge. Such information must never be issued without the prior agreement of the team's co-ordinator, even if it seems harmless. For example, what happens if a responder is asked if the blazing factory is close to a village, and, if so, what is the name of the village?" Assume that this information is not in the Fact File and that the journalist could find out but the spokesperson, keen to assist, happens to know the answer from personal experience. Whilst asking the journalist to hold on, and having ensured that the mute button on the phone has been depressed, the correct procedure is to obtain approval for the release of such information from the co-ordinator. In this instance, as the journalist could find out from other sources, there should be no problem. The data should then be written on the white board, to ensure consistency of information.

Very little information would be released like this because even the co-ordinator may be unaware of its significance and may have to seek guidance from the public affairs specialist in the main management team. What seems an innocent and harmless fact can be a major embarrassment to the crisis management team. Assume that a fire has broken out on a cargo vessel and that a responder has been asked what the cargo is. The necessary information is not included in the manual nor is it on the white boards but the responder, through his "day" job knows. Embarrassed at having to profess ignorance, he blurts out the answer to a very persistent journalist. Immediately, there is yet another crisis. The company crisis management team, fully aware of the nature of the cargo, have deliberately maintained silence on the topic whilst they seek additional informed comment from specialists on how to cope with the product if it escapes into the water, or affects human beings. Now, the company has lost its bid to buy a little time to decide how best to minimise the impact of any leak and seems ill-informed on how to cope. This is worse than professing to be ignorant, for a short time only, on what its own vessel was carrying.

Telephone responders soon realise that the types of questions that non-specialist journalists will pose, at least initially, are precisely those that they themselves would want answered if they were watching the emergency unfold on television. Indeed, subject to the evolution of the incident, some of the questions asked on the telephone could be put during a press conference or a television interview. Furthermore, many of the journalists will ask the same questions so the team's confidence grows. Another encouraging factor, for even the most nervous of responders, is that, because many questions are predictable, advisers can devise answers in advance, which gives confidence to the telephone team and shows the media that the company is competent and co-operative. This helps the organisation to convey its views and to deny some space and air time to its critics.

The media's changing perspective

The pace and character of media enquiries changes during an emergency. Initially, the quest is for relevant information on the incident itself. Questions will be the conventional ones of where, when, why, to whom and what? This is difficult for media responders as relevant information will be sparse. Appropriate background information must be offered which shows that the company is prepared and anxious to help, thus, hopefully, encouraging the journalist to ring again. This is followed by a period in which the emphasis shifts towards a more detailed investigation into the human aspects of the emergency. Additionally, "experts" are asked for their reaction, why the accident occurred and what they think about the company. The organisation must monitor these outside comments lest it needs to rebut any allegations but care must be taken to ensure that its observations do not merely draw attention to ill-informed remarks that otherwise would have been ignored. Occasionally, sleeping dogs should be allowed to slumber.

Journalists will now also be asking responders detailed questions about the company, especially if it is relatively unknown or foreign, has an indifferent safety record or is notoriously negative towards the media. If an organisation has shown itself to have treated next of kin badly or has appeared to be callous or complacent, the media will dig more deeply. Former and possibly embittered employees sometimes take the initiative and speak to newspapers and broadcasters. *I warned them that this would happen.* Finally, the emphasis switches to determining who was responsible for the accident and whether resignations or dismissals of the guilty are imminent. The company must not comment.

The lapse between the beginning of the incident and the quest to find out who was responsible for the emergency can be very speedy. For an accident at a remote location, it can be about 12 hours, but for rail crashes it may be significantly less. Given technological advances and increased media competition, the period will become increasingly compressed. Another feature of onshore incidents is that the "man in the street" is now encouraged by the main broadcasting stations to submit photographs and video footage for immediate broadcasting. Thus professional journalists may know more about the incident than the company.

The pressure on telephone media response teams fluctuates during the day. Massive initial demands for information may then slacken, relatively, whilst stories are produced. Then the numbers of enquiries picks up again, as journalists seek to collect more information. That said, the interest of overseas media, in different time zones, and more local radio and television stations, with regular deadlines, 24 hours a day, ensure that responders have few idle moments. This round-the-clock coverage poses another problem. Responders may be asked for a quick and immediate summary of all that has happened and, for someone who has been working for some hours, that can be a challenge.

ANSWERING THE PHONE

The telephone rings. What happens next?

The introduction

The responder answers with the agreed introduction. It might be *press centre*. Announcing the name of the company, if the call was routed via the switchboard, is unnecessary. If the calls are coming in direct, after the media response telephone numbers have been released, some companies require their name to be mentioned in the immediate response. Some also require their responders to answer with a very long introduction which irks the media and, foolishly concedes that there is a crisis. Possibly, the team may have been summoned to deal with any media enquiries relating to a minor incident which seems unlikely to develop but the company prefers, sensibly, to over rather than to under-react. For example: *This is Bloggs International crisis media management response team, Joe Brown speaking, how may I help you?* The more sensible reply might be *Joe Brown, media response team.* Why start by admitting a crisis is afoot?

Who is calling and who is responding?

If the caller does not immediately offer his name and affiliation, it should be sought and written down on the log sheet which is a modest record on which the responder should note such details and, very briefly, the nature of the questioning. Apart from providing the company with a list of callers, the system enables the organisation to ensure that all those who showed interest are told of any press conferences. Also, if a senior executive is about to undertake a radio or television interview, a glance at the log sheets will show the main topics of media interest and whether any serious allegations must be answered. Such information also assists in the writing of the press releases.

The journalist will ask the name of the responder unless it was offered when the phone call was answered. Some responders are reluctant to divulge this, fearing that their name will appear in the media. Unlike executives, the responders will not be named because that does not enhance a story. If a journalist includes a comment from a senior executive, it implies that he has the stature to be given an interview by the company at a crucial stage, which reflects well on the publication and on the journalist. Quoting a company spokesperson effectively admits that nobody more senior was prepared to talk to the journalist.

I'd like to do a broadcast interview down the line

Some responders fear that they will be asked for broadcast interviews. This is outside their remit. If invited, they should note the caller's name, telephone number, nature of request, programme and deadline by which an answer is required and pass it to the co-ordinator for attention.

What do you do when you're not involved in an emergency?

A candid answer will create problems. If, for example, a responder, dealing with an aircraft accident, admitted that he was a pilot, subsequent questions would inevitably cause difficulties. Equally, if the responder confesses to being a company chauffeur, that immediately detracts, however unfairly, from the information that is being offered, because all responders have the same information. So, if the telephone conversation develops in this way, the correct answer is *I'm a member of the telephone media response team: how can I help you?* If the questioning persists, the journalist should be told, politely, that if he does not wish to ask questions about the incident, the call will be terminated, as there are many other members of the media anxious to secure information.

How many of you are there, answering the phones?

The journalist may comment that there seems to be many people talking in the press room, so the emergency must be serious, and just how many are answering the phones? Such observations must be met with a firm assurance that company policy is to have too many, rather than too few people to help the media. The number of responders must never be given.

What information do you have?

The initial quest for information, which will be very scarce immediately after an emergency occurs, poses problems for the organisation and the media. Frustration may be very evident but, however inadequate responders feel at this stage, they must not agree with any criticisms from the media. The media response team member should offer all that is available on the incident, especially the holding statement or press release 1, and anything relevant from the Fact File. Indeed, throughout the emergency, journalists should be asked if they have the most recent press release. If the answer is no, it should be read out over the phone and responders should offer to dictate it verbatim but not too quickly, as few journalists have shorthand skills. It is wise to repeat any figures, so that there is no misunderstanding.

Reverting to the early stages of an incident, the responder should enquire whether the caller would like some additional background information on the company. This allows the company to take the initiative in selecting some favourable facts, but the chance was once lost when a spokesperson said that *the company was established about 100 years ago in a little village, just south of...* Responders should not ask *what information would you like?* This is an opportunity for the company to convey what it wants to offer: it also prevents the journalist, at least for a few moments, from asking a different question. This pre-supposes, of course, that the media team has adequate data available in the Fact File.

If all this enables the journalist to write an early, factual story, the company will earn respect for trying to fill the void and increases the prospects that journalists will return for more information. The organisation, by being prepared, is able to influence the flow of information, although, naturally, the journalist will still seek out other sources. At this early stage, journalists may know more than the company about the incident, or more than the company is prepared to concede publicly. Consequently, the media response team must be careful in refuting any stories: they may be true.

Ringing off

Responders should only ring off when no more information can be given or when the journalist insists on repeating the same questions or asking patently irrelevant questions. Even then, the caller should be warned politely, twice, that this is going to happen, as others are trying to reach the media team for information.

Using the press release

Few of the journalists ringing for information will know much about the industry or the company involved so the response team should be prepared to deal with some basic questions, especially on details or jargon contained in the press release. Responders must understand all the terms and facts contained in the press release, and how to convert any figures into different units, so that they can explain them to the media. If uncertain on the meaning of any word or phrase, they must seek advice from the co-ordinator before reading the release to the media.

The need to keep calm under pressure

Telephone media response team members must not lose their tempers because the media will always win a row. Some journalists, especially broadcasters, and frequently confronted by an immediate deadline, will be more insistent than those whose deadlines are more distant. Media responders must always appear calm, helpful and sensitive. They must not cut off the caller if the questions become difficult, nor must they fight the media or talk down to them. Equally, if they do lose their patience, they must ensure that they or their colleagues are not overheard. Mute buttons on telephones must be activated. *I've got a real *** on the line here.* Tact, diplomacy and care are essential qualities. How the company will be perceived by the outside world, through the media, will be determined by what it does to alleviate the problems and how it feels about the accident. Explanations are important and sometimes the words do not emerge as intended. *Accidents will always happen.*

When a series of difficult questions are put in rapid sequence, the responder, under severe pressure, can become repetitive. *How do you feel about the deaths of the three children? Can you hold on, whilst I find out?* Individuals often fall into the trap of saying that they will check everything. As teams become tired, they are increasingly vulnerable to excessive and undesirable candour so the co-ordinator must watch for signs of fatigue and replace the individual before any damage can be done.

Showing regret

Without even hinting at an admission of responsibility, responders must show regret at what has happened, and towards all the people involved. In this context, the words "only" or "just" can be very damaging. An executive, under pressure, said that *only five people have been killed*. In the context of those at risk, that might have been a small percentage but the apparently callous nature of the remark incensed the media. Many responders, keen to observe the rules that all that they say must be based on the Fact File, press releases and the white boards, reply, honestly, that they have no relevant information when asked how the company feels about many deaths! This is one occasion when it is legitimate to devise a sensible comment.

Knowledge is rather important!

Emergencies will not disappear, whatever the verbal skills of the media teams: the most that can be done is to improve a bad situation. Ultimately, knowledge is important for, without it, communication is empty. *We have no information whatsoever. There are seven of us here and none of us has been briefed.* The media response team must know some basic details of the company, emergency procedures and the location at which the emergency occurred. *What is happening at the scene of the incident now? Emergency procedures are being implemented and all that can be done is being done. What does that mean in plain English? I don't know.*

Responders must know about topics such as site evacuation, company and local authority fire-fighting and medical services. It is common practice, in many industries, to evacuate non-essential personnel. On being asked this, one media responder, showing admirable loyalty to his company, retorted angrily that all their people were essential.

The team must have up-to-date information and much will depend on the abilities of the co-ordinator to discover the latest news from his crisis management team and to brief his colleagues. Even when progress is slow, total candour must be avoided and team members must bridge to what they have, even if it means making some key points again. Finally, responders must know something about the financial implications of an incident and how to deal with the issue tactfully, bearing in mind that people and the environment come before any financial considerations. This was written after a hypothetical marine accident: *Company and insurance group spokesmen declined to comment on the extent of the insurance cover. This has worried environmental groups which have already claimed that the damage will be substantial. The company's silence on this crucial issue has increased market fears that the final bill may not be fully covered by insurance and shares dipped in early trading, pending a more positive statement from the company.*

The dangers of speculation and vague words

There will be great pressure on responders to speculate on the cause of the accident, possible developments and repercussions. After some hours of sustained questioning and, possibly frustrated by the slow internal flow of information, tiring responders may agree with a journalist's logic on what might happen next. *There could be more fires and explosions.* Another form of speculation, which carries its own penalties, is the view that all will soon be restored to normality. It seldom is! Speculating, especially on the cause of the accident, could lead to insurance and legal problems, and thus financial difficulties, apart from effectively pre-empting the results of the enquiry. Additionally, if the cause of the accident is something more fundamental than the speculation, the company could be accused of trying to conceal the real causes. Responders should also ignore any hypothetical questions.

Words like "assume", "think" "expect", "suppose", "imagine" and "believe" should be suffocated before utterance to reduce the risks of speculation. "Hope" is a useful word. *Bearing in mind that the missing men have been in the sea for four hours, do you expect to find them alive? I must assume that they are dead* is much worse than *we certainly shall not give up hope and that is why we are continuing with the search.*

Misguided humour

Although humour allows telephone media responders to release nervous tension, it is unwise to indulge it with journalists some of whom may not share the responder's sense of humour or may feel that it is inappropriate. Similarly, if a mute button is not pressed, the journalists may hear laughter and there might be scathing reference to this in an article or broadcast, casting great doubts on the company's humanity and professionalism. *What is your position in the company? I'm sitting down.* A story, written after an exercise, contained this accidental humour. *However, the water utility, one hour after the first sign of flooding appeared, was still unable to confirm that the disaster had been caused by a burst water main. A spokesman, declining to comment on any alternative explanation of the flood, said that water supplies had not been turned off as "we're in the business of supplying water".*

Other techniques

Sometimes, a caller might invent some "facts" hoping to hear a refutation of a detail, implying that the rest of the story is true. A response to this kind of question, which includes a "comment", should be along the following lines. *I cannot comment on the story that you have told me because I myself do not have the information. All that I can confirm is what I have already given you. I hope to have more information soon and we'll be happy to give it to you then.* The responder is effectively distancing himself from the company in saying *I myself do not have the information.* This tactic is a safeguard and can be used, with suitable discretion, on other occasions. For example, if the condition of the injured is not known in the press office, despite many attempts to find out, the responder could say that *at the moment, I'm sorry that I don't have any news beyond what I gave you but the injured, I'm pleased to say, are all receiving the best possible attention in hospital and I know that my colleagues are there with family and friends.* (Assuming that this is true!)

Many responders merely wait to be asked a specific question and then try to answer. During the conversation, which is not like a tennis match, with the questions and answers bouncing back in turn, the spokesperson should volunteer information that could be helpful to the journalist, whilst simultaneously making a strong point for the company, even if that were not the direct answer to the question. Examples of bridging are given in chapter 17.

Journalists will not necessarily know enough to ask all the questions that would either enhance their story or the company's case. Many know little about the sector and will welcome sensible advice. Consequently, the telephone responder should offer carefully-chosen but authorised background information whenever possible. If the journalist does not want such information, it will soon become apparent when there is an interruption and another question is posed.

If a journalist, oddly, fails to ask about injuries or fatalities, the information, assuming that its release has been authorised, must be given out. A failure to do so might suggest that the company was seeking to hide the information and, inevitably, the news will soon emerge from other sources. The inadequate journalist will then blame the company and relationships suffer. Within the context of the incident, the legal and insurance implications and the availability of information cleared for dissemination for the media, the golden rule is to tell the truth as fast as possible. Companies should lead with bad news and not wait for the media to either find out what they will discover anyway, or attempt to hide it in a welter of facts and figures.

During conversations, journalists may use phrases or words that are either misleading or incorrect. In such instances, the responder must interrupt with a firm rebuttal. For example, a marine accident might be compared to the *Titanic* and a small fire to the massive blaze at the Buncefield oil depot in Hertfordshire. Assuming that these comparisons are unjustified, such language must be rejected instantly, even before the journalist has stopped talking. It is easy to forget the main erroneous comparison by the time that the journalist has finished. Equally, any incorrect and damaging statements about the company must be refuted immediately. An uncorrected comment may be assumed to be right.

On the record

Responders should assume that everything said could appear in print or on the air and must never speak "off the record". Knowing when to do this, and with whom, must be left to professional media personnel. This approach helps to ensure self-discipline. What may prove more difficult to resist is the temptation to reveal something unauthorised, or a personal comment, to a persistent but friendly and patient member of the media. Saying, for example, *Frankly, off the record, I believe that the managing director has personally ordered a cut in the maintenance budget at the plant* does not mean that such information will be discarded by the media!

Defend the company, don't blame others and ignore claims that if only...

Responders may, effectively, be asked to defend the entire industry's safety record. Any such questions should be referred to the appropriate trade association: the responders' duty is to represent their employer and to use space and "air time" to the greatest benefit for the company. The company and individuals must always be defended. Even if there is a lurking suspicion of the cause of the incident, it must not be revealed. It is extremely unlikely that all the facts can be known, at an early stage, and discussing possible causes could have legal and insurance implications. In many countries, any incident has to be followed by an official and public enquiry and any premature comment from the company, publicised in the media, would be very damaging and extremely unprofessional.

Equally, any temptation to blame others for the accident or to suggest that if other groups, such as the coastguard or fire service, had reacted more speedily, should never be voiced. Such allegations merely provide the media with another angle to the story and this means that coverage will be sustained for longer.

Other organisations may tell the media that if their offer of facilities had been taken up, the accident might not have occurred or its repercussions would have been less severe. Such commercial opportunists surface occasionally and the temptation to comment should be resisted. If the company rejects the claim, the story might be sustained by a relatively ignorant press, convinced that lives could have been saved, whilst if the company admits that the concept should have been adopted, the same outcome might be achieved. A simple response could be that the organisation will consider any sensible suggestions for improved safety that might be implemented in the future but that, at present, it is too busy, dealing with the emergency. It is also possible, of course, that the company has already received and rejected any outside group's suggestion but the telephone media response team member will not know that.

The safety record

During an emergency, there will always be questions on the company's safety record. Information must be made available in advance, in the responder's Fact File, because the journalist, having looked at his "clippings" file, may be well-informed on this subject. Accidents tend to be reported so they often constitute a significant part of a journalist's "file" on a company. Defenders of the company must have supporting information for their assertion that the group enjoys an excellent safety record. *How many incidents have you had and have there been any injuries over the last ten years at the factory? We had an admirable safety record, until earlier today when we had the two big explosions.* Equally, even if the company spokesman has no detailed and authorised information available, any suggestion that safety work has been skimped, which might well violate the law, must be rejected firmly. Avoid this truthful but dangerous response: *I can't deny that safety has been downgraded to save money because I haven't any relevant information!*

Calling back, media kits, language and tone

Ideally, responders should never promise to ring back, as pressure will prevent it. This should be explained to the journalist, but any promise to return a call must be honoured. If the caller says that he will ask for the same responder next time, it should be explained that the phones are ringing frequently, and that anyone can help, as all team members have the same information. When appropriate, journalists should be offered media kits, consisting of the latest press release, background information on the company, the location of the incident and key personnel in the group. For television stations, relevant library film footage should be offered and it is becoming increasingly popular for companies to distribute video or DVD footage. Modern footage of a plant before the accident is ideal but old pics or footage should be avoided as this suggests that no modernisation has taken place for years.

Language and tone are important. Compare, for example, the implications of *I can't tell you that* with *I'm sorry, but I have given you all the information I have on that subject at present.* All technical jargon should be excised. If it is used, especially in a press statement, the responder must be able to explain it in day-to-day language. Similarly, all corporate speak must be banished. Frequently, journalists are assured that *corporate emergency plans have been activated* but responders are then unable to explain what this means in practical language.

Other serious questions

One new common question relating to the cause of some accidents is *you say that you don't know why the accident happened, so, logically, you can't rule out terrorism.* If an organisation does not deal with this question adequately, newspapers will use headlines like "terrorism suspected in factory blast". If a subsequent enquiry showed that poor maintenance was the cause of the problem, it could look as if the organisation was trying to hide its inadequacies. The problem is that terrorism cannot be ruled out so, logically, the prospect cannot be dismissed. A possible response might be *we do not know the cause of the accident but we have no reason, at present, to believe that it was caused by terrorist activity.*

Media responders will receive many different types of question, ranging from why the accident occurred, to compensation. Chapter 17 discusses many of these and offers some possible answers that might be offered by all company personnel confronted by the media. What follows is a simple summary of some of the key points and the list can form the basis of an assessment of the team members' performance after an exercise.

RESPONDING TO MEDIA CALLS IN AN EMERGENCY

What you must do before the phone rings:

- Establish the basic rules of response with the team leader and what phrase responders will use when answering each call
- Understand that it is your responsibility to answer the phone promptly and to pass calls on to the co-ordinator, or to seek his advice, only when really necessary
- Ensure that you have a copy of the Fact File, the first holding statement or press release and that you can see the white boards clearly
- Ensure that you genuinely understand what is written on the boards and in any releases
- Make sure that you realise that you can only use the Fact File, press releases, information from the white board and anything else authorised by the co-ordinator
- Be familiar with the company's emergency procedures and background details etc and know how to use the Fact File to maximum advantage

- Learn, from your co-ordinator, what the key messages from the company are and that you know how to convey them effectively

The phone rings...

- Pick up and answer the phone promptly, establish the identity and affiliation of the caller and fill in a log sheet
- Give your name and, if asked your role, say that you are a member of the telephone media response team
- Ascertain that the caller has the latest release and, if not, offer to dictate it or email it or point out that it is on the company's website
- Fill the initial void by offering background information on the company etc. from Fast Facts

The information to be disseminated

- Assume that everything you say will be printed or broadcast
- Give out official information only: disregard your own knowledge
- Refer overall industry questions to appropriate bodies
- Always give information that you do have, especially from the white board
- Assume that the journalist knows little about your industry, unless their affiliation indicates otherwise, so, explain tactfully what is necessary to ensure full understanding of the incident and the measures being take to minimise the repercussions
- Provide advice on details of press conferences if planned.

Style and tone

- Express regret at any loss of life or injuries or damage to the environment
- Always try to sound helpful, be calm and sympathetic
- Always defend colleagues and company
- Use non-technical language
- Ask media deadlines if relevant and show understanding of journalists' pressures

- Offer to make media kit or contemporary video footage available for media representative to collect

Techniques

- Make full use of all available information, especially from the Fact File and press releases
- Ensure you understand the question: if not, ask the journalist to repeat it or explain
- Outline the company's plan of action, even if not asked specifically
- Try to convey key messages more than once
- List positive initiatives or action taken by the company
- Create opportunities to convey key message by bridging *what's important to us now...*
- Know how to deal with the terrorist question
- Ensure that the question is relevant to your company: if not, see if you have the knowledge and authority to pass on the details of the third party
- Encourage callers to ring back as more information will be coming in
- Bridge, sensibly, from what you cannot say to what you can and want to say. It is not obligatory merely to answer questions and you can add comments to your answers which convey more positive information about the company
- If necessary, explain why you cannot give an answer
- Hold a caller, use the mute button and seek assistance when necessary
- Ensure that you know what you are talking about: do not be discredited by admitting ignorance on, for example, something that you have read over to the journalist from the white board
- Explain why, if you have to terminate a call, you are doing it
- Ensure that the journalists cannot hear any private conversation
- Know how to convey statistics sensibly from one unit into another
- Be able to summarise key points briefly for journalists with early deadlines
- Reject false analogies, colourful and exaggerated language, inaccurate premises, misleading or detrimental comments

- Refute serious allegations if possible, ask callers for source and inform the co-ordinator
- If in difficulties, refer to the co-ordinator
- Ring back if you promised to but do not promise often as the phone will seldom stop ringing
- Accept that some questions will be irrelevant or may even sound silly but do not condemn the journalist
- Be aware of what has been said by the company during radio and television interviews
- Press for more information from co-ordinator if necessary
- Explain to all callers that all team members have the same information

What you must NOT do when the phone rings...

- Refuse to give your own name or fail to ask a caller for their name and affiliation
- Reveal your job title, introduce yourself as a member of a crisis response team or say how many responders in the team
- Announce yourself with a long, time-consuming introduction
- Allow yourself to become involved in a long session in which the journalist fails to ask a question about the incident, opting instead to question your credentials

The information to be disseminated

- Use information that does not come from approved sources
- Use your own knowledge unless it is incorporated in official sources
- Give out unofficial information
- Miss the chance to use positive information because a relevant question has not been asked
- Withhold readily available information
- Give out information "off the record" or say, *between you and me*
- Speculate, respond to hypothetical questions or make "intelligent" guesses

- Offer to transfer media in-house specialists: instead, take details of enquiry and say that you will try to secure an answer. Transferring callers means that inconsistency of information occurs and control is lost and that a potentially key member of the crisis management team is forced to take an unnecessary call

- Discuss compensation

- Fail to express regret for any accident involving people or the environment

- Give your own opinion, however flattering the request may be. *You've been with the company for some years, I imagine, as you sound so knowledgeable, so I would really appreciate your advice on ...*

- Answer any questions of which you are unsure-check first with co-ordinator

- Comment on another company's business

- Say *I can't tell you that, for obvious reasons* and then prove unable to explain them

Style and tone

- Be trapped into defending the whole industry or blaming others for the incident

- Do not give an interview down the line

- Say "we have nothing to tell you"

- Use phrases like *at this moment in time* and vague words, like "think", "believe", "imagine", "assume" etc. which are close to speculation

- Use jargon or resort to corporate speak

- Imitate a politician by not answering the question or by defending the company against a charge that has not been made

- Boast: *our well-planned emergency procedures, a credit to the company, are working brilliantly*

- Lose your temper, ring off abruptly or say *no comment,* or admit that you're only a media responder

- Suggest that the journalists' questions are irrelevant, stupid or insensitive or that they are "asking the wrong question". There are no stupid questions, only stupid answers
- Be insensitive: *There will always be accidents in the manufacturing sector but government knows that business has to continue and that we do all we can to minimise the dangers*
- Be unhelpful: *you have an atlas, look it up yourself*
- Seem too cheerful, hailing comments as "brilliant" or "great"
- Appear anxious to terminate the call, especially in the early stages of an emergency, when there is little information on the incident itself or even say *I have nothing to tell you*, even before the first question has been posed
- Criticise journalists for their lack of knowledge: they might be testing you!

Techniques

- Miss the opportunity to give positive information, especially if the question has not been asked
- Spend too long on one call, especially one that is not progressing or one in which all the available information has been given
- Downplay an incident unjustifiably: *this accident is a fairly routine incident*
- Say that you cannot answer a question because it is technical or relates to operational or financial matters. If necessary, offer to find a reply for the next time that the journalist rings or explain why at present, an answer cannot be given
- Fail to explain some of the operational difficulties, such as shutting down a factory
- Lose the chance to explain the plan of action
- Promise to ring back
- Agree with journalists who offer suggestions or make criticisms
- Rush to expose any company problems, even if included in the three main sources of available information, unless the journalist asks
- Agree with a journalist's speculation, however plausible

- Discriminate against parts of the media: *you're a Sunday, you can afford to wait* or *you're a local, you're not so important*
- Say *that is all I have, so you'll have to ring off now*
- Ask whether the journalist has any more questions, as the answer will always be yes and no other calls will be dealt with
- Say, *I hope that answers your question,* as the journalist will then use that as an invitation to continue putting questions, with diminishing returns for the company, as other media people anxiously wait to speak to the responder
- Give the media their headlines: especially by agreeing with a journalist *we are fighting to avoid a catastrophe* and do not repeat a journalist's emotive word such as "baffled". The headline the following day will be "company admits, 'we're baffled'"
- Allow your private conversations to be overheard by the journalists
- Exude optimism unless advised by co-ordinator: you do not have an opinion. Avoid *there's no chance of pollution*
- Terminate conversations merely because the questions are difficult or pass too many difficult calls to the co-ordinator
- Make promises on behalf of the company that cannot be kept
- Refrain from answering because the question *can be answered at the forthcoming press conference.* The journalist may not be able to attend or may want a more prompt answer.

The flow of information and general responses

The team's effectiveness will depend not just on the skill of its members but also on the availability and flow of information. Incompetence in the crisis management team room can deny information to the media responders for transmission to the outside world. Here are some questions relating to the organisation and flow of information at the beginning of the incident and these, too, can be used to monitor performance during an exercise.

- Was the switchboard organised, did the operator know how to deal with calls before the media response room was set up and how to transfer calls when the team was assembled? Was the operator briefed on the importance of not putting media calls through to senior management personnel? Were early waiting callers treated to some inappropriately jolly music or did they have to listen to an answer machine or security person?

- Was the call-out system used effectively, were there any problems for the team in gaining access to the building? How quickly was the room set up, was the checklist followed, and was all the necessary equipment available? Were the phones tested?

- Did all team members know what was required of them at this stage and were they properly and promptly briefed?

- When the team was functioning, how quickly was information passed from management to the responders and then to the media? How quickly were answers to crucial questions, passed by the media responders to the management team, dealt with? How effective was the link person between the media response room and the crisis management team room? Did the management team regard the provision of information to the response team as a serious part of their duties?

- Was the necessary level of technical expertise available to the media responders, especially if the emergency developed unexpectedly or if it had lasted for a long time?

- Were all the roles clearly defined, so there was no uncertainty on responsibilities and delay in setting up the media response room? Were there sufficient extra support staff to assist in emailing etc if required? Were runners available to pick up message sheets or to undertake any other duty requested by the media response team co-ordinator and were they efficient?

- Did the telephone media response team co-ordinator have all the personnel, information and equipment needed?

- Was there sufficient space for all responders to work effectively, could they all see the board clearly? Was there sufficient space for the next team to sit and follow developments before they took over?

- Were the white boards, showing the latest information, effective? Were the colours difficult to read, was the writing too small or were the boards so small that they could not be read from the other side of the room? Did some specific topic boards remain bare, either because nobody had asked for data or the co-ordinator did not feel that such information was relevant? Was there a system to highlight new data on the white boards? Were entries on the white boards timed and was some original information crossed out and a new figure inserted?

- Was there excessive noise, too many people, too much movement in the room?
- Did the co-ordinator of the telephone media response team react to whoever shouted most loudly?
- Was the co-ordinator supine in pressing for information from the crisis control room so responders had no details to pass to media?

General responses

- Were any essential actions overlooked?
- Did the company act promptly to combat any particularly serious allegations?
- Were any major deficiencies in the systems apparent and was management properly informed?
- Were any affiliates advised of the emergency to enable them to react to local media enquiries?
- If more than one office was involved, was the co-ordination good?

CHAPTER 14

IN FRONT OF THE CAMERA AND MICROPHONE

This chapter discusses the physical aspects of a television interview and how to deal with many of the worries that can assail an interviewee. Representatives of small organisations, in particular, unable to finance a public affairs team, can secure a big advantage from a successful broadcast appearance. Some of the comments that do not relate to visual aspects are also relevant to all media questions during telephone conversations, radio interviews and press conferences.

A full understanding of the techniques should increase the interviewee's confidence, crucial for any successful interview. The interviewee is the expert but the interviewer could have more information than expected because researchers can contact other specialists. In the UK, the majority of people glean most of their news from television so the interview is an excellent opportunity to create a good impression. Surveys suggest that words and vocal elements contribute about 45 per cent of the emotional interest generated by an interview, whilst body language, including facial expressions, accounts for the remaining 55 per cent. When two US politicians participated in a debate, broadcast on television and on radio, audiences differed on who won, depending on whether they had seen or just heard the candidates.

An interviewee must seek to convey what he or his employers want to pass on to the different publics which constitute the audience. The purpose of what follows it to reduce the anxieties and potential distractions for the representative who may be facing the biggest challenge of his career and who has the power to influence the corporation's future.

BODY LANGUAGE

How to sit

Usually, the first picture that the viewer sees is of a sedentary interviewee and this influences the audience's perception. Formal standing interviews, relatively rare, will, like most sitting interviews, only reveal a head and shoulders picture. Lounging back or forwards in a chair suggests, respectively, disinterest or aggression. Moving around in a swivel chair distracts the viewer who ignores the words. Ideally, the interviewee's best position is to sit towards the back of the chair, but just slightly forward, looking alert but not hostile, and facing the interviewer. Body language must not undermine what is being said. Sitting cross-legged looks casual and can force the individual back in the chair, thus creating an impression of indifference. Having both feet on the ground removes another potential worry and thus, like other points discussed here, allows the interviewee to concentrate on the words.

Use of hands

Hands should not be used to make or emphasise key points as they can distract viewers' attention and a hand waved close to the camera can appear grotesque. However, a hand might be used, advantageously, if an interviewer denies the spokesperson the chance to respond reasonably. With a restraining hand, the spokesperson might say *please, let me finish my answer to your question*. If a producer sees an interviewee wringing his hands, for example, indicating anguish, the camera might reflect the gesture. A politician, explaining why he had resigned, had written "sorry" on his hand to remind him to apologise and this was detected by the camera! Even if the camera does not look at such manual manipulations, the interviewer may deduce that the topic under discussion is difficult for the executive. A tapping foot, too, may remain undetected by the viewer but it can betray the interviewee's nervousness to the presenter with potentially dire consequences for the line of questioning.

Use of the head

In daily life, people often nod to indicate agreement or to suggest that what is being said is being absorbed and will be answered. In a television interview, nodding to indicate that a point will be answered could be construed as indicating agreement with allegations against the company.

That said, if an interviewer is making serious charges against the company, a shake of the head indicates that the interviewee disagrees strongly and this might dissuade the interviewer from adding to the list of accusations. Some interviewers give themselves the last word or provide an unfair summary. A shaking head indicates that the company spokesperson, unjustly denied an opportunity to comment, dissents strongly and, as that is the last picture the viewer sees of the company individual, it is a powerful impression.

Smiling and where to look

Some people smile often whilst speaking. In a television interview, discussing an emergency, even those most prone to this habit are likely to assume a degree of gravitas that excludes smiling, but they should be careful.

Interviewees must never look at the camera, except when the interviewer is at a remote location and questions are received via an earpiece or headphones in a "down the line" interview. The executive should then imagine that the lens is a person because this makes the camera seem less impersonal. In a studio, interviewees must maintain close eye contact with the interviewer which creates some advantages. Speaking direct to a camera can induce interviewees to become pompous and stilted and jargon can dominate responses. As the interviewee is probably in the studio to put a human face on the company, this is undesirable. Using jargon may prompt the interviewer to ask for an explanation and this often derails the train of thought and is most likely to occur just when the executive is gaining in confidence.

Peering into a camera can have another effect on an inexperienced interviewee. Suddenly, the enormity of what is happening reaches the brain and, alarmed by the thought that the words are reaching millions of people and that the individual's performance could influence his and his organisation's future, the brain closes down. When it stutters back into life, the emerging words may fail to make sense. That is an extreme reaction, but the potential for such disasters can be reduced by maintaining eye contact with the journalist. The interview then is transformed from a national event to a reasonable one-to-one discussion between two human beings and the language is more conversational. However, studios are very busy places so the discussion will seldom become so relaxed that the interviewee fails to show the appropriate gravitas.

Few viewers realise what else is happening in the studio. Consider this: an interviewee has just been asked a difficult question which implies that factory inspection procedures have been relaxed, for financial reasons, and a food product has to be recalled because of suspected contamination after three people died. At that moment, a man carrying a monitor drops it on his toes with devastating but laudably silent consequences. If strict eye contact is being maintained with the interviewer, these events will hardly be noticed but if the eyes wander, the viewer, unaware of the counter attractions, will assume that the break in eye contact is prompted by the difficult question.

PRELIMINARIES

In the very beginning

The interviewee should not thank the broadcaster for the opportunity to appear as the broadcasters want the organisation to participate in their programme because they think it will be interesting for their viewers. Similarly, a courteous enquiry about the interviewer's health wastes valuable air time, shows a lack of professionalism and irritates the audience.

What do I call the interviewer?

Occasionally, the interviewee will be told to call the broadcaster by his first name but this is exceptional and the best advice is not to use any names at all. Using the interviewer's first name sounds wrong because few business people would know a television presenter. During the interview, the company representative may be addressed formally, as Mr. Bloggs. If the hapless Bloggs has used the broadcaster's first name, the contrast seems silly.

If a spokesperson is involved in a debate and wishes to comment on a remark made by another participant, he should use that person's first name and surname. Some senior broadcasters might resent any apparent familiarity. There is also the danger that, if the company representative uses the broadcaster's first name, that could lead to injudicious comments like, *John, you and I know that my company, as one of the world's leading pharma-ceuticals groups, does everything it can to protect human life and the environment.* This approach and the corporate boast could rile the inter-viewer, who resents being drawn into one side of the debate. Consequently, his next observation could be *what I and many others know is that your group has been accused of persistent disregard of environmental issues for many years and that today you have offered no evidence that this view is unjustified.* Similarly, interviewers should not be flattered.

What is the first question?

If it is practical, just before the interview begins, the spokesperson may ask what the first question will be. Some interviewers may decline to say, but, as both parties can benefit, most will try to co-operate. An interview which starts with the executive resembling an expiring fish is unlikely to yield sig-nificant information. Interviewers want to open up, not shut up, interviewees. The first question, even if it relates to the chronology of events, should be regarded as a prompt. So, whatever the question, the first response from the company should be to express regret that the accident has occurred, and, if relevant, to say how sorry the organisation is that there have been deaths and injuries or damage to the environment. After that, it is legitimate to reply to the first question. If the interviewee omitted to express regret at the outset and, instead, concentrates on the "what happened, when and where" type of chronological question, the comment on individuals may be made only when the interviewer, later, asks the specific question: this may suggest that the company is callous. Equally, saying sorry at the outset can inhibit an interviewer from being excessively aggressive.

Broadcasters will not reveal all the likely questions in advance as that would destroy spontaneity and deny them the opportunity to follow up any particular answer. No interviewer knows all the questions that will be put: a broad approach might have been devised, based on people, environment and other factors, in that sequence, but many questions could be deter-mined by the answers given.

Some companies believe that interviewers do not listen to answers: many journalists believe that interviewees, judging by their responses, do not hear the questions! Both participants in an interview should listen carefully and the company representative should try to respond to the questions. Some interviewees may criticise the question's relevance and then say what they want to say. This will appear to be an evasive tactic which will irk the interviewer and alienate the viewers.

How long should an answer be?

There is no definitive answer. The response should be "to the interviewee's satisfaction" but that might suggest that one answer could occupy the whole interview, although no interviewer would allow that. An interview is not like a game of tennis when each party has an opportunity, in turn, to return the ball as swiftly as possible. Most live interviews last for around three minutes, during which time the interviewer will expect to pose about six questions. Obviously, the longer the answer, the fewer the questions but that does not mean that the executive can deal with just one question, cheerfully weaving in the three key points unchallenged. A very long answer ensures that the viewer will forget what was said and may feel that it was designed to ensure that no more questions are asked as the company is guilty. However, most interviewers will intervene to clarify some of the facts buried in the verbiage or to ask another question. One test of a successful interview is when a viewer can recall any of the key points but this will not happen if the speaker fails to edit his answers and leaves the interviewer and the audience to determine what is relevant.

An interviewer will not interrupt an informative, well-presented answer which, effectively, provides some of the information that would have been solicited by additional questions: a long, rambling response will provoke an interruption or a new question. There must always be a determined effort to respond to the specific question.

A very short answer permits more questions and the benefits of free air time will be lost as the broadcaster dominates the interview. Additionally, the more questions that are put, the greater the prospects that the interviewer will alight on a difficult topic. Answers should also be full sentences, not phrases, so broadcasters can take good quotes and use them in their entirety. Phrases like "as I said before" should be avoided because, if the interview is recorded, the earlier comment may have been omitted.

Finally, interviewees should be careful when a very brief question is put because it denies them thinking time. The most difficult question is "why?"

TECHNIQUES

Some essential rules: regret, people, environment, and money

The order of priorities to be discussed is always people and environment first and property and other financial matters last. Compensation and *ex gratia* payments, essentially private matters, should not be discussed in public. The company must say, as soon as possible, how sorry it is that deaths and injuries have occurred or that damage to the environment has been sustained.

Bridging and adding points

A crucial skill is the ability to bridge from a negative or neutral point to what the company wants to say, even without an appropriate question. The executive enters the interview with a broad agenda which will incorporate the three basic points. *(See chapter 9)* Equally, the broadcaster will have an idea of the broad theme of the interview. Usually, there will be some overlap between the agendas but the problem arises when the company representative does not receive questions that immediately create the opportunity to make some of his key points.

Some questions are prompts and, whilst interviewees should always try to answer the questions, bridging to key points should be undertaken whenever possible. For example: *I cannot yet comment on the cause of the fire but what I can tell you is that, happily, all our personnel were safely evacuated within minutes thanks to our regular exercises at the site.* Apart from bridging, it is possible to add to the end of an answer. For example, the fact that the local fire service arrived promptly could be added to a response on whether the fire had been extinguished. *The fire is not yet out but the local service was on site in minutes and we're hopeful that it will be brought under control shortly.* Successful television interviews are not always secured by just answering questions as posed.

What if fatalities have occurred but this is the first time that such a tragedy has occurred? Boasting of a safety record that prevailed until yesterday invites the retort that this is now irrelevant and it could also sound callous. Having expressed regret at the loss of life, the company spokesman might then add *and one reason that we are so sad is that this is the first fatality that we have experienced in 30 years at the plant.*

Be yourself

Company spokespersons are selected on the basis of their real character and any assumed personality will soon crumble during the interview.

Don't try to avoid the question entirely!

Business people should not ignore the question: it may be appropriate to acknowledge it without responding in precisely the way that the interviewer wanted, but executives must not attack the question or the interviewer or claim to have answered the question before. If the question has been asked before, it may imply that the response was deemed inadequate. The interviewee has a choice; he can either repeat what he said before, implying that there is nothing more to offer, or he can devise a new response which might even be the same but in different words. A skilled interviewer will not allow a spokesman to avoid a serious question entirely. An animal rights protester was asked five times if she condoned damaging cars to further her cause and, on another occasion, a former UK Home Secretary was asked the same question 12 times.

Understanding the reasons for criticism

One approach may be *I can understand why people are saying that but I just ask that they understand my point of view.* This tactic must be used sparingly by the inexperienced lest their comments give way to tabloid headlines such as *Company admits: it was our fault.* This was not what was said but it could be twisted to mean this.

Attempting to re-word the question or answer a different one

Some experienced interviewees sometimes try to deal with a question that the interviewer has not asked but one with which they feel comfortable.

This can be dangerous for the inexperienced business executive because the broadcaster will be irritated by the attempt to take over the interview and by the suggestion that he does not know his audience. Here are some examples, many of which invite, and will receive, a stinging retort:

- *That really is an important question but an even more important issue is...*
- *Before I deal with that point, I think that I should just explain...*
- *I suspect that what you are really asking is...*
- *What I think viewers/listeners really want to know is...*
- *That's an irrelevant question. What's more to the point is...*
- *I'm surprised that you ask that when the real issue is...*
- *I cannot accept that that's the most important question which, surely, is....*

Some attempts at re-wording a question may be less challenging:

- *I'd like to broaden your question to include...*
- *I'm not sure that I can answer that question but I do know...*
- *I wish the answer could be as straightforward as the question, but this is why it's not...*

Challenging the relevance of the question or trying to shift the ground so obviously will merely rile the interviewer and must be avoided. Interviewees should not presume to know more about journalism and the audience's interests than the interviewer. There are no stupid questions, only stupid answers.

Attempts to continue with an answer

If an important point needs to be made, the interviewee must insist on continuing. However, this should be done only when absolutely necessary and executives must not imitate politicians who say *please let me go on, may I just finish*, or *you've asked me an important question so let me finish my answer.* Suffice it to say that an inexperienced interviewee would be well advised not to stray beyond: *That's an important question that you have raised, so please let me deal with it,* or *I am answering, but in my way, so please let me continue.* However, rather than saying *Let me make one more point,* the interviewee should just make it!

Coping with a long question that contains allegations or a false premise

The first reaction, on hearing a false premise or comparison, or an inaccurate statement, must be to shake the head from side to side, so that it is apparent to the viewer that the company rejects what is being said. This is important because interviewees may forget the misleading premise or basic allegation and only deal with the most recent part of the question. If the initially offending remarks are potentially damaging to the company, the interviewee should interrupt. This can be very effective but it requires courage. *I must stop you there as you have made a very serious charge against my company* or *I must interrupt as there is absolutely no comparison between what happened today and....* Then the executive must explain why the comparison, allegation or premise is totally wrong.

After this section of the question has been dealt with, the remainder of the question, if it was completed, may have vanished. Assuming that it was negative and contained more allegations, the interviewee must decide whether to let it all go and move on to the next allegation that he remembers. Alternatively, he can ask what the other serious allegations were so that he could defend his employers, which is a very bad idea. Preferably, assuming that the first accusation has been firmly dealt with, the interviewee should sit still, awaiting the next and, hopefully, unrelated question. Sometimes, if the first allegation is mild, it may be desirable to continue listening and then to select the first more challenging one that can most easily be dismissed. This then casts doubts on the others and may deter repetition. Because any allegations can prove damaging, on balance, the best tactic, usually, is to halt the interviewer as soon as possible and rebut the charge which may deter him from making other allegations.

Use of intonation and coping with aggression or interruptions

In everyday life, few people suddenly raise their voices a little or use pauses to dramatic effect, before making a key point. In a television interview, such ploys can be powerful. If, for example, a company had been accused of treating some employees unfairly, the response *that is not true* seems weak. The allegation demands more than a few carefully chosen words, delivered in the same tone and manner as more routine comments in the interview. Consequently, the comment *there is absolutely no truth in such an allegation*, made with emphasis on the word "absolutely" and delivered in a firm tone, with a little additional volume, can influence the viewers and interviewer. The former will realise that the speaker feels strongly on this issue and the interviewer may decide against pursuing this topic.

An interviewer may become aggressive to provoke a more positive reaction, to attack the organisation for its reaction, or because the time allocated for the interview is about to expire and he wants to put another question. The spokesperson should never adopt a similarly belligerent line which would ensure defeat, as the journalist is more skilled with the medium and the viewers' sympathy might no longer reside with the victim of the attack.

Pausing by the interviewee, asking for clarification of the question and moral responsibility

Any questions that prompt long pauses before a response will be construed by the audience as a clear indication that the interviewee is weak on that particular point and is struggling to answer. Equally, if losing eye contact on television occurs at the same time and the interviewee suddenly develops a passionate interest in the ceiling or his shoes, the impression of quiet confidence is destroyed. That may be unfair: perhaps the interviewee is merely thinking, but television is about perception. It is reasonable to pause occasionally before responding but the viewer must not feel that this is because the company has been exposed as vulnerable. Pre-prepared answers, delivered fluently and without pause, will sound insincere. Sometimes, individuals, hearing a question that they can answer, charge in at speed but most answers should be given at an even rate and be clearly enunciated. Some natural pauses should be made, even by the most skilled communicators. Frequently, many business people, in this context, find pausing to think very natural.

Some questions might not be sufficiently unambiguous to merit an answer without further clarification. Pausing, whilst working out the implications or meaning of the question could imply that the interviewee is in difficulty. That may be wrong, but perception matters so interviewees must seek immediate clarification of the question. Occasionally, the interviewee may decide against asking for clarification. *Do you accept the moral responsibility for today's emergency?* To ask what this means could invite some difficult questions and suggests that the organisation does not understand the concept of moral responsibility. Here is one possible response: *I don't know what you mean by moral responsibility in this context but to us it means ensuring that.... and that is precisely what we are doing now.* Alternatively, it would be acceptable to ignore the issue of the definition of moral responsibility and say what the company is doing to mitigate the effects of the accident.

Do not repeat the company name or key and damaging words

It is legitimate to say *all of us in XYZ Manufacturing have been shocked and deeply saddened by today's tragedy* but more frequent use of the organisation's name should be avoided. Instead, use words or phrases like "the company" or "the group". Similarly, it is very easy to repeat a key word used in a question. A fire might be described by the interviewer as a "conflagration". Under pressure, the executive might then repeat the word. Suddenly, the company is effectively confirming that what was previously a fire has become a conflagration.

An interviewee can unwittingly create difficulties for his employers in another way. An interviewer, noting that the company does not know the cause of an accident might say that the company is baffled. The spokesperson may then admit that, *yes, so far, we are baffled.* This will be repeated in newspapers so a safer reply is to say that an enquiry is under way, or will commence shortly, and, only when they have investigated fully, will the causes be known.

Don't ask the interviewer a question, blame the media or offer ammunition unnecessarily

Some interviewees ask broadcasters *why should we have done that?* It seems evasive and journalists can respond with a stinging retort. Another ploy is to ask the interviewer if he has read a particular report: this is a waste of air time and may be seen as unfair by the watching public who know that broadcasters seldom have time to read massive reports. Some over-confident interviewees ask if a response answers the question. The journalist may well reply that it does not. Worse still, some executives may blame the media for the problem under discussion. *The problem is that you people in the media…* The instant reply would be on the lines of *the media has not…. but your company…* Sometimes interviewees offer information that has not been sought and which is neither immediately relevant nor necessary but which could cause difficulties for themselves.

Don't defend the entire industry

Many interviewers will wonder why an industry has so many accidents. The executive may challenge the basic assumption, if it is grave and untrue, but it is wrong to use valuable airtime defending the entire industry. The executive is there to communicate what his employers wish to say about the incident and must not be seduced into discussing others' responsibilities. *I cannot possibly comment about the entire industry, but, as far as my own organisation is concerned…"*

Do not waste time defending the company against an allegation that has not been made and a variation on a question

Some politicians defend themselves against unmade allegations as this is doubtless easier than challenging a valid assertion or accusation. Business executives must not do this. A variation is to answer a question that has not been asked but it provokes the response you *are answering a different question. What is your response to my question?*

Do not respond to hypothetical questions and do not lie

It is easy for the interviewer to speculate. *If your school bus had overturned and crashed into the queue of waiting children, it would have been a major tragedy, wouldn't it? It did not and I'm not going to speculate on a hypothetical situation.* Some companies, wrongly, may be unjustifiably economical with the truth but this will usually be detected and the organisation will suffer accordingly.

Criticising other parties

Some organisations, keen to deflect criticism, may allocate at least some blame on to others. Equally, the interviewer may effectively invite the company to implicate others. After a shipping accident, for example, the question might be: *If the government had implemented the Jones recommendations, some 30 miles of beaches would not now be covered in oil, would they?* A response might be: *It is not for me to comment on government policy but I'm delighted that nobody was injured and that the clean up has already begun.*

The media enjoy a public row between two organisations as it adds an additional dimension and prolongs the story's life. Even implying that another group was partly responsible for the accident can pre-empt the outcome of an official enquiry and there could be legal and insurance implications. If subsequently, the company is formally found guilty, the media will argue that, by accusing others, it was seeking to hide its own culpability. Furthermore, if another organisation is implicated by the group at the centre of the accident, air time will be increasingly devoted to the allegations.

Dangers of using examples from other industries and citing overall industry problems

Occasionally, companies use examples from other industries. Great care should be exercised if the purpose is to indicate that other sectors have similar safety records or adopt similar proposals on dealing with an emergency. An airline official argued that his company's aircraft were maintained more often and carefully than the interviewer's car. The retort was that the private car did not carry hundreds of passengers or travel at 30,000 feet. What is preferable, if necessary and if pressed, is to admit that a particular industry, involved in the emergency, can be potentially dangerous which is why some specific safety measures have been adopted and why the personnel are trained so intensively.

In a different context, the worst crisis for many companies is to announce substantial redundancies. Such news, of course, may have little impact nationally, unless the numbers are significant or the company is well known. However, whatever the extent of the likely coverage, it may be appropriate to say that *it's very sad that so many people have had to lose their jobs but, my organisation, like so many in the industry, has been forced to take this unpleasant step because of the context in which all the companies in this industry have to operate.* In this way, whilst expressing regret, the company shows that it is not alone in having to make redundancies. Sometimes the interviewee might even claim that, without these dismissals, many more jobs would have to be lost in the future.

Avoid flippancy and humour

Few interviewees are flippant on radio or television and many show a degree of gravitas that suggests that an emotional breakdown is imminent. However, sometimes adrenaline can prompt individuals to speak and behave in ways that, in "normal life" would horrify them. During a press conference training session, after a fictional industrial accident, a spokesperson avowed that his company had a safety record. When pressed for details of this record, he said that it was on the record. Later he argued that the media were wrong to be so questioning about the incident because *more people are killed on the roads each day and I don't see you making a fuss about that.* One company employee was asked if there was a bar on the ship. *Yes, there's a salad bar.*

Use of notes

Using notes on television looks bad and suggests that the company representative is nervous or ignorant. One of the rare occasions on which notes might be employed relates to personnel numbers. Interviewers will ask about the number of people present at the time of the accident and how many have been accounted for, are missing, injured or dead. This can be difficult so a reply might be *the situation is changing fast and I don't want to give misleading information, so let me tell you the figures that I was given just before I came to the studio.*

CHALLENGES

What if I don't know the answer to a question?

If a company spokesman does not know the answer to a sensible question, he should admit it. A deluge of irrelevant information will merely prompt the interviewer to say: *And the answer to my question is?* If a spokesperson does not know the answer to a question, the only response must be along the lines of *I'm sorry, I don't want to mislead you, I don't have that information.* A bland refusal to deal with the question will raise suspicion so the interviewee must explain why he cannot respond. Usually, an interviewee's rehearsal will have anticipated virtually all the questions, but occasionally, the unexpected can be asked. Saying, for example, that I'm *sorry I can't explain that because I'm not an engineer,* may suffice in some circumstances.

Sometimes, professing ignorance could reveal the company as uncaring or worse. Consider the questioner who asks *what is the condition of the people evacuated to the village hall?* Clearly, if this has not been anticipated by the company and its advisers, some dismissals should be imminent. However, the question must be answered. What follows may be the least harmful of various alternatives. In such an instance, it is legitimate for the individual to distance himself from the company: *I myself do not know their latest condition, as I have been involved in other aspects of today's terrible tragedy, but I can tell you that my colleagues are currently with them and doing all they can to make them comfortable. We are also arranging for their relatives to visit them.* The key here is that others from the company are with the victims. If they are not, then the company must not lie but it is inconceivable that any organisation would not be involved in looking after the injured. In this instance, having commenced on a serious negative, the company has bridged successfully and has introduced a key fact, through "adding on" that arrangements are being made to assist relatives to visit the injured.

No speculation and why did it happen?

Two negative points, often related, refer to speculation and the cause of the accident. Companies must never speculate, especially on the possible cause. The problem created by being asked the cause of the accident can be dealt with by saying *It's much too early to know the cause* or *I don't want to mislead you and at the present, the causes are being investigated* or *an enquiry has been set up and I don't want to pre-empt the results of their work.* Even if the cause of an accident appears to be obvious, it is financially and legally totally wrong to admit it. There may be other reasons for the accident. Few emergencies are caused just by one factor. Secondly, "confirming" the cause of the accident virtually pre-empts the outcome of the official enquiry and admitting the cause of the accident may violate insurance cover.

One new common question relating to the cause of some accidents that can be asked of telephone responders and broadcast interviewees alike, is *you have just said that, at this stage, you do not know why the accident occurred, so you cannot rule out terrorism?* Failing to exclude such a possibility could lead to headlines like "terrorism suspected in factory blast". That could sound like an attempt to avoid responsibility if a subsequent enquiry reveals that poor maintenance was the cause. However, terrorism cannot be ruled out so, logically, the prospect cannot be dismissed so a possible answer might be *we don't know the cause of this accident yet, but have no reason, at present, to think that it was caused by terrorist activities.*

Commenting on remarks that have not been seen or read

Spokespeople must never comment on remarks that they have not read, seen or heard. The interviewer might have invented a comment or misunderstood a remark. The company then has to fight another group or individual and the media will have additional copy as a new variation develops on the basic theme. A possible retort is *I myself have not heard/read/seen those remarks.* It is then important to continue, assuming that it is relevant, *I would be very surprised if these comments were made because...*

Pausing by the interviewer, the calm after the storm and flattery

A spokesperson should be on his guard if an interview has been particularly difficult and then the questioner suddenly becomes more reasonable. A taxing topic might be about to be raised and the restrained demeanour is to lull the interviewee into a false sense of security. Some interviewers will deliberately leave a pause after an observation, that the executive will feel obliged to fill the silence with another comment, possibly going further than before, merely to fill the "space". The interviewee should not continue speaking unless it is to repeat the answer that has been given before, assuming that it was satisfactory to the spokesperson. Some interviewers, seeking to relax the company executive may include a flattering remark about the individual and this, too might herald the approach of a particularly dangerous question.

Interviewers going outside the agreed parameters of the interview

If some interviewers stray outside the agreed area of discussion, merely refusing to deal with the question can seem evasive. So a spokesperson should point out that he agreed to appear to discuss the emergency only and cannot comment on other colleagues' responsibilities.

Correcting an error

Some senior executives, rather than admit having made a mistake, although aware that they have erred, opt, absurdly, for consistency. On one occasion, a shipping executive said during television training that his company's vessel, which had sunk, was carrying 4,200 containers. The correct figure was 3,200 but, foolishly he sustained the error. The journalists checked with the authorities and decided that the vessel was over-loaded which was the likely cause of the accident. Making an error is probably most executive's greatest fear and many, consequently, have doubtless rejected the potential for good offered by television or radio.

An error, detected by the interviewee or the interviewer, during a live or recorded broadcast

If it is unimportant, it should be ignored. If it is serious, the interviewee should say something like *I think that I just said X and Y: what I meant, of course, was A and B.* Another possibility is that the interviewer will notice an apparent error and invite the speaker to correct it.

A serious but undetected error in a live or recorded broadcast

A live interview should be watched and recorded by the individual's colleagues and, surely, at least one will detect the error even before they have access to any recordings. All interviewees should tape their own contribution. The company should contact the broadcaster immediately and seek air time for a correction, although such a request is unlikely to be granted.

The company must also telephone contacts and distribute a press release, apologising for the error, giving the accurate information, and then post it on its website.

Can you guarantee that such an accident will not happen again?

Many company personnel rush in with such assurances but, if machinery and human beings are involved, nobody can give such a guarantee. A suitable response might be *Neither I nor any one else could give such a guarantee but what I can tell you, categorically, is that we shall be doing absolutely everything to minimise the prospects of such an accident occurring again.* A slick interviewer might interrupt and remark *so it could happen again* before moving on with a new question. In such circumstances, the spokesperson must be resolute and continue or repeat the suggested full response.

Agreeing with the interviewer

Occasionally, corporate representatives may agree with what seems to be a sensible suggestion from the interviewer and so commit the company to significant costs. Superficial suggestions often have an immediate appeal in a crisis but seldom prove to be appropriate after more detailed consideration. *That is an interesting idea and it may be considered by the enquiry.*

Repetition of an old and regretted quote and a personal question

Sometimes, an interviewer may confront the spokesperson with an old and potentially dangerous quote from the past. *It was a stupid thing to say, I regret it and have long since apologised, so let's not waste time on that.* As before, with a personal question, explain why there will be no answer. *My own salary is not relevant here and has absolutely nothing to do with our overall expenditure on safety.*

Never walk out

Some executives, having started to leave the studio in disgust, then turn to bandy further words with the interviewer before making a final exit. However irked, executives should never leave an interview prematurely as it suggests that they cannot cope. Walking out will make news and will be long remembered, to the detriment of the individual and his organisation. Keeping cool under attack and making basic points will win some viewers' support, especially if the interviewee is seen to be the target of unfair treatment.

WORDS

Words, corporate-speak, jargon, clichés, lists and statistics

In daily life, words like "think", "believe" or "imagine" are used with little regard for their precise meaning but in an interview, the journalist will soon pick up on these apparently tentative words which imply some uncertainty. Another word in this category is "only". If, for example, the chief executive of a water supply company, with millions of customers, says that "only 14" people have been taken to hospital it will be widely assumed that he meant that a very small proportion of those at risk were in hospital. However, for those whose relatives are in hospital, it sounds as if the organisation is uncaring. When discussing bad news in a television interview, words like "sadly", or, if there is some good news, words like "happily" can be inserted. Age, especially of equipment, vessels and installations is usually construed by the media as potentially dangerous and thus a *prima facie* cause of an accident. Paradoxically, new is apparently synonymous with untried, experimental and inexperienced.

Using corporate speak, jargon and clichés, such as "at this moment in time", can be disastrous. The prime objective is to communicate clearly with the audience and to portray the company as caring and human. Many professional broadcasters imagine that they are talking to an intelligent teenager over the fence and that helps to eliminate jargon. If the interviewer does not understand what is being said, and has to seek an explanation, the speaker's flow is halted and the theme may be difficult to recover. *What happened? In accordance with our well-rehearsed contingency plan, the emergency procedures were implemented immediately and we can confirm that the prompt action has succeeded in arresting the progress of the fire.* Interviewers will want to know what this means in plain English. How many people are at the plant and are they all safe, how many fire tenders are on scene fighting the fire etc.? Furthermore, the expression, "we can confirm" is hardly one that is normally employed when discussing, say, a question on where the family might spend Christmas.

Clichés can be most irritating and may divert viewers' attention. Unacceptable words and phrases include *you must understand* or *you must realise* or *you must trust us*. The response is predictable. Interviewees should also avoid *draw a line in the sand, time to move on, lessons learned, I'm not here to tell you, I'm not in the business of, like, sort of, you know, no problem, as I said before, if you like, crackdown, the fact of the matter, making clear, move on, do you know what I mean, brilliant, fantastic, at the end of the day, regroup*, etc.

Statistics do not work well on television or radio so should be used sparingly. If essential to the story, they should be put into a context: for example, *our delivery trucks last year travelled the equivalent of twice around the world without an accident*. Similarly, interviewers will intervene immediately if they hear that the spokesperson is about to offer a list of points, and, even worse, if such a list is preceded by numbers or the dreaded a) etc.

Finally and briefly, in a word.. and the end of the interview.

Many interviewers often preface their last question with "finally and briefly" or "in a word". If it is impossible to respond briefly and to do so could create problems, the interviewee should say that the subject is too complex to answer briefly but then skilfully insert a key point, by bridging, which will be the last comment the viewer hears. The interviewer will terminate the discussion, usually with a word of thanks but this should be met just with a polite nod, not a deep sigh indicating relief. Smiling, out of politeness, must be avoided, as it looks inappropriate in the context of an emergency. The strong desire to leave the studio and to return to the real world encourages spokespeople to rise from their chair prematurely but if either the camera or the microphone remains functional, this can have a damaging effect on the recently concluded interview! Therefore, interviewees must remain seated, saying and doing nothing, until it is confirmed by one of the studio staff that it is "safe" to leave.

What if the broadcast version of a recorded interview is misleading?

Most companies merely seethe with indignation, vowing that they will never again be involved with the media. Unless the injustice was truly massive, a correction will not be broadcast so companies wrongly believe that nothing can be done. If a significant injustice has been perpetrated, action should be taken but being treated badly by one broadcaster does not justify ignoring the entire media. Such a boycott could damage the company. When complaining to the broadcaster, it is helpful to have an early transcript of what the interviewee actually said.

A misleading account could result from a failure to understand a point, or, relatively rarely, from a deliberate attempt to portray the group in an unfavourable light. In the first instance, whenever circumstances allow, and this is particularly relevant in a more relaxed press interview, the company spokesperson should ensure that the interviewer fully understands any technical points. Equally, the use of phrases such as "the most important aspect is.." will help the journalist to understand the company's perspective. Where the broadcaster either edits what has been said, apparently maliciously, or pulls quotes out of context, it is desirable to write directly to the chief executive of the broadcaster detailing the complaints and the letter should be copied to the regulatory authority. Sometimes, an apology might be broadcast but, even if this does not happen, possibly because the complaint is not deemed to be sufficiently serious, it is still worth writing. In some cases, the production team will be rebuked for their unprofessional conduct and this may deter such behaviour in the future. The wronged organisation can draw attention to the "true facts" by letters from the chief executive to all relevant newspaper and magazine editors and a comment should also be posted on its website.

SUMMARY

Monitoring the performance of individuals, in training or in a real incident, is important and the following lists can be adapted to create a checklist.

Do

- Record you own interview in full so that a transcript is always available
- Wear "appropriate" clothes for television
- Devise three key points and work them effectively into the interview promptly

- Plan a quote or soundbite and inject it as soon as possible
- Decide on the worst possible question and how to respond
- Select a piece of new news to include in the interview
- Ensure that the company is taping the interview in the office, if it's live

- If possible, ask what the first question will be
- Re-iterate the parameters of the interview, as agreed earlier, if necessary

- Remember that everything is on the record
- On television, sit back, comfortably, control your hands and do not cross your legs
- Shake your head, when really necessary, to indicate disagreement
- Always look at the journalist, not the camera, the ceiling or your shoes
- Take care with your body language

- Treat questions as prompts
- Respond as a PR person, not an expert in…
- Always think of the public's reaction to what you are saying
- Express regret for…
- Remember that people come first, then the environment and finance nowhere
- Emphasise the role of the emergency services
- Ask for clarification if you don't understand the question

- Answer to your satisfaction, as succinctly as possible, in full sentences
- Bridge and add on information, especially to make the key points
- Use volume and intonation to indicate what is really important

- Correct any serious errors you make
- Eschew technical language, jargon and statistics
- Refute misleading analogies or inaccurate descriptions
- Interrupt if the interviewer is listing many allegations

- Beware of pauses by the interviewer
- Expect interruptions from the journalist who may be running out of time
- Remain calm and beware of flattery
- Always remember that you are the expert, not the journalist

- Explain why you cannot answer a question
- Avoid misleading parallels
- Use words like "sadly" and "happily"
- Contradict an unfair summary or incorrect interpretation of a response
- Ensure that you finish important answers

- Stay silent and still after the interview until told you can leave the studio
- Complain if a recorded interview is edited so your words are severely distorted

Do not

- Wear clothes or jewellery that will distract viewers' attention
- Wear clothes that carry your name or that of your organisation

- Follow the interviewer, who, off camera, can lean to left or right in his chair
- Wave your hands around, nod at the wrong time or cross your legs
- Smile inanely and consistently
- Peer down the camera lens
- Call the interviewer by his name or as Mr..

- Use one-word answers
- Speculate, especially on the causes of the emergency
- Be flattered into saying what might have gone wrong
- Repeat the company name frequently

- Repeat "dramatic" words used by the interviewer
- Say "no comment"
- Be flippant or try humour

- Respond to a speech, comment etc, that you have not seen or heard
- Bluff
- Use examples from other industries unless carefully planned in advance

- Use weak words, like "think", management speak, clichés, jargon or statistics
- Admit to being baffled etc, using words uttered by interviewer
- Waste valuable time defending the sector
- Use exaggerated language about your organisation or lie

- Go outside the agreed boundaries of the interview
- Reveal the causes of the accident, even if a view has been formed
- Give information on compensation
- Waffle because air time is too valuable

- Ask the interviewer a question
- Agree to implement an interviewer's suggestion
- Be condescending to the interviewer or show any dislike for the media
- React in hostile fashion to difficult questions or a persistent interviewee
- Challenge the validity or relevance of the question
- Leave the studio prematurely

CHAPTER 15

TRAINING, TESTING AND EXERCISES

Many UK companies offer basic training in crisis communications but potential clients should select only organisations able to demonstrate relevant experience. To be effective, training, which often includes role playing and instant analysis, must be followed by realistic exercises to ensure that an individual, team or company can cope with the media during an emergency.

TRAINING

The nature of specific training will depend on what the company requires but the objectives of media-related sessions should be:

- To enable participants to understand and to respond to the media effectively during and after an emergency, backed by a workable plan which meets the company's objectives and the media's needs. The emphasis is on advance planning, including internal organisation, especially in collecting and distributing information, and on a practical approach to communicating the organisation's messages to the public and other key sectors, via the media.

At the end of the training, depending on which aspect is being taught, participants should be able to:

- Create an effective internal system of collecting and distributing information

- Prepare information in advance, to assist in an emergency

- Respond effectively and promptly to the media in an emergency, thus minimising damage to corporate reputation
- Write an effective press release
- Deal with telephone calls from the media
- Give effective interviews on radio and television
- Organise and present a successful press conference

Because it may be difficult to envisage some emergencies and the chaos that ensues, some courses begin with videos/DVDs of real crises before detailed presentations on the topics chosen by the client, in conjunction with the trainer. During the sessions, frequently illustrated by real events, participants are asked questions and these, together with instant role-playing, illustrate and emphasise key factors.

Who should be trained?

Organisations must decide how they would cope with the media's demands during an emergency and then arrange training for their relevant staff. For example, senior management might need to learn how a crisis management team functions, with particular reference to the speedy collection of accurate information and its prompt transmission to the telephone media response team and thence on to the media. Senior managers may also need to learn how to undertake a successful radio or television interview or mount an effective press conference. More junior personnel might need training on how to write a press release or how to respond competently to media telephone calls.

TESTING

Instant testing on the different aspects of media response is essential during a training session because it can highlight weaknesses that can be overcome before the end of a course. One major problem facing many executives is nervousness and this can be addressed by mounting some initial tests which are preceded and followed by analysis and advice. By using examples from outside the participants' experience the basic rules of media response become clear and participants are given experience in mastering a brief quickly. Some subsequent testing and exercises, of course, are based on the participants' industry and realistic scenarios are essential.

Broadcast interviews, writing press releases and mounting press conferences

Even in training, most executives are nervous at the thought of undertaking a broadcast interview, especially on television, in front of their colleagues. In addition, the realisation that this could be a real incident one day induces more nerves. A skilled interviewer can easily make a nervous business executive look silly. Foolishly, some consultants do this, which may only confirm a participant's prejudice against the media, and then they try to "rebuild" the participant's confidence. This may not be possible.

In the real world, business people, expressing regret at the consequences of an incident, and trying to explain the measures being taken to minimise the impact on people and the environment, are unlikely to be treated aggressively by most interviewers who want to secure a story. If a participant has previously been severely embarrassed in training, he will probably perform badly.

Company personnel, facing the cameras, for a series of interviews, must be confident. This can be achieved by asking them to choose any non-work related topic for their first interview. Their choice is not revealed to the interviewer until five seconds before the camera goes live. Business people know that the interviewer, even if hostile, cannot have done any homework that could destroy them immediately. Having had this injection of confidence, the subsequent interviews, one of which, at least, will be based on the participant's company, are less difficult. Each is preceded by detailed advice, as would happen in the real world, but, although successive interviews become more challenging, the interviewee becomes more confident.

Broadcast interviews, press releases and press conferences can be based on a specific and realistic incident but, before participants are required to perform, they are given basic tuition on each of these topics and more specific advice on the scenario they have been given. Later, their press releases, interviews or press conferences are analysed carefully. After these sessions, based exclusively on external incidents, many training groups then use company material as, hopefully, some of the basic rules of communication will have been absorbed by this point.

Incidents for a scenario

Many different scenarios can be used to test press release writing, press conference organisation and broadcast interviews. Typical ones could include a serious accident at a busy road junction after the introduction of traffic lights, sexual abuse in a boarding school, food poisoning in a hotel or a major explosion at a factory after an employee revealed previous correspondence with his erstwhile employers in which he forecast an accident because of a lack of maintenance. All this may sound sadistic but the trainees are given time and detailed advice in advance of being "examined", as would happen in the real world.

Details of the scenario will be confined to one sheet of paper on which is noted the participant's name, and fictional company name and his job title. The "success" of the test does not depend on the participant's recollection of all the details. Indeed, participants are invited to make up any relevant and sensible information but they are reminded that such an approach might open up a new and undesirable line of questioning. The second section offers information about the incident but is brief enough to allow the participants to grasp the essentials and to organise what must be conveyed quickly. The final section suggests some key points that the organisation may feel should be made to the media.

Whilst the participant may know what to say, in for example, a television interview, inexperience may mean that he is unable to insert a key point or cannot react sufficiently quickly to a major challenge. A press release may fail to put the incident into a relevant context and a press conference may reveal inconsistencies between the participants. Later, detailed analysis can rectify many of the problems that emerged from the performance.

A specific example of a scenario

You, Ivor Kure, are the chief executive of Whatever Hospital in Sussex.

An 80 year-old man was left, unattended, on a hospital trolley for five hours. He was unconscious, following a fall at his home in sheltered accommodation. A junior triage nurse assessed his condition and decided that he was only a "medium priority". The patient subsequently died, having suffered a massive internal haemorrhage. He had not been treated but he had been checked "fairly regularly" by nursing staff who claim that his condition had remained "stable". A hospital spokesman said that "it would appear that the patient was not seen by a doctor as quickly as he should have been" and that "there were a lot of people waiting in A&E as it was a bank holiday weekend". He added that there was never any indication that the man's condition was life-threatening or that a sudden deterioration could have been expected. An internal enquiry has been initiated, after this, the second such tragedy at the hospital in the last three months. A grieving son has demanded a public enquiry and is threatening legal action.

Your task is to defend the hospital by:

- Expressing your horror and regret
- Stressing that the results of the enquiry will be made public
- Claiming that you are determined to ensure that changed procedures will avoid such a tragedy in the future, as far as humanly possible

Without trivialising the appalling incident, or making a judgement in advance of the enquiry, you may or may not want to admit that the services at the hospital are under significant and sustained pressure, whilst stressing that this, of course, is no excuse for what has happened. Bear in mind that some of the viewers/newspaper readers may be waiting to have an operation in your hospital and that they are the ultimate audience you are trying to reach. Significantly, this is the second such tragedy in recent weeks. An allegation might be that you said then that you were taking action to ensure that there was no repetition. Now there has been another fatality in similar circumstances, so how can anyone believe you now? Is it not time for you to resign? Other problems include the fact that the man was 80, which, surely merits some attention inside five hours, the comment that the triage nurse was a junior and that there were no signs that the man's condition was life-threatening. If he was not checked over a five-hour period, how did anyone know that?

EXERCISES

Regular exercises, based on realistic and properly researched scenarios, are essential extensions of training. Without such exercises, always carefully monitored, it is impossible to determine the success and relevance of the training and the adequacy of individuals, equipment, systems and the interaction of all the elements. Even if each part of a company's overall response team is trained, it might be necessary to ensure, firstly, that the different parts work well individually and, secondly they function well together. These objectives can be achieved by exercises.

Exercises may involve just a few people, for several hours, to test a single function, such as telephone media response, or they can be major international drills involving operational and media testing over several days. These necessitate major planning and the participation of hundreds of people, from many organisations. Whatever the level, most participants agree that once a carefully planned exercise has commenced, artificiality vanishes, replaced by a sense of urgency and realism.

Major comprehensive exercises should only be staged when the individual components have been adequately trained and tested separately. The larger exercise is concerned not just with the performance of all the individual parts but also how they link together, especially in relation to the telephone media response team and with outside organisations. The company's media response specialists might have to liaise with their counterparts in different organisations, but all must tell the same story, lest the media detect exploitable differences.

Personnel can practise their roles, which may differ sharply from their routine work and, because no two emergencies are ever identical, experience is important. The turnover of personnel within emergency response teams is often high, reflecting transfers, promotions, retirements, resignations and redundancies. Regular, if localised, exercises allow new team members to gain experience and to forge new personal relationships, especially as their members will rarely work together in the "real world". Additionally, in large companies, the work of the public relations people becomes more widely known, and hopefully, better understood.

In some exercises, ignorance on company policy, or even an absence of policy, can become apparent, especially if an organisation has never previously thought through the implications of an emergency!

Exercises enable companies to ensure that all individuals involved in emergency response are competent and reliable. Incompetence in a real emergency could have very serious repercussions, so these people must be moved from the job in which they failed. Realistic exercises have seen men reduced to tears and women trying to escape from the pressure by hiding in cupboards.

Specific purposes of a media-related exercise

Before discussing the nature of exercises, and how to organise them, it is useful to note that, apart from testing the performance of individuals and teams, and their interaction, in relation to the media, an exercise enables a check on other key factors, including:

- Call-out procedures of all team members and advisers, especially out of hours
- Internal security, personnel access to sites out of hours and travel arrangements
- Access to, and suitability of, telephone media response room and equipment
- Setting up of rooms for telephone media response teams
- Understanding how to use equipment
- Alerting management and testing their ability to communicate and organise
- Liaison with other media teams, possibly in other organisations
- Facilities for press conferences and radio and television interviews
- Ensuring that access to the site is controlled and that non-media personnel do not speak to journalists
- Handling media at different locations, including site, office or hospital
- Provision of facilities for media and a location for a press conference
- Testing practicality of media Emergency Response Procedures Manual and Fact File

Organising an exercise

The objective of all exercises, irrespective of their complexity, must be stated in advance. The exercises, based on plausible and difficult scenarios, must be monitored honestly and carefully, to determine whether the intentions have been met. Without honest monitoring, holding an exercise is pointless.

Timing and participation

After some basic training has been carried out, an exercise should be mounted without any prior warning and, ideally, as staff are going home or during the night, which will test call-out procedures, travel arrangements, security and the ability of team members to gain access to the building. If individuals, aware that an exercise is to be mounted at a specific time, "cheat" by arriving early or ensuring that some equipment is in place, the value of the exercise is diminished. Some key individuals, knowing that an exercise is planned, suddenly go on holiday. This may be realistic as emergencies can develop during vacations, but if the exercise is the first undertaken by the organisation, the presence of important members of emergency teams can give confidence to others. If key individuals frequently vanish before an exercise, fearing that their inadequacy will be revealed, they should be replaced.

Precautions

News of the scenario might escape to the outside world, where it might be construed as reality. To avoid alarm and the spreading of rumours, the following action should be taken just before a major exercise:

- Notices should be posted at all the entrances and exits to offices or installations. After the exercise has commenced, arriving staff and visitors should be told that an exercise is in progress
- Telephone switchboard operators should be told in advance and given a brief pre-prepared release, so that they can respond to any callers who believe that there has been an accident
- Security staff should be notified. In some early morning exercises, before the telephone media response team has assembled, some security guards have alienated the media with an impressive blend of arrogance, rudeness and ignorance
- Every exercise must be given a name and all related telephone calls must begin and end with the code name

- The exercise co-ordinator must compose a phrase, in advance, so that, if a real emergency occurs, participants understand that the exercise has been terminated

- Care must be taken to ensure that if the media hear of the emergency, they realise that it is an exercise. All press releases must be clearly labelled EXERCISE....

- If outside telephone numbers are to be used, they must be checked carefully to ensure that they are accurate. All participants must understand that only these numbers can be used

- All role players, including visiting journalists, must wear security badges, know the name of the exercise, how it will commence and finish and how it will be terminated if a real emergency develops. They must have a list of organisations and numbers of those participating, a reliable telephone and an approximate time-table. Role players, perhaps representing the local emergency services, should have "job descriptions"

If the exercise is restricted to an internal phone system and involves only the media response, with all personnel convened in just three rooms, one of which will be occupied by the visiting journalists, much of the above can be safely disregarded but all conversations must begin with the name of the exercise and all press releases issued during the exercise must be labelled appropriately.

Who should be involved in a media exercise?

The identity of those who are involved will be determined by the nature and purpose of the exercise. A crisis management team may be involved, to test the flow of information from that office to the telephone responders but external presenters can substitute for this team if necessary. Apart from the telephone media response team, telephone operators, security staff and administrative personnel should know what is required of them in a real emergency, so it is wise to involve them occasionally in exercises. Links with other company press offices around the country, or even abroad, should be tested regularly and those organisations with close links to other groups must be organised so that the media cannot detect and expose any inconsistencies. In some emergencies, company media responders need up-to-date relevant information from an experienced media person at the site. This function can be role-played from the office during an exercise.

Types of exercise

A major in-house one-day exercise

All the main elements of media response can come together in a day-long exercise. A carefully scripted and detailed scenario is prepared and a number of situation reports and new challenges or news items are injected during the exercise. A session of this complexity involves perhaps 30 participants, 10 journalists, sometimes in different countries, a film crew and two presenters. Telephone responders and a crisis management team participate and the latter provides the former with information, especially in relation to particularly difficult media questions. The senior team also devises strategy, writes press releases, undertakes broadcast interviews and mounts two press conferences during a very intensive day.

The participants, confronted with a developing and realistic scenario, must respond as they would in a genuine emergency. As the scenario unfolds, through the situation reports, the management team must decide what information may be passed to the telephone response team for dissemination to the media. New developments are conveyed to the crisis management team and some additional aspects of the emerging crisis may be invented to test specific responses. The media's seriously challenging questions are passed to the crisis management team so they can devise appropriate replies.

Such an exercise may last for up to six hours, without a break. This tests the company's ability to sustain consistency, especially when new telephone response team members are introduced. Few individuals can do this important work for such a long period as the pressure is unyielding. The final session is devoted to a detailed discussion involving all participants. Even if a company's performance is poor, comments must be judicious because sustaining confidence is crucial. Any serious misgivings can be communicated separately and later, in the consultant's report.

This type of exercise allows all aspects of media response to be tested. Those involved can see the interaction between the participants in, and information given by, the telephone media response team and management involved in press conference and broadcast interviews. The pressures are substantial but this concept has been used very successfully for testing companies in the UK and overseas, notwithstanding the difficulties imposed by different cultures and languages.

A "larger version" of this type of exercise, favoured by multinational groups, can be staged by using a longer scenario, involving more organisations and hundreds of role players in different countries. Such exercises, sometimes lasting days, are, of course, very expensive and take many weeks to organise.

A debate

One inexpensive form of exercise, which minimises disruption to routine work but helps to assess individuals' understanding of emergency procedures, is a debate. Members of the telephone media response team are summoned, in accordance with call-out procedures, which is the first test of the system. Ideally, the venue would be the media response room, so the company can determine how long it takes to set the room up, with the necessary telephones etc. before being able to take media calls.

When this has been done, the person chairing the debate then gives the team some limited information on what has happened, according to a scenario. The team is then allowed a few minutes to draft a holding release, even if that was not their responsibility in a real emergency, and the chairman then asks the team what else it would be doing at this time, before accepting calls from the media.

The scenario unfolds gradually, with the chairman, effectively acting as the world's media, asking questions and posing new difficulties. There might be a nasty and unexpected twist in the plot or it might involve removing the team co-ordinator, to see how his sudden absence affects performance. Simulated telephone calls from journalists could then be enacted, with the responses, based on the Fact File and the limited detail on the accident, carefully noted and then discussed.

Most of the calls would be made from in-house personnel, if the chairman wants others to contribute, but some should be made by members of the media response team. Because they are then required to think like journalists, they develop an understanding of the pressures that the media face and they devise questions that they themselves might receive in a real emergency. This should give them confidence and demonstrates that many questions can be anticipated. This process can continue for as long as desired but, if the maximum benefit is to be derived from the exercise, someone must be designated to take notes, not least on how long it took to set up the room and equipment.

There are disadvantages to this simple exercise. There will be no opportunity to check the flow of information from the incident control management room to the media response team and any damaging media allegations cannot be relayed to a more senior level. Nor will it be possible to test the approvals system for press releases. Finally, there is a danger that the in-house personnel will not be very effective journalists but at least all involved, especially team newcomers, have some practice.

A more detailed exercise for the telephone media response team

In this type of exercise, the course presenter gives each of the two teams copies of press releases and puts up information on the white boards or flip charts in their room. Massive details for a short exercise of this kind are unnecessary but an outline scenario is essential so that the presenter can improvise around the basic situation if necessary. The teams also have copies of the Fact File. Some journalists, usually based in the same building, then ply one of the two teams of responders with questions over the phone.

The exercise is divided into a number of sessions and during the intervals between these periods, the presenter can analyse the response to the media calls, which have been recorded. He also gives advice throughout the exercise, putting new information, from the scenarios, as necessary, on white boards. He will also consider how the media reaction might develop in the next session and how the team can respond most effectively. Having different sessions allows one team to answer the phones whilst the other, accompanied by another presenter, listens to their responses and discusses the performance.

During the exercise, as in other forms of testing, greater variety is introduced by the wide-ranging roles that the journalists undertake. It is important to subject the response teams to varied calls from different parts of the media. The journalists can employ unexpected tactics to secure information and can mix fact and fiction. They can also co-operate to provide greater pressure than their modest numbers would otherwise allow. As the exercise progresses, the presenters might give the journalists more information, in addition to what is contained in the press releases, which prompts a new range of questions.

This type of training exercise can be mounted quickly, easily and inexpensively. The main requirements are a sensible scenario, a bank of phones in a well-organised room with white boards, or flip charts, the facility to record proceedings, some professional journalists and two experienced trainers. Ideally, the number of participating journalists should outnumber the responders to create pressure, more-demanding questions and to create greater frustration. Having at least one "spare" journalist allows them, in turn, to write running stories during the exercise. They can also write stories during the intervals and these are read out at the end of the exercise when a senior journalist and the trainer assess the teams' performance.

In this type of relatively informal exercise, the press releases are written in advance, to line up with the developing scenario, and the fact that there are distinct sessions. What follows is a typical North Sea oil industry scenario outline and some typical press releases. Gradually, some of this information will be given to the media response team and, depending on the circumstances, some facts may be "leaked" to the participating journalists. This example has been chosen because the scene is offshore, which complicates communication, and the incident is likely to last longer than many onshore emergencies. Other organisations can adapt what follows for their own exercises. The scenarios for four sessions and the linked press releases follow.

Session 1

The time is 12.30 pm on the morning of 12th May and the weather is fine with excellent visibility and little wind. The semi-submersible rig ... is drilling for a group of companies for which ... is the operator, in block ... in the North Sea, some ...miles off the ...coast. The nearest town,..., is ... miles from the rig and is ...flying time away. The nearest offshore installation is ..., which is ... miles away and is operated by ... The flying time to it is ....

Drilling commenced on ... and has reached ... feet, against a target depth of ... feet. This is the first time that ... has drilled in the area but it has used ... Drilling Company and this particular rig on previous occasions in other parts of the North Sea. Its overall experience is limited, having drilled only .. wells in the last .. years. There are ... people, including five women, employed by a catering contractor, on the rig. ... are at work and ... are resting, as a three shift system is in operation. There are ... oil company personnel on board and the remainder are contractors. Suddenly, without any warning, there is an explosion and fire in the drilling area. This is all that is known: there is no information on injuries or fatalities.

Session 2

The fire spreads quickly and personnel not involved in fire-fighting and essential communications go to muster stations. The coastguard is alerted immediately and organises helicopters and rescue vessels. The offshore installation manager orders all non-essential staff, numbers unknown, to evacuate. This leaves an unspecified number still on board, including the medic, some fire-fighters and the radio officer. The original number on board at the time of the accident is confirmed at 80. The operator also organises onshore-based doctors to fly to the rig or to the standby vessel, depending on circumstances... The weather is calm so the standby vessel,..., is able to pick up all the non-essential staff, including five women, from the lifeboats. They are subsequently taken off by helicopter and are being flown to shore, via a nearby platform. They are all fit and well but a count reveals that nine men are unaccounted for.

Session 3

Subsequently, the bodies of three of the men are discovered on the rig and two more men, seriously injured, are also found on the rig. Four remain missing and as the weather forecast indicates that conditions, now deteriorating, are expected to worsen, the search and rescue operation intensifies. The fire was put out within an hour and although the damage to the rig was severe, the helideck is still operational and the injured men, suffering from serious burns, were lifted off by helicopter at 15.00, after initial treatment by the medic, and taken to ... hospital at.... Their condition was described by the hospital as "serious". There is a delay in contacting the next of kin of those who were killed as they came from Turkey.

Session 4

The bodies of the four missing men are found. Two were on the rig and two were in the water. This means that the death toll is seven. Furthermore, it is now apparent that the early and unconfirmed reports that there was some oil pollution around the rig were accurate. It also seems that the spill is worsening and speculation develops that the cause of the explosion and fire was a sudden increase in pressure whilst drilling. The operating company arranges for assistance from the Southampton oil spill centre but stresses that the spill is modest and that the remaining men on the rig are investigating how to curb the oil flow. Because the coast is only .. miles away, and as the wind has changed direction, some oil has already reached a local holiday resort beach and there are reports that some oil has also contaminated a local bird sanctuary. A former employee of.., speaking to local media, has claimed that he left the company because of their "cavalier attitude to safety". The Health and Safety Executive are about to begin an investigation into the accident. The damage to the rig is now more extensive than earlier thought and there is no question of an early resumption of drilling.

Press releases

Here are press releases that might be distributed in each of the sessions. Each release, which would be self-contained and on company-headed paper, (see chapter 11), would be dated, numbered and timed and would also include the name and number of the media contact person. Such details are shown here only on the first release.

Sample press release 1

Date: Time: Contact: Tel. no.   Email: Website:

EXERCISE ******

INCIDENT IN UK NORTH SEA

.., the operators of the rig, .., currently drilling on block .., in the UK sector of the North Sea, some .. miles off the .. coast of .., near .., confirm that an incident which occurred at about 12.30 has disrupted normal operations.

No details are known yet but the company is doing all that it can to ensure that the incident is brought under control as soon as possible.

Air and sea support services have been alerted and every action is being taken to assist those on the rig. The precise number on board at the time of the incident is not known at present, but it has accommodation for 85 people. The weather is fine.

Offshore personnel are trained in safety, first aid and fire-fighting and all participate in regular drills and emergency exercises. Some medical facilities are available on the rig and on the standby vessel, the .., close to the rig. Both have helidecks. The rig is well-equipped with modern lifeboats and the standby vessel has fast liferafts.

The rig, owned by.., of .., and built in 19.., is a semi-submersible and commenced drilling for .. on this block on ... Drilling stops automatically if an incident could threaten safety, but it is not yet known if the rig was drilling at the time of the incident.

Further information will be made available as soon as possible.

end

Notes for editors

.. is an exploration and production company, based in ... It was established in 19.. and now operates in .. countries. It has been involved in the North Sea since 19... The company has not had any previous serious incidents. Currently, .. is producing some ..,... barrels a day of oil equivalent, from sources around the world but the bulk is derived from ... The company has offices in .. and .. and at .. locations overseas. It employs about .. people, of whom about .. work overseas.

Sample press release 2

EXERCISE * * *

ACCIDENT IN UK NORTH SEA

.. regrets that an explosion and fire occurred at about 12.30 today on the rig.., which was drilling some .. miles off the .. coast of …Currently, nine men are missing and an intensive search has been mounted by the emergency services. There are no reports of injuries. Eighty people were on board at the time of the accident and non-essential staff were safely evacuated to a nearby platform before being flown to the shore. A specially-trained fire-fighting team remains on the rig, which is equipped with deluge systems.

The weather is calm and shore-based emergency services have been alerted and assistance is also available from the.. platform, which is .. minutes flying time away. The standby vessel, .., is on site and assisting. Some medical facilities are available on the rig and both the rig and the standby vessel have helidecks. The rig is well-equipped with modern lifeboats and the standby vessel also has fast liferafts.

The company is doing everything possible to ensure that the incident is brought under control as soon as possible and is grateful to the emergency services and others who are helping.

Further information will be made available as soon as possible.

The number for next of kin to ring is: ...

end

Sample press release 3

EXERCISE * * *

THREE KILLED IN UK NORTH SEA

.. deeply regrets that, following an explosion and fire on the rig .. at about 12.30 pm today, three men have lost their lives. Another four are missing and an intensive search is being carried out on the rig and helicopters and vessels are looking offshore. Two injured men, suffering from serious burns, were lifted off by helicopter, after initial treatment by the medical staff on the rig and taken to ... hospital at.... Their condition was described by the hospital as "serious". Sixty non-essential staff have been evacuated safely and are now back on shore. All are fit and well.

The fire on the rig, which was drilling some.. miles off the coast of .., was extinguished within an hour. Although the damage was severe, the helideck remains operational.

..'s chief executive, .., speaking from.., the nearest onshore location to the rig, said "all of us in the company are deeply saddened at today's tragic accident. We send our condolences to the relatives and friends of those who lost their lives and to those who have been injured in today's tragedy. I am ensuring that everything possible is done to look for the missing men and we all hope that they will be found safe and well very soon".

The number for next of kin to ring is: ...

End

Sample press release 4

EXERCISE * * * *

SEVEN KILLED IN UK NORTH SEA TRAGEDY

.. confirms, with the utmost regret, that seven men lost their lives following a fire and explosion at about 12.30 today, on the rig .., which was drilling .. miles off the .. coast of ... Additionally, two men have been seriously injured and are now in .. Hospital. The death toll increased when two of the missing men were found on the rig and two in the water.

..'s chief executive,.., speaking from .., the nearest onshore location to the rig, said "my colleagues and I are shocked and deeply saddened by today's tragedy. We send our condolences to the relatives and friends of those who lost their lives. We also are thinking of the injured men and wish them a speedy recovery. Our main task now is to investigate the causes of this appalling accident and to co-operate with all the authorities in the investigation, which has already started, to ensure that this kind of accident never happens again. We are very grateful to all those who have been assisting us today: it has been very sad for all of us."

Earlier, 55 men and five women were evacuated safely and returned to shore this afternoon. All are well and uninjured.

The fire on the rig was extinguished within an hour. Eleven personnel remain onboard the rig but they are expected to be lifted off very shortly, as the weather is deteriorating. The helideck remains operational. Some crude oil is leaking from the damaged well and the company is co-operating with the authorities and the Southampton oil spill response centre to combat pollution. Equipment is already being moved to ..., as a precaution.

The number for next of kin to ring is: ...

End

CHAPTER 16

MONITORING PERFORMANCE

Checklists, relating to specific functions, included in the relevant chapters, can be adapted to monitor performance. Heavily-edited reports and stories based on the performance of teams and companies in exercises follow. Without candid and informed monitoring and appraisals, exercises can be a waste of money.

The more detailed an exercise, the more important it is that it is monitored by experienced observers whose role is determined by the nature and objectives of the exercise. If the exercise is based at more than one site, observers should be positioned at all locations. Their main task should be to concentrate on aspects where improvements are needed and they, like company responders, must log all their activities for subsequent analysis. Whether in-house staff, or preferably, experienced external consultants, observers must be in place before the start of a major exercise, to note how quickly team members arrived, their initial action, and whether all the necessary equipment was in place.

Observers should lead the debate immediately after the exercise and comments must be candid but not hurtful. After the debrief, observers should write a detailed report. Ideally, these observations should be compared against pre-prepared checklists. This allows comparison with other groups and with the company's previous performance. If the company fails to act on the report, the value of the exercise is diminished, future training will not be taken seriously and the morale of those participating, many of whom will be "volunteers", will be undermined. Apart from determining whether the basic objectives of the exercise were met, observers should note the lapsed time that passes before key decisions were taken because the efficient flow of information is fundamental. Delays in the provision of information can be noted and compared against times taken by other organisations, especially in the same sector.

The role of consultants

Experienced consultants can play a significant role. Exercises mounted, monitored and assessed by a company's own staff can prompt misleading views on the levels of competence. Unless carefully scrutinised, using objective tests, the only criterion against which the exercise can be measured is a subjective assessment of performance against that attained last time but how does the company compare against the rest of the industry? Lacking external advice, there is no real answer. Consultants put a company's performance into a context, can be less inhibited in their comments than employees and bring a depth and variety of experience that cannot be achieved in-house. Additionally, without infringing confidentiality, consultants may recognise a particular problem in the client company that has been solved elsewhere.

REPORTS AFTER MEDIA EXERCISES

Reports must be candid and prompt: it is pointless to organise a major exercise and then portray the performance as being much better than it was. If this were to happen, and the company then faced a real emergency, it could justly turn on the course organisers and condemn them for misleading the company on its state of preparedness.

In an exercise, observers may ring the media telephone response team themselves, to determine the reaction to a particular point or to set a trap to test the results of the earlier training, so what follows is based on presenters' own direct experience and detailed discussions, carried out during and immediately after the exercise, with the journalists. Because the performance of the media telephone response team is influenced by the effectiveness of the crisis management team and the response team co-ordinator, this section begins with a very abbreviated version of one report on the crisis management team. Most of the comments here reflect on what went wrong but this does not mean that most companies fail: indeed, most do well after training.

The crisis management team

Much depends on the ability of the crisis management team not just to manage the crisis but to ensure that the media response team is provided with timely, accurate and confirmed information.

- The crisis management team leader, calm, quietly confident and interested in all aspects of the crisis, controlled and inspired his team. He always had time to check press releases and was interested in what his more junior colleagues were attempting. He and his team understood the importance of disseminating information rapidly and accepted advice on some aspects that had media-related implications.

- The crisis room remained relatively quiet all day so working conditions were acceptable and there were many fewer "interlopers" than usually occurs.

- The "secretary" arrived within 16 minutes of the team being assembled.

- Within four minutes of her arrival, the first "report" was completed but it was unclear if this was a holding statement for the media responders or a situation report from which the media advisers could draft a press statement. Some "genuine" releases only reached recipients late in the exercise and there was some inconsistency in the information offered. This was evident towards the end of the afternoon, when, for totally valid reasons, temporary silence was being maintained on a fatality, whilst others were confirming it to the media. The fault probably occurred in another participating country but the "home" team was handicapped.

- There was some internal debate about releasing the details of the fatality and this was probably caused by the team's ignorance on the procedures of passing on this information to the next of kin.

- The confirmed cargo figures, carefully checked and approved, were "corrected" later!

- Because of the significant co-operation and a sensible division of labour, the company could anticipate and research answers to unasked questions.

- Alerting the local company on how to cope with the media, when the survivors came ashore, was handled well and an expert was available to assist.

- Because of the excellent teamwork, it was possible to find out what the company was doing and to present a positive picture of planned action.

The importance of timing

Many reports, such as the first one below, are based on logs kept by observers; this one is included to demonstrate the importance of timing.

10.20   First call to the media response team. Put on hold by the operator. Minutes of cheerful music then silence whilst she checked to see if the team could take a press call. Some minutes later, no, the team was busy. *Could someone call me back? No. It's important, I need to talk to someone now. Hold on.* More cheerful music. Eventually, a responder admitted that he was the training manager but I refrained from capitalising on this error. What was my source for the claim that one of his company's vessels was involved in an accident? A shipping contact but I refused him more details and told him journalists don't reveal sources. He contended that there was no incident but then admitted that an unconfirmed report suggested that something "potentially very serious" had happened. Passed me on to the media team co-ordinator who also asked me to identify my source. Refused. He conceded that there was a security alert on a company container vessel. No more information available.

10.38   Phoned again, the operator who tried to fob me off, claiming that I had already called. Are media calls rationed and by what right does the operator decide who calls and how often? Persisted and after more music, spoke to girl who revealed her daily occupation. She wasted time denying me basic information on the number of personnel on board, (POB), details of the ship and any terrorist threats that the company had received. Pointed out that, in the time she had taken trying to silence me, she could have found out the POB and size of the vessel. She ignored this, implying that information would only be released when it suited the company. Her querulous attitude would have persuaded me to go elsewhere for information in real world. Under severe pressure, she passed me to a colleague, an inexperienced outside consultant. All the information I wanted would be revealed in 30 minutes! Meanwhile, nothing except port of discharge.

10.50 Next call on behalf of a quality paper. Music, then connected to the consultant. He could not tell me much about whether there was a fire or explosion because he was "a long way from the incident". What does that say about the company's communications? Eventually, told me that normal crew was 26 and that nine were still on board. Pushing hard, discovered that the vessel was 40,000 dead-weight tonnes. Didn't know whether all the cargo had been discharged but conceded that emergency services, including fire, were on site. The vessel had a good safety record "I think". Identity of cargo owners unknown and ignorant on any previous terrorist threats. Desperate to curtail the call as he had to write a press release and was working alone.

11.10 A much happier consultant returned my call, confirmed that there had been a bomb threat, that there was no fire or explosion and that nine essential staff remained on board. The vessel was only 4,000 dwt. Language problems might explain the discrepancy with what I was told earlier. The vessel had discharged its cargo completely but he did not know how much bunker fuel the vessel had been carrying. Offered to fax me a press release which arrived at 11.26. Apparently, the threat was contained in a phone call to the company's head office.

11.18 As a broadcast journalist, pressed hard for an interview. Again put through to the consultant but insisted on speaking to a senior manager. Reluctantly transferred. He agreed down-the-line interview but we had to restart as he told me, "on air" that all would be clear in a press release. He didn't understand interviews but answered well with sufficient detail. The vessel was being searched and nine personnel remained on board. Contradicting earlier comment, he confirmed that some containers were still on the vessel which was alongside the jetty but other ships were in the area as it was difficult to move them at short notice. The company had not received any such threats previously and had improved security lately.

Language and culture

Language and culture can be major obstacles to fluent communication especially as big incidents attract major media attention, particularly from the English-speaking world. The extracts that follow are based on an exercise held abroad.

I cannot recall a media response team that suffered so badly from three basic factors. The responders' command of English was poor and often led to misunderstandings and premature finishes to phone calls. Secondly, their culture did not allow them to be particularly co-operative or to take the initiative as often as desirable and it was significant that not one of the responders, all of whom were very junior, used an external phone in their jobs. The inclusion of even one experienced person would have given other team members more confidence. The third factor was nervousness that influenced their efforts and led to premature efforts to halt conversations.

Doubtless, reflecting language problems, one shy responder failed to react to the allegation that "this is a particularly old vessel." One girl said that it was quite safe and that she had been on the vessel...This might have been a positive point but it left her vulnerable to detailed questions about the ship, which her colleagues could not answer etc. etc. Many responders lacked a basic understanding of the company beyond their own day-to-day activities. This meant that, reluctant to take the initiative, they were unable to imagine the scene at the accident and thus to "paint a picture".

Nervousness, particularly at the beginning, meant that they were telling journalists that they lacked some basic information when it was available from the boards or in their information sheets. Too many responders, and the second team, awaiting their turn to man the phones, congregated in front of the white boards so some responders could not see the updated information. The second team added to the noise level which was too high and induced fatigue.

There was no speculation, despite pressure, and the team was polite and calm and their performance improved steadily but if the journalists had been obliged to write stories before the press conference, which was handled very well, they would have reflected substantial corporate confusion.

Unfortunately, the response team co-ordinator arrived too late for a full briefing although he was offered advice during the afternoon. However, he spent too much time in the crisis management team room and not enough with his team. One simple solution would have been to ensure that there was no spare chair in the crisis room! Presumably, his continued presence in the crisis room was, partly, to ensure that some of the questions posed on the message sheets were answered. He always seemed involved in discussions but the responses were slow.

He emerged occasionally, to give his team some information, but this meant that there was nobody to assist them on an *ad hoc* basis. Collecting and sifting message forms, advising individuals on specific points during and after calls, reassuring them after calls, dealing with "difficult" journalists himself, ensuring that the board information was accurate and that responders were aware of the latest news and that they understood the latest press release and trying to make sure that all members of the team had a fair turn on the phone, was, therefore, not carried out effectively. He failed to appoint a deputy.

The media response team also suffered because no "simple and previously agreed phrases" had been conjured up to pass to the media. For example, in the continued absence of the co-ordinator, there was no phrase that could explain ownership of the company so the team seemed ignorant on a basic matter. Usually, the responders offered the press release but there were some problems in conveying the difference between the actual POB and the theoretical maximum, as printed in the Fact File.

Some responders were prematurely confident, assuring callers that, despite the absence of information, there had been no injuries! One deliberate error by a journalist, on the number of passengers and crew, was corrected. Biggest problem was lack of speedy and relevant information, such as a telephone number for next of kin. The responders were annoyed by their lack of basic information.

Why bother to have an exercise?

Even if a company holds regular exercises, their success depends, inevitably, on the systems devised and the personnel involved. What follows is a report on one such drill.

> This organisation staged exercises so often that some obviously bored specialist staff behaved unprofessionally. Some key staff had organised to be replaced by more junior colleagues. Consequently, response team advisors did not always understand their responsibilities. The leader was on holiday and his deputy had "more-important" work to do. The responders started badly: no Fact Files available. Instead, the response team's technical adviser referred to brochures and technical sheets-totally inadequate, in terms of their complexity, layout and language. Responders could not be expected to find the relevant section, absorb the unaccustomed detailed information speedily and then translate that into accurate day-to-day language for the media, all done whilst the journalist waited.

> Throughout the exercise, the picture conveyed was of a company talking to itself, with a near arrogant disregard for the outside world's requirements. Charged with finding out some basic information and hearing that the media was pushing hard on some elementary aspect on which there was no information, one press officer said "tough". That same person, an adviser to the response team, clearly well-informed technically, was more concerned with showing off technical knowledge, often irrelevant, rather than providing answers to important but non-technical questions.

> The company showed a potential for self-inflicted wounds reflecting disinterest, inexperience and a lack of leadership. Easily the worst part was in dealing with allegations made by a single issue pressure group which had claimed that, according to one of the company's own studies, its technology damaged the environment. Instead of refuting

this firmly and promptly, the company researched the allegation closely so there was a long delay during which time the organisation was crucified. The company contended that a prompt rebuttal would have encouraged journalists to ask how the organisation could be sure that the claim was untrue. If the denial had been delivered strongly and authoritatively, the media would have been satisfied, at least in the short run, whilst more technical ammunition was fashioned.

The media response team advisers, penalised by a lack of a division of labour, tried to solve too many problems simultaneously, resulting in their neglecting some basic issues.

Some companies hold regular exercises but...

Many organisations hold regular exercises, partly because of the turnover of staff and their possible lack of availability on a crucial day. The comments below reflect the fact that many individuals, in any exercise, are new to the task and that the role of the telephone media response team is crucial.

Initially, much confusion in the media telephone response room, partly because the co-ordinator, new in the company, did not understand the system. A poor start was exacerbated by his inability to take command and to allocate jobs. Colleagues complained that his ideas, not those laid down in procedures, nor suggested by the presenters, would lead to duplication, whilst other personnel lacked sufficient work. Confusion over who should write up information on the board. The co-ordinator, incorrectly, thought that answers to media-raised queries, coming back from the crisis room, should be given only to the responders who received the initial media call. So valuable time, that should have been spent understanding background material, was lost in an unnecessary debate over jobs.

Responders told journalists that they lacked information which was in their Fact Files. More intelligent personnel became indignant. Gradually, the team began to work well together and the co-ordinator learned quickly. Noise levels were kept down and big effort made to ensure that all responders understood the Fact File and press releases but they needed more time.

The first statement to emerge from the crisis room, confusingly, was described as a "reactive statement". Would have been more sensible to begin with press release number one. Issue of "reactive statement" caused problems in numbering the "proper" press releases. Two, 45 minutes apart, were both numbered one.

The oft-repeated phrase "informed by the captain" suggested that the information could not be corroborated and as incident occurred 100 miles off the coast of the most technically advanced country in the world, this was a regrettable impression. Table space occupied by each responder was tidy and spare copies of all relevant documents were laid out carefully. At least one responder, despite being repeatedly reminded that he could only use authorised information, revealed the nationality of the personnel on board the vessel which he could not have known except through personal knowledge.

The co-ordinator stopped one call that had lasted more than three minutes, even although the questions were neither repetitive nor irrelevant. Apparently, the topic at the time of the alleged cut off was the responder's unfortunate and imaginative admission that the company was on "red alert"!! The problem posed by this confession spread quickly but there was no collective attempt to deal with the repercussions of such a comment. The responders were rotated sensibly but they argued that the flow of information from the crisis management team was too slow. Was genuinely essential information reaching the telephone people sufficiently quickly? Asked about the weather, one responder said, *I don't know, I'm in France, not in America*, where the fictional accident had occurred. Responders tried to curtail calls prematurely.

A request for a radio interview was handled well but first question ended with a comment about terrorism. The interviewee said, "that's correct", implying that terrorism might have been the cause. Then painted a good picture of what was happening and that the crew was well trained. However, the phrase "act of terrorism" was used again by the interviewee and was met by the response of *I'm not terribly concerned about that*. Phrase "at this moment in time" used so frequently, it was surprising that the interviewer did not scream.

During a television interview, the participant said, *as we have already said in our press statement.* Knew nothing about the extent of the injuries on the second vessel involved in the accident and failed to bridge to more positive matters. Weak, especially on the evacuation of non-essentials, but that could reflect lack of self-confidence and knowledge. As a lawyer, probably reluctant to say anything until it's cleared.

In the first press conference, the response on compensation for next of kin was inadequate and it was unfortunate that some of the worst news seemed to have been held back. In both press conferences, the chairman rejected attempts at interruptions before reading his statement. Foolishly, refused to reveal his name and compared his vessel to the *Titanic!*

Another day, another exercise

The co-ordinator briefed her telephone media response team at 15.05 and the holding statement appeared 15 minutes later. A more experienced and confident co-ordinator would have used the whole of this period to ensure that the team was familiar with the Fact File. In her first exercise, she lacked the clout to secure important information from her senior colleagues in the crisis management team.

Early calls to the media telephone response team revealed some serious gaps in their knowledge of the company and the location at which the accident had occurred, although some of this information was in the Fact File. At this early stage, when the company's stance would influence the media for the remainder of the emergency, it was disappointing that responders did not say *hold on, please, I'll see if I have that information readily available....* They seemed reluctant to offer background information unless it had been requested.

Respondents lacked precise information on the number of people at the site but were slow to say that *typically, it would be about...* One responder guessed that the fire started after 4.00 am. Unfortunately, the incident had already been confirmed in a press release as having started some time before! Responders, ignorant on what happened at the site, made silly guesses that the media could have exploited dramatically.

One routine response, *I have no information on that* from someone whose main intention was to end calls as swiftly as possible, became so monotonous that one journalist came close to asking him for his name.

After about 30 minutes, the board was beginning to be filled up with information but later in the afternoon, there was no information on the emergency vehicles on site. The company lacked the imagination on how to handle a minor but important official. It was unwise to tell the mayor that a new press release would be issued shortly and he would have to wait. The role-playing mayor was treated badly by the crisis management team who terminated the conversation whilst the official was still speaking. This was conveyed to the journalists who used it to full advantage.

Told by one journalist of the "disgraceful" treatment of the mayor and asked for a comment, the chairman of the subsequent press conference said that he was not interested in the media's opinions. After a journalist's attempt to seek clarification of the figures of injured and missing, one authoritative panel member's clumsy intervention raised doubts on who was chairing the press conference and antagonised the journalists. The team was poor at offering details of its own fire-fighting facilities and their reply on the vexed issue of whether the missing man was on site was confusing.

The media were told that the building where the accident happened was 100 metres by 50. Earlier the media had been informed that it was 200,000 square metres in area! One hostile panel member informed the media, brusquely, that if they wanted to know the condition of the injured, they should contact the hospital. The chairman agreed that the consequential costs *could overwhelm us.*

And finally...

Some members of the telephone media response team had difficulty in suppressing their experience and knowledge. Early, when details about the incident were sparse, few responders offered background information. There was some useful anticipation of likely questions by the media co-ordinator, who had a good rapport with his team and the crisis management team. The board writing was well done and the room well-organised although some in-boxes would have prevented the inevitable chaos as the exercise progressed. Occasionally, there was a failure to anticipate questions that would be prompted by comments in the press releases.

There were no examples of speculation but the biggest problem related to the fate of the officer's wife. How to cope with this sensitive issue spoiled one television interview when the company man looked visibly uncomfortable as the point was pressed and his reasons for not answering the question were unconvincing. Regrettably, the interviewee failed to maintain eye contact with the interviewer and he was poor at editing his own answers.

At the press conference, team members did not correct the chairman's error when he said, *lives had been lost.* It was also unfortunate that he admitted, *we are a little bit distressed.* He should have involved his team more. Even by the end of the press conference, the company had not been able to confirm basic information. Bizarrely, the chairman invited the media to pray with him for those involved suggesting that he had a moral superiority over the journalists!

Some comments on specific training

Television

Although * was fairly fluent, his initial failure to maintain eye contact could be a problem. In the afternoon interview, he failed to bridge satisfactorily, thus allowing the interviewer to ask at least 12 questions. Furthermore, he failed to express any regret about the dead and injured. * appeared sceptical about the whole exercise and although competent and looking right on camera, he was dismissive in his interviews. *seemed competent in front of the camera and looked suitably grave when the occasion demanded.

Telephone response

The team's performance was disappointing, given their combined experience and status within the group. Despite being told to make maximum use of background information, they ignored this advice just when it was necessary to win the support of the media if they wanted journalists to ring back. The responders' main objective seemed to be to terminate calls as rapidly as possible. The approach was far too negative.

As the information came in and as the team's confidence grew, they were a little more forthcoming but some responders were ignorant on the company's activities. Nobody was prepared to take a chance on what the group chairman felt about the incident. This might have been a good time for the co-ordinator to organise a short time-out, to agree a sensible comment but nothing happened. One journalist's erroneous assertions that there had been a number of serious casualties were denied but another responder allowed a journalist to claim that there had been a fire and explosion but later interrupted to make a correction. Once again, responders did not use the Fact File. Some responders lapsed into corporate speak as they tired and there was the usual inconsistency on numbers of people involved.

Press conference

The chairman made a bad mistake in not reading out the latest statement, thus forcing the journalists to read the release later. *I'm not at liberty to say* used frequently by several members of the press conference team would have provoked some interesting questions in real life. The team was good on compensation and when denying that complacency might have been a factor in the accident but they were not sure on how to deal with the issue of sabotage.

Finally, here is a blunt appraisal of one company instructed by its parent group to have an exercise.

Without doubt, this was the worst performance I have ever encountered. I shall remember this day's efforts as encapsulating virtually all the errors it's possible to make and this group invented some new ones. In real life this effort would have led to genuine disaster and, frankly, I doubt if the company would have survived. The blend of ignorance and hostility was truly impressive.

STORIES WRITTEN AFTER EXERCISES

Ideally, all major exercises should incorporate communication with the media. This is essential because, ultimately, however successful the operations undertaken to minimise injury and environmental damage, the company's reputation will suffer unless this is conveyed to the outside world. The only genuine way to determine the success of an exercise is to hire professional journalists to ring the company's telephone media response team, during the exercise, and to ask questions of them and of senior management at a press conference before writing a story.

Restraints and advantages

Some organisations opt to hire journalists at two separate locations which is useful if different languages or cultures are involved in two different countries. This practice is also used when the company is operating two "information centres". Such an approach usually fails, from the company's perspective, because skilled journalists can soon detect inconsistencies in the information being given by the two different teams of responders and this will be reflected in their stories which will imply corporate confusion and incompetence. Big companies, confronted by major disasters, operate just one media response centre.

In most instances, hired journalists can only use information obtained from the telephone media response team. Specialist journalists are often used by different sectors of industry and may be allowed to use their knowledge of the sector, as this could happen in "real life". Additionally, such journalists are allowed to pass on such information to their colleagues in the exercise and to explain any technical issues. Because the number of journalists involved is modest and because their sources are usually limited to asking the company's media response team questions, they are encouraged to share interesting pieces of information secured from the company and are invited to exploit any inconsistencies. Competition between the journalists is suspended in favour of putting maximum pressure on the media response team. More pressure comes from the fact that the journalists will each represent different parts of the media during the exercise. So, for example, a tabloid paper will be more interested in whether there were any females working at the site that has just blown up whilst some papers will show interest in the financial cost and the commercial consequences.

This allows the journalists to be more imaginative and enables the media response team to have some exposure to different parts of the media, their different objectives and styles, in a relatively short time.

Occasionally, the external organisers of an exercise will employ a limited number of individuals to act as spokespeople for other groups, such as hospitals and police, but this is seldom successful as they can undermine an exercise which, after all, is intended to test the host company.

Finally, the course presenters, charged with ensuring that the media response team and the journalists are working towards achieving the exercise objectives, can pass on interesting information to the journalists, or, if necessary, can invent a new rumour, solely to test out the reaction of the response team. In that way, the exercise remains flexible and efforts can even be concentrated on a particular individual. Unscheduled but imaginative interventions can also be made if a media response team is becoming complacent.

Stories and analysis

Some journalists will write scathing stories but this is not encouraged as it can undermine the confidence of the volunteers who constitute the media response team. However, articles, like broadcast interviews and press conferences during training, should allow the team to be taken to the edge of the cliff and to be shown the rocks below, whilst being held back securely. The immediate debrief should allow discussion of the stories and some debate on the more major errors, without, of course, identifying the culprit. That said, if some major mistakes have been made and the company has been negative or arrogant towards the media, the stories should reflect this and the hired journalists are usually allowed to speculate on the likely reaction to an organisation's reaction to the accident.

Many course participants take exception to headlines and attack the journalists but they seldom compose the titles to their own pieces. Company personnel, conditioned to accept that their organisation always tells the whole truth, often react critically when hearing an adverse comment in the story. Another point not always understood by responders is that they cannot influence the lurid language used. A fire might be promoted to a conflagration and smoke, the constituents of which cannot be identified by a company, which, in itself will appear puzzling to the media, might become a toxic brew or even a cloud of death. Ultimately, stories after exercises can show management what is important to the outside world and how easy it is to attract adverse comment. What follows demonstrates that the absence of a company response or a careless remark can have a very negative impact.

SHIPPING COMPANY IS SILENT ON MYSTERY CRUISE LINER EXPLOSION

According to local reports, at about seven o'clock this morning, an explosion rocked the cruise liner **, some ...miles south of the Azores in the Atlantic. **It is thought** that there would have been some ** people on board the ** year-old vessel, **one of the oldest still in regular service.** The owners of the vessel, ** **specialise in economy-level cruises for pensioners.** The vessel, **described by one shipping expert as an "elderly rust bucket",** sailed from Southampton on **.

The vessel is registered in **, known in shipping circles as a **flag of convenience** state, **because its safety requirements are more lax than in other maritime nations.** Its vessels' **crews come from Third World countries,** which, according to one former passenger, created problems as they had **little command of English.**

** **were unable to add anything to this early report, even after nearly five hours.** They could not say **if anyone had been injured, whether an evacuation had begun or whether there had been a fire. Nor could they reveal whether rescue vessels or helicopters had been despatched and they were unable to comment on the extent of on-board medical facilities.** One spokesman thought that some Super Puma helicopters, **identical to the one that crashed off Norway last week, with the loss of 12 lives, might be on their way to the apparently stricken vessel.**

According to local weather forecasts, the weather in the area is expected to deteriorate later in the day and this will further compli-cate any rescue attempts.

A shipping expert **speculated that a fire might have started in the engine room, as a similar incident had occurred about four years ago,** when two crew members were killed.

The company's failure to communicate is already causing uproar. **Relatives of the passengers are angry that they cannot find out what happened and EU members of Parliament are calling for the shipping authorities to come down hard on what one MEP described** as *this cowboy company. Society demands that companies are very open on these occasions. **, for whatever reason, has ignored next of kin, officials and the media, and, above all, for all we know, its customers. We have a right to know. We have no idea of what happened and this is totally* **unacceptable.**

A spokesperson for the company, admitting that he did not know what had happened, nevertheless argued **that the safety record of its vessels was excellent but was unable to provide any supporting evidence for the claim.**

This latest apparent fiasco could prove to be a serious blow to the company that has already been **forced to sell assets and lay off staff worldwide** in recent years because of serious financial problems. Industry sources say that ** is a **little-known and introvert company. European cruises contribute about ** of its profits,** according to informed sources, so this reverse and the **resulting negative publicity could be catastrophic to the group in its efforts to survive in an increasingly competitive market.**

If this story had followed an exercise, the company could take action to ensure that its systems were changed. However, if this incident had happened in "real life", such an article would have hastened the company's demise. Because of the company's inability to communicate, the journalist used his knowledge and experience to invent sensible quotations from other people and to "editorialise". By ignoring demands for information, the company, effectively, has encouraged the journalist not just to go to other sources, but to speculate.

Analysis

After a piece like this, few informed potential passengers would select this company for their next holiday but so much of the negative coverage could have been avoided by sensible communication from the company. It has not even been confirmed that there has been an accident!

It is thought

Why cannot this information be confirmed? Words like "thought", "believed" "felt" merely imply a lack of certainty and add to the appearance of incompetence. If the company genuinely lacked information, it would have been useful to explain why it did not know what had happened and what it was doing to find out and take appropriate measures. In any event, it could have provided some indication of the numbers of passengers on the ship.

One of the oldest still in regular service

Even if this is true, it may well be that excellent construction and regular maintenance means that the vessel is at least as good as more modern ones. Furthermore, there are strict rules imposed by international authorities that are designed to prevent sub-standard vessels from work. When was this vessel last inspected?

Specialise in economy-level cruises for pensioners

This implies a rather discreditable operation, planned to provide minimal facilities for those who cannot afford anything better. The company could have corrected this view if it had bothered to speak to the media.

Described by one shipping expert as an "elderly rust bucket"

The company's failure to comment has prompted the journalist to seek other sources. Was this "shipping expert" someone with a vested interest in criticising the cruise liner owners?

Flag of convenience...because its safety requirements are more lax than in other maritime nations.

This allegation might have been true several years ago but it is now widely regarded as wrong.

Crews come from Third World countries…with little command of English

This suggests that "Third World" crews are less efficient or skilful than those from, for example, Western Europe. However, there is a dearth of personnel from this region and, in any event, crews from "Developing nations" are competent and employers usually insist on their speaking good English.

Were unable to add anything to this early report, even after nearly five hours.. if anyone had been injured, whether an evacuation had begun or whether there had been a fire. Nor could they reveal whether rescue vessels or helicopters had been despatched and they were unable to comment on the extent of on-board medical facilities.

This, of course, is the most damaging comment and portrays the company as uncaring, callous and incompetent.

Identical to the one that crashed off Norway last week, with the loss of 12 lives, might be on their way to the apparently stricken vessel.

This, of course, is a further negative comment, especially as it is not even certain that there is a need for evacuation. The company spokesperson, doubtless irked by his ignorance, has speculated. Furthermore, there is no comment that, notwithstanding the Norwegian accident, the Puma is one of the safest of helicopters.

Speculated that a fire might have started in the engine room, as a similar incident had occurred about four years ago

In the absence of comment from the company, the journalist has found someone to help him add detail to the story but the comment is just speculation. Did a "similar" incident occur? This wording suggests that the current incident has been confirmed!

Relatives of the passengers are angry that they cannot find out what happened and EU members of Parliament are calling for the shipping authorities to come down hard on what one MEP described as this cowboy company...

Inevitably, politicians and others will use such a story to advance their own interests and this is legitimate. In such incidents in "real life" relatives of passengers thought to be involved in an accident can become justifiably angry at the lack of information as was shown after a ferry accident in Egypt in 2006.

That the safety record of its vessels was excellent but was unable to provide any supporting evidence for the claim

This can happen in "real life". Journalists will not merely include such comments without supporting evidence.

Forced to sell assets and lay off staff worldwide

If this is true, is it because the company had changed its role? It may be that it had to take this action, because like other companies in the sector, its trading position was being undermined by poor market conditions over which it had no control.

Little-known and introvert company

If the company has made no effort to communicate with the media in "normal times" and offers little information about itself in the emergency, it must be assumed that it is little known and introvert.

European cruises contribute about ** of its profits

This may be true but would the journalist have looked for this "fact" if he had been plied with useful information from the company?

Resulting negative publicity could be catastrophic to the group in its efforts to survive in an increasingly competitive market.

After this story, and, doubtless many others, it is doubtful if anyone would want to cruise with this company.

CHAPTER 17

QUESTIONS, ANSWERS AND ALLEGATIONS

This selection contains possible questions and some potential answers but they should not be regarded as "model" answers. Spontaneous answers, in an individual's own words, are always preferable to slick, intensely-rehearsed responses. The replies merely suggest a method of dealing with questions.

Sometimes, of course, these suggested responses might be irrelevant, inaccurate or untruthful and organisations must never lie to the media nor seek to mislead journalists. This chapter shows that many questions can be anticipated and answers compiled in advance. Some of these questions will prompt organisations, which have not had to confront emergency-related issues, to devise answers to issues such as compensation or *ex gratia* payments. An organisation should not be damaged because an interviewer or a journalist can make it look inadequate. The company should know how to deal with a fair but difficult question and how to avoid appearing ignorant or uncaring. Few business people are in regular contact with the media and, when the pressure is enormous, it is easy to make serious errors because of the powerful combination of stress and ignorance of media techniques.

It is impossible to separate the questions that might be addressed to each business sector or even type of media responder, so, in the main, they are presented, loosely, by topic. Patently, journalists can always ask more questions, whatever the subject, so the following is but a selection of the more obvious.

EARLY IN THE EVOLUTION OF THE INCIDENT

You say that there has been an incident. What is an incident?
We define an incident as an event that disrupts routine operations at the location, so it could be something minor, which doesn't have any impact on people or on the environment and we hope, of course, that this incident proves to be a very minor one. Meanwhile, can I tell you something about our organisation?

What happened and have there been any casualties?
The incident only occurred *about* * minutes ago, so I'm sorry that I really don't have any more than I have given you/which is in our first press release, which you say you have/which I'll read out to you, but perhaps I could tell you something about the company and its activities in the UK and overseas? OR At this early stage, we don't have all the details, but what I can tell you is... OR Before I respond to that question, I must tell you that, tragically, * men lost their lives earlier today, because of the fire/explosion at * and I'm sorry to say that another * people have been injured. They have been taken to hospital and our local representatives and the police are working together to inform the next of kin as soon as possible. . All of us are shattered at what has happened and we're so sorry for the families involved. The good news is that everyone else has been accounted for.

Where and when did it happen?
At the moment, we have very little information about what happened and all that I can tell you is, as our first press release indicates, is that there was an incident on/at * at about *, earlier today.

What was happening at the site at the time and was production shut down promptly?

How close is the site to the nearest residential area?

Will local people be evacuated?
Such a decision will be taken by the local authorities but we're working closely with all the services involved.

*How much * was produced at the factory/refinery/stored in the depot before the accident and what proportion is that of total UK supplies?*

Does that mean that there will be a shortage?

What is made at the plant and what is that used for?

What was the weather like at the time of the accident and could it have contributed to the accident?
It was ... at the time of the incident and it's much too early to say whether that was relevant but it may be one of the many factors considered by the official enquiry.

PEOPLE

It is now two hours since the explosion on your offshore oil platform/factory/depot/vessel but you still cannot say how many were on the site at the time and whether all have been accounted for. Why not?"
I'm sorry that I can't give you the precise number yet as our main objective is to evacuate all those involved to safe refuges and as this operation is still continuing, I can't offer specific figures and I don't want to mislead you. What I can say is that there were some * passengers and crew on the vessel/ there was accommodation for * people on the rig/platform/ that, usually, there would be about * people on site at this time of the day. We can't give you precise figures on casualties, but we can confirm that *...

Does the figure of those on site at the time of the accident include contractors and company personnel?
Contractors would have been working at the site at the time, but I hope to have the numbers later.

*I understand that * men have been killed. Can you confirm this?*
At this stage, I have no information on the number of casualties, beyond what I have already confirmed. OR As I have said, tragically, we know that some people have lost their lives but the police have asked us to withhold all details until the next of kin have been informed and I'm sure that you can understand, then, that there is nothing more that I can say at present. OR At this stage, I am sorry that I have not received the details, as my colleagues are actively concerned in assisting at the rescue. You'll appreciate that the accident only occurred * minutes ago. However, unhappily, there have been some fatalities and I know that some people have been injured.

We are working closely with the emergency services, especially the police, and all are doing a magnificent job in very difficult circumstances.

Has anyone been injured?
I'm sorry, but so far, I have no information on the number of casualties, beyond what I have already confirmed. However, the emergency services are on their way to the site and should be there at about * OR within the next few minutes OR the emergency services arrived within * minutes of the alarm. In addition, there is a standby vessel, close to the rig/platform, 24 hours a day, 365 days a year. It has fire-fighting equipment and some medical facilities, designed to offer immediate first aid. It also has a helipad so, if necessary, and depending on the circumstances, a helicopter could land and take off any injured.

What was the nature of the injuries?
I'm sorry but I can't give you any details, but happily they are not life-threatening/but sadly they are very serious.

Is everyone accounted for?
I'm sorry, but, at present I myself don't have any information on that. However, the emergency services are on their way to the site and should be there at about *. Meanwhile...

The missing men have been in the water for some time. Realistically, their prospects of surviving must be minimal, don't you agree?
Many factors determine survival times, such as the temperature of the water, the age and state of health of the men and what they were wearing. There are examples of people surviving for this length of time and we remain hopeful, which is why the search is being sustained.

Have the next of kin of those killed/injured been informed?

What is the telephone number for the next of kin to ring?

Where, precisely, were the casualties working at the time of the explosion/fire etc?

How long have they been working for the company?

What clothing would the missing men have been wearing?

What are the nationalities of those killed/injured or missing?
I'm sorry but I cannot comment on this until the next of kin have been advised. I'm sure you'll understand the reasons for this, especially as we have a number of different nationalities working for us at the site/on the vessel.

When will you be able to give details of the casualties?

Where are the injured being taken for treatment and when will they reach there?

Will you transport the relatives, at your cost, to the hospital?

What advice can you give to local residents/next of kin?

What do you say to the local people?

What measures are being taken to ensure that the local people do not suffer if they inhale the smoke/drink the liquid, touch the chemical etc?
You must ask the authorities that question although, of course, we are co-operating in any way that we can.

THE CURRENT SITUATION AND FACILITIES AT THE SITE

What is happening at the site now?

Are the emergency services on the site now and when did they arrive?

Is the fire out/when do you expect it to be extinguished?

Who is fighting the fire?

What fire-fighting facilities are there at the site and what role do your firemen play?

Is it fair to expect amateur fire-fighters to tackle such a blaze?

Our on-site fire-fighters, all volunteers, train with the professionals and participate with them in regular exercises. Incidentally, I must point out that, currently, the fire is not sufficiently serious to prompt evacuation of the site.

What is the extent of the damage so far?

Did you have any medical facilities at the site? If not, why not?

How would the personnel be evacuated?

What is the capacity of the lifeboats? Is there one place for each and every passenger and, if not, why not?

I understand that there is only one entrance and exit at the site and that it is blocked. If that is true, what are the implications for extinguishing the fire?

THE IMPACT ON THE ENVIRONMENT

Has there been any pollution and if so, how will you combat it?
I'm pleased to say that there has been no pollution OR there has been some pollution and our own experts and the authorities are co-operating in devising and implementing a plan to minimise its impact.

What products are involved in the pollution and what is their effect on people and animal/fish life?

What are you doing to minimise the environmental impact of this accident?

What are the constituents of the smoke from the stricken vessel/the depot/factory?

What was in the containers that fell to the bottom of the ocean/blew up?
(Because it is important to have answers to the inevitable follow-up questions, the organisation may opt to remain silent on these crucial questions whilst it is investigating fully, but procrastination has its limits and a long delay will be construed as incompetence.)

Will the company's insurance cover be sufficient to offer sensible compensation to all those who have been adversely affected by today's disaster?

Who has insured the vessel/factory/depot etc and for how much?

How much will the clean-up cost?
We haven't considered that. Our objectives are to rescue the people involved and ensure that they receive the best available medical attention and to minimise the impact of any pollution.

Was anti-pollution equipment available at the site and if not, why not and will you ensure that adequate supplies will be available at all your sites in future?

There must have been a delay as you had to source it from some distance. Will you change your policy in future?
I'm sure that this, and many other issues, will be considered by the investigating team.

What kind of oil/chemical/liquid has been spilt and how much of it will evaporate?

How do you collect the oil/chemical/liquid that has been spilled?

Will you be using dispersants, and, if so, what kind? Are they toxic?

What are you doing to minimise the repercussions and to prevent the oil/chemicals/ dangerous material reaching the coast?

When do you expect the oil/chemical/dangerous material to hit the coast?
It's difficult to tell even whether it will reach the coast because of the wind speed and direction and currents, but we and the authorities are working very hard to prevent such an eventuality. We hope that nothing reaches the shore but equipment from * is being moved into place at * to minimise the extent of any pollution if necessary.

CAUSES OF THE ACCIDENT

Why did this accident happen?
At the moment, it is impossible to say. Nobody knows. It's too soon. A number of official enquiries have already begun/will soon commence work, and I can't and don't want to pre-empt their conclusions on why this tragedy occurred. We are very keen to find out precisely what happened and we shall then take whatever action is appropriate to ensure that, as far as possible, such an accident will never recur.

Yes, but you must have some idea?
As I said, "it's much too early to say". .

I realise that you can't say much about * but, as someone who has been in the industry for * years and is widely respected/ who has been recommended to me, what do you feel about the causes?
As you say, I've been in the industry for some time and it is precisely because of my experience that I can tell you that, at this stage, we cannot possibly know what caused the accident.

I realise that at this stage, you cannot say what caused the disaster, but what kinds of things could have caused....?
It would be wrong to speculate and I don't think that it would be very helpful to comment on what could go wrong. Suffice it to say that we are well aware of the potential dangers in.... and that is why we place safety at the very top of our list of essentials and train our personnel to....and carry out regular training and exercises. We must wait for the enquiry to tell us what happened and there is no more that I can say on that subject now.

Let me re-word the question. How could an accident of this kind happen?
I cannot speculate.

I'm not asking you to speculate on what happened on this one occasion. I'm asking you, as an expert, what factors could cause such an accident.
Working in this sector is an inherently and potentially dangerous activity, which is why all of us in this industry pay so much heed to safety. However, because the operations are so complex, it would be irresponsible of me to begin to discuss the factors that could cause an accident. I'm sorry, but that's as far as I can go.

You will have heard a radio interview earlier today when a member of the crew/personnel on site said that the cause of the accident was....How do you respond to this?

Yes, I did hear that interview. We must acknowledge that the man who gave the interview had just had one of the most traumatic moments of his life and we must await the enquiry's report.

I imagine that the cost of today's accident must be in the millions. Does that sound about right to you, as an industry expert?

At this stage, nobody in the company has given any thought to the costs, direct or consequential. Our efforts are concentrated, one hundred per cent, on saving lives, rescuing and treating the injured and minimising damage to the environment.

You have just said that you don't know the cause of the accident, and that we must wait for the results of the various enquiries. That must mean, that, as you don't know the causes, you cannot rule out the possibility that this was the work of terrorists?

You're right: we don't yet know the causes, but, at present, we have absolutely no reason whatsoever to believe that this was the result of terrorist action.

But it remains a possibility?

As I have just explained, there's no reason to believe that what happened was the result of terrorist action, but, if you have any evidence that it may have been, we would be pleased to consider it and to pass it to the appropriate authorities. We've not had any terrorist threats and have no reason to believe that this was the cause of the accident. (Many executives fail to offer this kind of answer so there could be headlines like "terrorism suspected in factory blast". Later, that could sound like an attempt to avoid responsibility if the enquiry rules that a lack of maintenance was the cause.)

How old is the factory/ plant/vessel?

The factory/plant/vessel was built/constructed in * but it has been maintained to the highest standards and exceeds the minima laid down by government and has always passed all the official inspections.

Does your company have sufficient experience to run this kind of operation?

It's been suggested that your company has cut manpower levels and maintenance. Could this have had anything to do with the accident?

Who do you blame for this accident?
At the moment, we don't know why it happened, and we shan't until the enquiry reports, so there is no question of blaming anyone or anything at this stage.

COMPENSATION AND EX GRATIA PAYMENTS

Questions relating to compensation occur frequently at press conferences and the response must be handled very sensitively but firmly. The specific questions can vary and may include some of the following:

Can you tell me what is the death in service benefit?/ How much compensation will be paid to the next of kin and how are the figures determined?/ How soon will payments be made?/Your salary is about *. How much will be offered to the next of kin of those who were drowned/burned to death/lost their lives?/Will the compensation for next of kin be generous, at American levels, or mean, at European levels?/As an officer from western Europe and a rating from the Philippines both sadly lost their lives in this shipping accident, will the next of kin receive the same compensation?
Compensation is a confidential and private matter that concerns only the individuals and the company so I shall not be commenting further except to say that we shall behave responsibly and do our utmost to ensure that payments will be made speedily. (Any figure could be ridiculed by the media as inadequate. No sum of money can compensate for the loss of a loved one. The response must never refer to any international agreements or nationality. Responders must not be trapped into discussing the basis or extent of compensation as this could suggest that a person from a developing country is less valuable than, say, an OECD citizen. If payment differs it does so because of the relative incomes and rank and has nothing to do with nationality.)

Will you pay reasonable ex gratia sums to those whose lives have been disrupted by today's accident?

We shall be treating all reasonable requests for *ex gratia* payments sympathetically. Those involved should either ring us on **** or visit the claims office, which will be open tomorrow at **. We certainly don't want anybody to suffer because of this accident and perhaps I should also add that we are....

RESIGNATIONS

As the person responsible for maintenance in your company will you resign if the enquiry finds that the accident was caused by inadequate maintenance?
I'm confident that maintenance will not be seen as the cause of the accident so the question is hypothetical. (Alternatively, unless the question is directed at the chairman of the press conference, he should intervene. *There is no question of my colleague resigning.*) (If the subsequent report does accuse the head of maintenance as being neglectful, his future can be discussed at that time but, by then, the media interest will have faded.)

As chairman of this company, will you resign because of what has happened?
That is a matter for my colleagues to decide but if the report clearly cited a failure for which I was responsible, I would, of course, consider my position.

REPERCUSSIONS ON THE COMPANY

What effect will the accident have on supplies of products/services/power to the local community/country?

What is the reaction of your senior management to this accident?
Everybody in the company is deeply saddened by what happened today to our colleagues and our senior managers are doing all they can to minimise the impact. Three board members are already on their way to the site.

Will your chief executive go to the scene of the accident?
He is already playing a strong co-ordinating role, leaving the on-site work to his technical colleagues but he may well go to the site later.

What do you think will be the impact on the company's cash flow/share price/profitability etc. of this accident?
Frankly, all our efforts are concentrated on minimising the impact of the emergency on individuals/ the environment, and we're not considering the impact on our finances in any way. If, however, this question is important to you, I can try to find out and ask one of my colleagues to ring you back. (This approach is only recommended when talking to serious financial journalists from respected and influential specialist publications.) Otherwise, omit the last sentence and complete the answer with the following: If you are interested in this aspect, I suggest that you ring us again in a few days. Meanwhile, is there any information that I can send you about the company, including our annual report and interim results? Our website has some information that may help you.

How badly damaged is the facility and when will it be able to resume production?
It is much too soon to make any sensible evaluations. All our efforts are being concentrated on looking after/ looking for/ the people/safeguarding the environment.

What punitive action do you expect the government to take against your company/the industry?
This was the first accident we have had in more than * years at the site but I cannot speculate on what the government may or may not do.

How significant was this vessel/pipeline/refinery/terminal/factory/asset, to the company?

What was the capital cost of the rig/platform/terminal/plant/vessel/office block?

Will insurance cover the cost of re-building or will you close the site down?

Would you yourself live close to this site, now that this disaster has occurred?
I am happy living where I am but, if I had to move, certainly, I would consider this area.

Will you buy back local properties of those who want to move away from what they now regard as a very dangerous plant? That was the offer made by a big oil company after a fire threatened a number of homes.
I would dispute the description of the plant that you ascribe to the local people. This is the first serious accident we have had for * years so I personally see no reason to buy back any properties.

Obviously, you are keen to learn all you can from this accident to ensure that such a disaster never happens again. I imagine, therefore, that you will automatically be implementing all the enquiry's recommendations or might you reject some of the recommendations?
The enquiry has only just started and we don't know what they will recommend. Whilst I am not prepared, at this stage, to say that we shall automatically implement each and every recommendation, we've never ignored any official advice in the past and I'd be surprised if we did in the future. You will understand, however, that I am not prepared to commit the company to something that I have not even seen. Perhaps I can remind you that the system allows the company to discuss the recommendations with the authorities so we must all await the report.

Do you expect to be prosecuted for corporate manslaughter?

Do you expect to secure new licences to operate in the future?
The enquiry has not yet completed its investigations but we are confident that we shall not be held responsible for the accident.

SAFETY AND HEALTH

Which organisation will be carrying out the investigation?

What will be the main focus of the investigation?

The North Sea/shipping/transportation/manufacturing industry has a really bad safety record. Why do things go wrong so often?
I totally reject the premise in your question, but I can't speak for the industry and, if you want information on that, I suggest that you ring the trade association. However, what I can say is that for our organisation safety is, and always has been, of paramount importance. We have been

involved in this country for * years and this is our first major accident, which is another reason why we're all so sad.

What is your company's safety record?
It compares with that of the best in the industry. We have been involved in * different countries, carried * million passengers/driven * million miles over the last * years and I'm pleased to say, we have had no serious injuries or fatalities in that period. We operate * vessels/vehicles that, together have travelled the equivalent of * times around the world in the last ** years without any fatalities.

Some medical experts say that the local people are now more likely to contract cancer in the future. Are they right?
The accident has only just happened and it is obviously much too soon to be making such dire and alarming forecasts. I'm not a medical person but I understand that many specialists have already ridiculed this suggestion.

What specific measures did you take at the site to avoid an accident of this kind?

What fire-fighting and medical facilities are available on the site?

How close are the nearest houses/schools etc?

Why was such a potentially dangerous plant located near industrial and residential property?
We are not complacent, but this was the first serious accident at the plant in * years. Furthermore, it was operating safely for years before the surrounding area was developed. Additionally, we meet and exceed all the regulations relating to safety and environment and keep the local community fully informed on all developments.

Is it right that such a vessel comes so close to a centre of population carrying such a dangerous cargo?
We're not complacent and we certainly regret what happened but we must put this into context. It is the first serious accident we've had at the port in * years. Furthermore, many hundreds of vessels have visited the port without incident over that period and, of course, we and our colleagues in

the sector meet and exceed all the regulations relating to safety and environment. That said, we shall learn what we can from the official report.

Has there been a similar accident at this plant or at any plant like this in other parts of the world?

Why is an office block located in the middle of such a potentially dangerous plant?

How were the personnel evacuated?

What safety measures are on the installation/at the factory?

When was the plant/vessel/installation last inspected and by whom?

How often are training exercises/drills carried out at the site and who participates?

How detailed is an aircraft inspection before it flies across the Atlantic?

What is you safety budget?
Like so many large companies, we don't have a safety budget as such because safety is an integral part of all our operations. We never, ever, skimp on safety.

If this accident had occurred at a different location/time of day, the impact would have been catastrophic?
Happily it didn't and I won't speculate on what might or might not have happened.

Do you accept moral responsibility for this accident?
We all mean different things by moral responsibility but I can tell you that we and the emergency services have reacted swiftly to minimise the impact of today's sad accident. Those who needed treatment were evacuated to local hospitals within minutes, all our staff who are not involved in assisting the emergency services are off the site and currently there are * fire-tenders on site, as well as many other emergency vehicles. We are doing all we can to help the people involved and are making plans to... The whole company

is deeply saddened by what has happened: my colleagues and I know some of the people involved and everyone is doing what they can to minimise the impact of this tragic event. Subsequently, we shall all be studying the enquiry's report, to see what can be done to ensure that we learn all the lessons of this accident.

Can you guarantee that this kind of accident will not happen again?
No, I cannot because our industry is a potentially dangerous one and we all know that, in every industry, despite training and testing, human beings can make mistakes and equipment can fail. However, we shall be doing everything we can to minimise the chances of this kind of accident happening again and, if it is appropriate, we shall be discussing the results of the enquiry with other companies operating in our sector, as well as with the Health and Safety Executive. We want to learn from today's accident.

Can you put your hand on your heart and say, with total honesty, that your company could not have done anything to prevent today's accident?
In some ways, that is an impossible question to answer for the simple reason that we are all human beings and we all make mistakes, including the media. Furthermore, we don't yet know why the accident occurred. What I can say is that we have always done everything we could to avoid accidents. Our safety record over the years bears this out.

*I understand that * happened. That seems the most likely cause of the accident doesn't it?*
It may seem like that to you, but it certainly doesn't to me. My colleagues and I have worked in this sector long enough to know that it is highly complex and it would be unwarranted and irresponsible, at this stage, to guess on the causes of the accident.

SHIPPING ACCIDENTS

Many of the questions listed earlier in this chapter are relevant to the shipping sector so are not repeated.

What was the vessel's route and cargo?

How many people were on board and how many were passengers and crew?

Was a pilot on board and did he have the ultimate responsibility at the time of the accident?

Aircraft carry black boxes. Why don't your vessels? Is it a question of cost?

Name one innovative safety measure that you have initiated in the last five years.

What is your company's policy on drugs and alcohol on board your vessels?

Do you carry out independent, surprise inspections?

Has anyone ever be found guilty after an inspection and, if so, what happened?

Was the tanker double-hulled? If not, why not?

How often has the master done this voyage?

Did a navigational error cause this accident?

What type of crude oil/cargo/liquid was being carried on the tanker/ container vessel and will it dissipate quickly into the atmosphere?

Why did the vessel drift? Why did it not have auxiliary power to allow it to drop the anchors?

Was another vessel involved?

Who owns the vessel and where are they based?

Has the vessel ever been detained in a port for safety reasons?

With whom is it insured and for how much?

ALLEGATIONS, ACCUSATIONS AND USEFUL PHRASES

A company involved in an accident may be attacked by an "expert" or even a former employee, alleging that he warned the organisation some time ago that an accident was inevitable because of poor maintenance etc. The group must be aware of any such accusations, in advance, and have a response, however inadequate, when media calls begin. A company should consider all the skeletons in its cupboard. A simple question might relate, for example, to the safety record of a plant or vessel, and whether similar plants or vessels have been involved in accidents in the past. Many questions can arise indirectly from eye witness comments, claims from trade unions, allegations that some companies had the technology, that, if it had not been rejected by the "victim" company, lives could have been saved etc. Here is a brief selection of quotes, questions and allegations:

This is our worst nightmare and we've been saying for 15 years that something like this would happen.

Environmental experts query tanker's course.

No one told us how dangerous it was to live here.

Tug 'could have saved vessel if crew had stayed'.

Experts say that this site/vessel/plant was too old and should have been closed down/withdrawn from service many years ago: was that a factor in what happened today?
I don't know who these "experts" are but if they are experienced, they will know that what really matters is maintenance and training of the staff. We've not stinted on either.

Was the delay in summoning aid to avoid expenditure?

Why did the master of the stricken vessel define his position incorrectly?

The vessel was 20 years old, had a flag of convenience and was manned by a Third World crew. Marine experts say it was an accident waiting to happen. They're right, aren't they?
I don't know who these "marine experts" are but they are wrong in leaping to such conclusions. We maintain our vessels scrupulously to meet all inter-national regulations and countries offering so-called "flags of convenience"

now demand some of the highest standards of safety. Developing World crews are often amongst the best available and vessel maintenance is one of our top priorities. Frankly, such allegations are not only out of date, they are just plain wrong.

Your organisation is a small company operating in a potentially dangerous environment and in a sector where the government continues to impose more costly safety regulations. You can't really afford to operate safely, can you?

I must correct you. Our company is part of a large, experienced group and we certainly can operate safely in this country. We can only operate if we have all the right licences and approvals from the government and we're inspected regularly. We've been operating in this country since 19** and the accident today was our first ever involving a fatality, which is why we are all so sad.

You've lied or misled us in the past over * years. Why should we believe you now?

That is a serious charge. I'd like to discuss it with you at another time to ensure that, if such an incident did occur in the past, and it may have been a simple misunderstanding, it isn't repeated. What I've told you now is true and has been confirmed by senior management.

One survivor said that it was only a matter of time before an accident occurred as training and maintenance budgets have been cut.

I'm unaware of these remarks so cannot comment on them but I'd be amazed if they had been said because, as all my colleagues at the site know, we've never cut maintenance or safety training. Safety remains at the very top of our list. That's why we run regular training and emergency exercises and why trade union representatives sit on all our local committees and make a valuable contribution. I'm completely unaware of any adverse comments coming from those committees.

(It is a favourite ploy of journalists to claim that someone has said something critical, or a report alleges something negative about the company etc. However, the responder must always refuse to comment on a report, quote, speech etc. of which he has no knowledge. The journalist may be making something up or has misunderstood a point. Assuming that the responder is not aware of the allegations contained in the journalist's claim, the first part of the reply should be that the responder has not heard/seen ...etc. ..so cannot comment .. but then surprise should be expressed...because...and then a trenchant point should be made, if possible, which casts doubt on the allegation.) Here are some more examples, with the first part of the answer omitted in some instances:

The local MP has demanded that this site should be closed down permanently. What do you say to that?
.......because today's accident at the site was the first there in * years. Furthermore, as the local community knows, we have won awards for safety at this plant and we shall be even more vigilant after today's accident.

Do you expect the plant to re-open as there is so much hostility towards you now from the local community?
Frankly, I myself am unaware of the reaction you have described but I readily accept that our excellent relationship with the local people has been tested and we are very sorry that they have been inconvenienced. However, we shall be apologising to them and seeking their views whilst assuring them that we shall do everything possible to avoid a repetition of what happened today. We have also...

Experts say that this site/vessel/plant was too old and should have been closed down/withdrawn from service many years ago: was that a factor in what happened today?
I don't know who these "experts" are but if they're experienced, they will know that what really matters is maintenance and training of the staff. We've not stinted on either.

Eye witnesses/survivors say that there was panic and that nobody seemed to know what to do.
...Because we hold regular drills at the plant/on the vessel/rig/platform/site and our personnel are well trained and experienced in all the necessary procedures, it's significant that, happily, the vast majority of those involved were all evacuated safely, although of course, we were deeply saddened that....nevertheless, the enquiry may consider the point that you have made but I am very confident of the outcome. OR My information was that there was some initial uncertainty, which is very understandable, but that

staff/crew/passengers soon acted responsibly and safely in line with well-tested procedures.

The widow of one of the men who was killed told me that her husband always said that your company skimped on safety and that, from the very outset, an accident was likely. What do you say to that?
….Because we maintain the highest safety standards and never, ever, do anything that jeopardises the lives of our colleagues. We encourage a very open culture and if any worker had a grievance or worry on safety, there is a simple system for reporting it or, if the individual prefers anonymity, that too, is catered for. Indeed, some of the improvements made in recent years have resulted precisely from such suggestions.

The mother of a survivor has claimed that her son used to work at the plant but that after complaining about lax safety procedures, he was sacked.
….Because it would not be in line with company policy, so I can't think that that allegation represents the full story. However, it is a serious charge and if she gives me the details, I'll ensure that it is examined.

The head of the local fire service has claimed that he was only alerted some 30 minutes after the fire started and that, if he had been called earlier, he and his men might have saved not only some lives but also the main building.

….Because I know for a fact that the fire service was called within minutes and that they were on site very promptly. We have an excellent relationship with the local fire brigade, and, indeed, all the emergency services, and they participate with us in our regular exercises to ensure that we all work together as effectively and efficiently as possible.

This plant is not all that significant to the group: did management take its eye off safety here whilst it was dealing with more important matters elsewhere?
I reject that entirely. We take safety seriously at all our plants and at this one, for example, in the last few years, we have done….and invested…. I am the plant manager here/the plant manager and I/he could produce 100 staff who would tell you that the allegation is absurd.

Critics have pointed out that, following the major fire that devastated the depot/trading estate/factory etc such sites should not be sited so close to residential areas.

I know that this is an issue that is now being discussed. However, we must wait for the full report on the incident before deciding, in conjunction with the authorities, what action, if any, is needed. However, I must emphasise that inland depots/plants of this kind, operated by many different companies, have had had a very good safety record over the years but we are not complacent.

In recent years, you have made thousands of people redundant. Surely, this has had an impact on safety?

Regrettably, like so many companies in this and in other sectors, we have had to make people redundant because of the economic situation and, of course, none of us wants to have to do that. However, I must stress that at no time has safety been endangered by this and we would never allow that to happen.

Could the long hours that the crew have to work have contributed to the accident?

You have what some in the industry call a United Nations crew. Can they all communicate in English and could the problem have occurred because of a failure to understand English?

I believe that's most unlikely. It's a prime requirement that all seafarers working for the company speak good English and they are tested before being offered employment.

You say that you put the lives of employees/passengers/crew above all else. As you don't know the cause of the accident, it could be an equipment or mechanical failure, why don't you ground all your aircraft of the same type/shut down production at similar sites, withdraw similar vehicles and plant using the same equipment/ to prevent similar disasters?

Currently, we have no reason to believe that such action is required and the authorities agree with us because they haven't told us to take such action. Furthermore, we are not alone in using *: it is used across the industry globally and has proved very safe for many years.

Being realistic, surely, the reason that you are not prepared to do this is because a high proportion of your net revenue comes from that oil field/aircraft/type of plant/procedure/vessel?

I totally reject your allegation that we put money ahead of people. We never jeopardise safety and taking risks with peoples' lives would be totally indefensible, morally and, for that matter, commercially. Like many companies in the industry, we have used this type of equipment/aircraft, etc. for * years without a serious accident.

Next of kin have been complaining to us that they cannot contact the company and that no information is coming from you. What will you do about this?

I'm sorry to hear this, as we set up a highly-trained personnel response team within * minutes of knowing about the emergency. We also gave out a specific telephone number for next of kin and the media has kindly repeated that number, which is ********. My colleagues have been very busy dealing with calls but if you've any names or numbers of next of kin who have phoned you, because they can't contact us, I'll gladly pass on the details to my colleagues who will try to ring the people involved. We have also put some relevant information on our website. www*****

One source told me that your company had always put profits ahead of safety.

This company puts safety above everything. I wouldn't have worked here for * years if I felt that it did not operate to the highest standards. If we're just talking about the cost of safety, and that alone, and I stress that, having an accident is much more expensive than maintaining a good safety record.

You pressured the contractors to complete the job, to secure earlier revenue, to meet the target date or to keep costs under control.

Your contractors are not subjected to regular safety inspections and are not required to meet your standards.

Your vessel was in the wrong lane at the time of the accident./ The vessel/vehicle was going too fast for the conditions.

The hours worked by your employees on ferries, trucks and trains, are too long and must be a contributory factor in the accident.

You are calling off the search prematurely because it's expensive.

Your chief executive is not going to the scene of the accident because he is too busy, believing that making money is more important than peoples' lives and he hasn't even made a comment on today's disaster.
That repugnant suggestion is totally wrong. He has been busy co-ordinating the massive rescue effort, especially with the various authorities. In fact, he has expressed his deep regret in a number of broadcast interviews and in our press releases. (Assuming that this is all true!)

This aircraft/vessel/truck etc has a history of malfunctions yet you continue to use it/them.

You pay your drivers extra for being ahead of schedule so that encourages them to take risks and that is why today's disaster occurred.

All your claims about evacuation times are based not on the average passengers but on young and fit staff who know much more about escape routes. That's right, isn't it?

You delayed telling us about this accident, hoping that we wouldn't find out.

Some board members had sold large numbers of shares, so even they lacked faith in the company.

Your company only operates old vessels/aircraft and the average age of your fleet is significantly higher than that of the industry/most of your competitors.

You failed to keep the local people advised of what was happening, despite all your expensive PR campaigns trumpeting the idea that you were a listening company.

You say that, knowing what has happened, you won't make changes in operations procedures. Surely, that is most irresponsible?

I don't know where you got the idea that there will be no changes. If we gave that impression, we apologise and I must assure you that we shall consider the enquiry report very carefully.

If you hadn't reacted so slowly in securing help to cope with today's disaster, many lives could have been saved and the reason for the tardy response was that you wished to save money/were too arrogant, had no plans in place.

You knew that the vessel/aircraft/machinery/equipment was faulty, yet you did nothing about it.
That is a serious charge and I am totally unaware myself of any evidence to back your claim. I would like to see your evidence.

Working through the night in these circumstances was almost inevitably going to lead to an accident and it did.

SOME USEFUL PHRASES

Some of these phrases will be equally helpful during interviews or press conferences, but, for convenience, they are arranged in relation to a specific situation. Some of them can be found above or elsewhere in this book.

When expressing regret

When under pressure and feeling emotional, some executives retreat into corporate speak. This sounds callous and spokespersons should use words that are at once human, understood immediately by a mass audience and worthy of being quoted directly in the media.

We are all deeply saddened by what has happened. My colleagues and I lost some close friends today. Our thoughts are with the relatives of the deceased and those who were injured.

When dealing with a comment of which the company spokesperson has no knowledge

See above OR Yes, I have seen/heard that report and I would like to say immediately that...

When asked to discuss the financial implications of the incident

Frankly, at the present time, we haven't had the desire or time to consider that. All our efforts have been concentrated on... OR *Money is the last thing on our minds at the moment.* OR *That, doubtless, is important but, at the moment, our priority is...*

Why did the accident happen?

It's much too soon to know/tell. OR *As you know/as I have explained, an official enquiry has already started/will soon start its investigation and I have no intention of pre-empting its findings.* OR *Nobody knows at the moment and I certainly don't want to mislead you.*

What kinds of factors could cause such an accident?

Operations on such a site are very complex and there is no point in my attempting to guess what might have happened. That would be speculation and I shall not speculate either now or in the future.

When the interviewer starts with a question that does not deal with people and/or environment

Before I try to answer that question, let me say immediately that we are deeply saddened at what happened today and that... OR *I shall answer your question, but, first of all, I must bring you up to date with some new and sad news. I'm sorry to say that ...*

When the interviewer lists many questions and does not allow the interviewee to reply adequately

Those are questions that we want answered, too.

When the interviewer has made a serious error or has made/quoted a serious allegation

I must refute that with all the experience and knowledge that I have gained in * years in this industry and in this company. OR *Please, just let me correct the comment that ...* OR *I really must emphasise...* OR *Before you go on, please allow me to correct you on a very important point...*OR *No,* *that is definitely not the case...OR I can understand that point of view but let me tell you what is really...*

When the interviewee lacks some information

I'm sorry that I myself haven't got that information at present but I know that my colleagues...,meanwhile, what I can tell you is that...OR Let me explain, why, although I should like to help you, I cannot. OR It might just help if I explained.. OR I can understand why you feel that, at this stage, we ought to know...Let me tell you, briefly, why...OR You've raised an important point and it should be addressed by someone who has the full details. I'm sorry that I haven't so I can't help you. OR I know that time is precious to you as you must meet deadlines, so let me explain that, for legal reasons and client confidentiality, which, I'm sure you understand, I cannot help you on that specific point.

When an interviewee or a press conference chairman is being interrupted

You've raised an important point and I would like to give it the answer it deserves, if I may. OR Please, before you continue, let me deal with one very important issue that you raised there...

Refuting comments

That may sound a good suggestion now but its ramifications must be studied before any such action is taken. OR There is absolutely no question of...OR Of course, we shall...OR Let me try to put all this into a context...OR I'm surprised that such an issue is raised because... OR I hadn't heard that before, but if you can let me have details, I shall certainly... OR Yes, we did do that and let me explain why...OR We certainly hoped that... but sadly.. OR The experts in the emergency services now tell us that...

When the company passed out incorrect information

I'm sorry if there have been any doubts/misunderstandings, so let me try to.. OR That was wrong and I apologise. What is the real ... OR The sad truth is... OR Thanks for the chance to...OR Let me try to clear up any doubts/misunderstandings/false perceptions OR *Let me try to explain why some confusion may have arisen...*

General

*We are absolutely determined to...*OR *As chairman/chief executive/managing director, I am totally committed to...* OR *really must pay tribute to...* OR *What ... did today was truly heroic and should be recognised as such...*OR *I would like to express my own deep regret, and that of the company, that...*OR *Let me give you a promise now. I shall ensure that...* OR *What is particularly sad is that...*OR *That certainly was the case but since then...*OR *Happily, there have been some positive developments since then...* OR *What is even more important is...* OR *The good news is that nobody has been hurt and that everybody has been accounted for.* OR *Happily, the fire has now been put out and...*OR *I'm pleased to say that...*OR *It certainly is complicated so perhaps...*

CHAPTER | 18

DID THEY REALLY SAY THAT?

These comments, based on thousands of responses, are included as a warning of what pressure can do to the nervous, the inexperienced, the untrained and the complacent. The potential repercussions need little elaboration.

A simple remark from a key figure can have severe repercussions in a crisis. A shipping master, who, after a real accident, decided that he could better co-ordinate the rescue of his passengers, still on the stricken vessel, from shore, evacuated himself in a helicopter. He then tried to deflect criticism by arguing *I said abandon ship, what more do they want?* Allegedly, many years ago, a senior transport executive implied that fires on the underground were *something we have to live with* and *fires are not our top priority.* When under pressure, a very small minority of interviewees can make mistakes that seem extraordinary to an audience, most of whom have no concept of the stress that can be felt. A lack of information and nervousness can cause major difficulties and whilst some nerves are necessary to avoid complacency, they can overwhelm the inexperienced.

Local comment

Of course, former employees, members of the local community and others can make potentially serious comments to the media. Consider this remark, injected into an exercise, made by a "victim".

> *I don't know what I'm going to do: my husband has been killed, my house is badly damaged and I've got to stay in this draughty cold hall until the poisonous cloud has gone and my house has been repaired.*

All my medicines are at home and I really don't know what to do. The company won't help me and I can't afford any extra expense, not at my age. My husband always told the company that one day there would be an accident because they cut maintenance and he was right. Close it down now. Since they got rid of so many jobs, it doesn't even employ many locals now.

Organisations that ignore local opinion or ignore the possibility of serious issues developing with one or more of its audiences will pay a heavy price sooner or later as frustrated individuals suddenly find that their opinions are being sought by the media.

Dangerous quotes made to the media during exercises

Some tired individuals will say something that they will always regret, such as *some level of mortality is acceptable,* but the possibility of such remarks being made can be reduced by removing fatigued team members. Untrained responders can wilt under pressure, even within minutes of being exposed to a television camera, a jangling phone or journalists at a press conference, and say something that reflects badly on the organisation. This, once again, underlines the need for realistic exercises and also the need to omit personnel, who are unhappy with the company, from all teams. Another cause of "odd" answers reflects responders confusing the persistence and direct approach of the journalist with bad manners. Journalists must be direct: they have deadlines to meet and work in a very competitive industry. Few are deliberately bad-tempered as this seldom prises information from a company representative.

Safety

- *Six people have been killed but that's life.*
- *I lack the information to refute the view that safety has been down-graded.*
- *Frankly, our safety record is not that good.*
- *We have an excellent safety record and in 24 hours, I should be able to prove it.*
- *We had an admirable safety record until the explosions.*

What we think about the media

- *We're at war with the media.*
- *I'm not allowed to speak to you: I'm too busy saving lives.*
- *The press always twists the truth*
- *Get off this media line. I'm here to deal with journalists' calls.*
- *I've had enough of this: I'm here to answer sensible questions.*

Ignorance

- *It's as if we're not here. We're told nothing.*
- *Frankly, I'm not responsible and you cannot rely on what I say.*
- *I'm as frustrated as you are: I've no information at all.*
- *I can't comment except to say that the company is in trouble.*
- *I can't confirm or deny anything. I'm a bit confused myself.*

Speculation

- *What I'm giving you is official speculation.*
- *The people are trained in safety procedures, or I assume they are.*
- *I guess they're dead.*
- *Were six lifeboats enough? I expect so.*
- *It could have been caused by an operational error.*

Press releases

- *A new press release is being prepared, but, like the others, it won't say anything.*
- *What does that mean in our release? God knows!*

Really?

- *If we issued releases whenever employees were hurt we couldn't operate.*
- *We're a little bit distressed as some people have been killed and others raped.*

- *Sixteen people have been killed but it could have been worse.*

- *The dead man has had heart attacks before, but never one this serious.*

- *The oil leak is fuelling the fire, so there's no need to worry about pollution.*

Mistakes in front of the camera or microphone

Interviewers can convert an error into a disaster. This does not imply that all interviewers will immediately concentrate on a nerve-induced error in real life but some "unfortunate" remarks which seem patronising or evasive will compel a challenging response from the interviewer. An interviewee accused the presenter of being unfair for criticising his company for the problems they encountered on their new vessel's maiden voyage. *Remember what happened to the Titanic!* The reply was predictable. *Are you saying that your company and naval architects have learned nothing in 100 years? Your competitors have made significant progress in this period.*

A hapless regional manager, who had criticised his colleagues in Head Office, sought to justify his criticisms. The greater the effort he made, the more foolish his colleagues appeared. This excruciating interview could have been avoided by simply claiming that such banter between Head Office and the regions was normal as the relationship was competitive but co-operative.

Sometimes, an interviewee is desperate to trumpet the virtues of a safety record. To do this whilst surrounded by blazing fuel tanks constitutes something of a challenge. Even if the accident was not the company's fault, it is wise to show some regret for what happened. Without this comment, the interviewer will be potentially hostile and when told that *we have an exemplary safety record at this depot and....* the response, obviously, was *you might have had but that is hardly relevant now as this disaster is now enveloping the whole neighbourhood.* Some senior personnel behave clumsily in front of the media, because they hate journalists. *Your company has seen a steep rise in the numbers of personnel seriously injured over the last few years. Why? That's typical of you media people. I really don't know where you get this kind of false information and then you condemn us for what hasn't happened.* The scribe responded: *The figures come from page 23 of your annual report. You might like to have a look at them and then let me have an answer to my question.*

Sometimes, the most innocent of approaches can conceal a very serious question. In some countries the ownership of shipping companies is a vexed issue so one senior executive, after a very friendly and thus deceptive beginning to his training television interview, was asked about this. After a few embarrassing moments, he waved his arms across his face in surrender and said that the interviewer had won.

The most innocent question can embarrass even the very senior directors. One was being interviewed after a fictional fire. He was asked three times, in a long interview in front of the cameras: *Will your company, one of the biggest in the UK, make prompt ex gratia payments to those who have been seriously inconvenienced by your accident and who have a reasonable case?* When asked for the third time, he offered the same inadequate combination of useless words, corporate jargon and evasion. Immediately after the interview, asked why he had not given an answer, he said that to have agreed would have opened the floodgates to numerous claims. The interviewer said that he had anticipated that so he had included the word "reasonable" in his question. The second defence was that the executive did not know company policy on this issue. He lacked the mental agility to devise a policy so his failure to reply sensibly to a serious point had implied that his company was mean and uncaring and viewers might have boycotted his company's products.

The need to plan has been emphasised heavily throughout this book. One example, when an interviewee failed to carry out some basic research in advance, would have had very serious consequences if the interview had been on national television. The scenario was that some customers, using one of the company's aerosol products, had suffered burns. The company's defence was that full instructions, on every aerosol, exceeded the requirements of the law. The interviewer, who had bought one of the aerosols the day before, noted that it lacked any instructions. The offending canister was held up to the camera at an agreed point and the hapless company representative was asked to point out where the cautionary words appeared. *They are not there but this must be a very old aerosol and I can assure you that any that you buy now carry the necessary words. You must have a very old container. No, I bought it yesterday, in my local supermarket.* The interviewee then flustered but should have said something like: *I am astonished that such an old aerosol was still available because it's some time since we introduced full warnings on our aerosols. I'd be grateful, if, after the programme, you give me details of this purchase so we can investigate immediately.*

CHAPTER 19

EFFECTIVE ROUTINE LINKS WITH THE MEDIA

Throughout the book, there have been references to the role that an effective media relations policy can also play in day-to-day life. Companies can use press releases, broadcast and print interviews and press conferences to publicise their activities in "peacetime" and much of what has been written can be adapted. This chapter is more general and discusses how an organisation can develop a routine relationship with the media and concludes with a section on how to make an effective presentation.

A routine media relations policy allows an organisation to learn about the media. A successful relationship with the media can also aid the company's commercial prospects whilst simultaneously allowing the media to understand something about the organisation. A peacetime plan may mean, for example, that the chief executive gains some experience of television interviews and how to conduct a press conference, whilst his more junior colleagues will learn how to write and distribute a press release. All this can also be enormously helpful in troubled times.

A modest media relations plan, in relation to day-to-day activities, resembles a reasonably-priced insurance policy. Even small organisations should consider how they could advance their standing in the community by having good links with the local media. Very modest organisations can suddenly be exposed to the media: for example, a small local company, but which, in the context of the town in which it operates, a big employer, may have to make many workers redundant. On one occasion, a journalist wanted a financial figure that the media relations contact could not provide but he quoted a range which suited the scribe. Later, the same journalist phoned his contact relating to possible redundancies. He was told that the story was untrue. Instead of running it, with the claim that it was false, the story was never written.

Devising a media relations campaign

Why maintain good relations with the media?

A constructive media relations policy has financial implications beyond its costs: it can support marketing plans and other commercial objectives economically. It can also assist, albeit indirectly, in other policies, such as government relations and links with financial institutions.

Securing the support of senior management and organising a budget

Senior management's support is fundamental. Senior personnel must be seen as endorsing plans and prepared to devote time and effort when they have a role to play. They must also ensure that the person who talks to the media is fully informed and enjoys their confidence. Without this support, objectives will not be met.

Identify the media co-ordinator and lay down some basic rules

The position of media co-ordinator need not be a full-time position but someone should be named as the sole link with the media. This allows that individual to accumulate relevant experience whilst ensuring that no careless comments from other employees reach the media. That is not censorship but the lesser of two evils because someone lacking direct access to senior management and ignorant of the media can easily create major problems. The nominated person should not be on the verge of retirement, partly because he may be less than totally committed, but more particularly because such an appointment prevents continuity in the post. The company is buying experience by creating the position which would soon vanish with the individual. If the appointee lacks knowledge or experience of the media, he should attend a specialist course.

It is also necessary to determine what information can be released to the media and under what circumstances. Unless this is agreed, the co-ordinator will always be asking senior management for decisions and that could lead to friction. Equally, the extent to which the co-ordinator can act independently must be agreed.

Naming the co-ordinator and telling all staff of the appointment

Once the appointment has been made, whether it is full or part time, senior management must inform all employees and instruct them that all media-related issues must be referred to the specific individual. He must also be invited to sit on all appropriate committees, have access to relevant information and be told of any events that might arouse media attention. This may sound obvious but experience shows that key officials are often denied access to relevant documents or information. If such material reaches the press, the hapless media person can look stupid if interviewed by someone who has the document or some "secret" knowledge.

Decide what information is relevant to the media and tell the staff

As this chapter is concerned with routine business, the company is probably looking to disseminate good news. Consequently, new contracts or new investment in plant or machines, additional jobs and new appointments are prime material. One easy way of alienating colleagues is to provide the media with information and to deny it to staff. They may be approached by friends who have seen the report in the local paper and then the employee has to confess ignorance. All external communications, such as press releases, must be disseminated amongst the staff who may also offer ideas for media coverage.

Draw up a list of relevant media

The co-ordinator should draw up a list of interested or potentially interested media people, possibly, if relevant, by subject interest, and ensure that it is maintained.

Decide on a programme

The organisation should be seen as proactive. If the co-ordinator is only part-time, this is more important because such matters will otherwise always be relegated in the list of tasks to be done. Within this programme, should be included events, interviews, site visits and other initiatives such as lunch with the company executives.

Other aspects

Subscribing to a news-cutting agency allows the company to see what is being said about it in the media and transcripts should be obtained of all broadcast interviews. The co-ordinator should also read, or glance at, all industry-related publications. A weekly summary of points of interest should be sent to management.

Methods of creating publicity and disseminating news proactively

- Updating the company's website
- Press releases and presentations at industry conferences
- Visits to relevant exhibitions covered by the media
- Active participation in trade groups, specific institutions etc.
- Phoning selected journalists, lunches with the media co-ordinator or key officials
- Site visits for the media, briefing meetings, interviews, press conferences
- Company newsletters/newspapers/brochures/magazines/videos/DVDs
- Provision of material, including maps, photographs, executives' biographies etc.

Factors contributing to good media relations

- Responding promptly to media and honouring promises to ring back as requested
- Providing good access to company officials
- Offering the maximum available information and background material
- Showing an understanding and regard for media deadlines
- Keeping in contact with the media, even when little is happening
- Ensuring that the contact list is up to date
- Providing accurate and confirmed information
- Not going "off the record" unless the journalist is known and trusted
- Trying to know as many journalists as well as practical

MAKING SUCCESSFUL PUBLIC PRESENTATIONS

This section identifies some of the problems and offers advice that should reduce the prospects of failure. Having the opportunity of making a public speech, like being invited to participate in a broadcast, is an opportunity to communicate with many people at little or no cost, apart, of course, from the time spent devising and presenting the paper. Invitations to business people to participate in broadcasts are often accepted with minimal consideration. One reason for hasty acceptance is probably the thought that little effort or planning will be required. That, of course, is wrong. The prospect of making a public presentation, at a conference, for example, often prompts the opposite reaction.

Apart from nervousness at the thought of appearing in front of a large live audience, there is the worry that preparing the paper will occupy much valuable time. However, rejecting the request should only be taken after careful deliberation. Many of the audience may be relevant to the organisation which, alone, might be a good reason for accepting an invitation. Unexpected opportunities can follow from just one interested member of the audience. Perhaps the company wants to defend a position or to be identified with a particular viewpoint? Clearly, a public presentation can improve a company's profile and a speech can persuade some listeners of a particular point of view. No experienced speaker expects to win over total support for a controversial stance but some listeners may be converted who might have remained hostile if they had not heard the presentation.

As with television interviews, some basic questions have to be answered, apart from the fundamental one of "is it wise, on balance, for the company to participate?" For example, will the organisation's representative be the only one addressing this particular topic? Are any other speakers opposed to the company's views? Is it better to confront them or should the invitation be rejected because it could cause the company more difficulties? Who is organising the conference and do they have a good reputation for attracting a large audience? Will the media be present? Who is the best person in the organisation to present this paper? Responses to these and other questions will determine whether it is wise for the company to participate. If the decision is taken to appear, much work has to be done.

The opportunity to persuade individuals of a point of view, to understand the company's thinking or "just" to raise an organisation's profile merits detailed planning to achieve full advantage from the opportunity. The perception of most companies is not derived from their technology or profitability, but from the overall impression that their employees create. If a company decides to accept the invitation, it must confront the task realistically. Too often, lazy, unthinking speakers dig out an old presentation or agree to speak on a topic with which they are unfamiliar and consequently spend most of their time trying to justify why they have not addressed the topic on which they were billed to appear. A frequent cause of major irritation at some conferences has been the habit of those speakers, who, asked to discuss the future, allocate 90 per cent of their allotted time to the distant past and then, foolishly, waste the remaining 10 per cent trying to explain the relevance of what had gone for ever to the future.

A successful conference presentation will, therefore, reflect detailed planning on a number of key factors, including the size and nature of the audience, preparation of the paper, the physical presentation, the use of visual aids and the venue at which the meeting will take place.

Selection of the speaker

The first task is to determine who should represent the company. That person will require not just knowledge of the topic but also some experience and skills in presenting. To some extent, the latter can be acquired with some hard work and practice. Clearly, a diffident speaker will be less likely to impress or convince his audience than one who exudes confidence without being complacent. A speaker must appear natural, carry authority, conviction and confidence and be enthusiastic on his subject. Even the most clearly-enunciated views, but expressed quietly whilst the speaker is studying his shoes, will be lost on a bored audience.

All this may necessitate practice as many people are nervous in public and quiet and introvert in private. Such individuals, required to speak in public, must act to impress an audience, who, after all, neither know nor care that the speaker is also quiet in "real life". Indeed, they may construe the lacklustre performance as an indication of a lack of enthusiasm for the topic. A presentation will be accepted more readily if an audience is convinced by the speaker's words, backed by analysis and facts, relevant to the topic, and supported by his demeanour. A business audience will not appreciate a sustained haranguing but will also soon tire of a quietly-spoken and apparently diffident personality who appears disinterested in his own presentation.

Nervousness

Public speaking resembles participating in a dramatic production. There is a stage (the conference hall) a script (the speech), an actor (the presenter) and an audience. One common problem for potential speakers is nervousness which can mar an excellently prepared speech. However, some adrenaline is essential, because, without it, a speaker can appear arrogant which can alienate an audience. The trick, not easily mastered, is to be sufficiently apprehensive, without being over-confident. One popular method of inducing self-confidence favoured by speakers is to convince themselves that they know more about the topic than all, or certainly, most of the audience, otherwise the roles would be reversed.

The knowledge that a paper has been well researched, which includes assessing the nature of the audience, and its delivery rehearsed, will expel some of the nerves. The impact of nerves can also be mitigated by taking deep and long breaths. A young economist, giving his first-ever full day lecture to a paying audience, noticed that the room was beginning to spin round after only two hours out of the scheduled seven. Sensing that he was about to faint, he asked for a window to be opened and, whilst this was being done, he sat down and emphasised a point that he had already made. Swiftly his head, and the room, returned to their normal positions and he resumed without any further problem. At his next appearance, at another venue, the same problem occurred, at precisely the same time but he followed the precedent. This cured his nerves and he was never troubled by this problem again, despite appearing regularly on live television.

The audience

A speaker must know, in advance, the nature of the audience and their expectations. On one occasion, an OPEC minister was due to speak in London, just after a crucial meeting of his organisation. Instead of discussing what had happened, a large and expectant audience was profoundly disappointed to hear him speak for about 45 minutes on the supply and demand for firewood in his country. One way of alienating an audience is for the speaker to announce that he is not going to speak on the topic billed in the programme. If an individual feels unable to discuss what has been offered, he should not accept the invitation, or, if necessary, delegate a more relevant colleague.

It is necessary to determine not only the subject matter that the audience is expecting but the level of understanding that the majority will have. If it is a technical conference, jargon may be acceptable but, of course, if it is a more general grouping, its use will ensure failure.

If the audience is likely to be international, the presenter should try to establish the extent of their command of English. If instant translation is to be offered, speakers must eschew technical jargon and colloquial expressions. Equally, speakers must show some sensitivity and understanding of the culture of the country in which they are appearing. Once, at a conference in the Middle East, a local official asked a British speaker to stop whilst he erased the tape recording of the most recent remarks. Above all, if addressing a multinational audience, humour should be used with the greatest possible care, and, preferably avoided entirely if there is any doubt about its likely reception.

Knowing something about the nature of the audience helps reduce nervousness. Does the audience consist mainly of workers from the speaker's trade or industry, or of friends, customers, strangers or politicians? What do they want to hear from the presenter and why has he been asked to speak? Experienced speakers know that, on some occasions, an audience will be looking for a solution to a problem or an insight into a relevant topic. Knowledge that this is being done can also boost confidence.

Despite diligent research and the involvement of the event organisers, it is not always possible to make a correct guess on the nature of the audience. On one occasion, just as a presenter was about to speak, a steward told him that they had identified a "trouble-maker" in the audience but that there would be no problem as he would be watched closely and ejected at the first sign of trouble. Experienced speakers can sense whether the "academic" level of the paper is appropriate from the "feel" of the audience within a few minutes and can adjust if necessary, up or down. However, adjusting takes skill and experience and, in some cases, is impossible.

Attendees expect a speaker to keep to schedule. Presenters must not over-run as this will irritate the audience and other speakers. In particular, audiences do not appreciate being delayed when food or drinks beckon. This is not just a greedy desire to consume: it is also a time for networking which is an important reason why business people attend conferences, workshops and seminars. Above all, the speaker must remember that the audience does not have to listen to him. In some countries, if bored, listeners will walk around the room, often talking quite openly. There can be few more disheartening experiences for a speaker which also pose a few problems for the chairman.

In summary, the speaker should establish:

- The type of the expected audience, including numbers, age group and experience
- What is expected of the presentation, in terms of length, style and content
- Whether the audience will have heard of the company or the speaker
- Their level of understanding, familiarity with the language and jargon
- What can, realistically, be conveyed to them, in the limited time available
- Their likely attitude to the speaker's stance on the topic
- Who else is on the programme and whether there will be a debate or questions
- Whether the media will be attending. If yes, that is a danger and an opportunity
- The audience's prevailing mood: after-lunch speakers must be lively

If the audience's reaction to the topic being discussed is likely to be negative, the speaker must:

- Present both sides of the case
- Argue with facts and conviction, whilst acknowledging that others may differ

Preparing the paper

Notes, text or nothing?

Some advisers suggest that a paper should be prepared at one sitting to ensure continuity and consistency. Others recommend that, if time permits, thoughts should be jotted down over a period and that the final version should only be compiled close to the date of the presentation so that the latest developments or thinking can be taken into account. That said, much will depend on the speaker's preference, the time available and the assistance and input of colleagues. An early decision on the likely key points will assist in the editing of ideas and in the selection of points for the final draft. Most audiences cannot recall more than a few points from a 30 minute presentation, so, as in a broadcast interview, repetition of say, three key points is desirable. The speaker should also indicate their importance by telling the audience that they are significant and the main theme of the paper should be emphasised throughout. This emphasis can be stressed by a change in tone, or it might be preceded by an obvious pause.

Whichever approach is adopted, parallel consideration should be given to devising or finding adequate visual aids to illustrate key points. If, for example, statistics are to be used, they should be as up to date as possible, and, if they are elderly, the speaker should say why. Statistics should be easily understood and read from an uncluttered visual aid and, above all, be relevant and as contemporary as possible.

The presentation may be memorised word for word but this is not recommended. Apart from the huge effort and time involved in such a feat, it could easily destroy spontaneity. Furthermore, it may not fit the audience's mood, link in with what has previously been said or be relevant to any occurrences since the paper was prepared. Possibly the silliest practice is for the speech to be written out in full and handed to the audience who then sit, diligently following the speaker whilst he demonstrates why he will never become a television news reader.

Some skilled speakers can make lucid and interesting presentations without any notes, relying on their experience, knowledge of the subject and keenly aware of the logical approach in what they intend to say. This option is not recommended for most company personnel, especially in a formal setting. However, those who do have the necessary skill, understandably, always sound more spontaneous and less contrived than their colleagues.

Many speakers favour the use of notes, possibly on cards or on a laptop. Such notes provide confidence in case the brain stops functioning and composing such notes, in itself, helps to fix the structure of the presentation in the speaker's mind. Experienced and confident speakers may well opt for writing out some brief notes, possibly on cards, and then improvising around key points and this is the preferred option. Finally, on some occasions, the presentation may be put on "invisible screens" like autocues, placed in front of the speaker. These allow him to look around, addressing each part of the audience in turn.

Whatever method of preparation and presentation is selected, the speaker must be familiar with the material. A UK government minister once grabbed a speech on his way to a function and, some time later, when on his feet, he turned to page five, all that he saw was the cryptic message, that, in words that lose something in the translation, from that point on, he was on his own. He was lost.

The material must be presented logically, so the audience can follow the theme. Whatever method speakers employ, their material must be organised so that the presentation sounds natural and spontaneous. From that perspective, whilst some rehearsals may be desirable for all except the most experienced speakers, if only to determine timing, excessive practice can destroy spontaneity.

Because the eye has difficulty in taking in more than four or five words at a time, reading from a typical length horizontal line is difficult whether what is being read is the speech itself or just notes. What is recommended/ by some consultants/ is a system/ of writing out a speech/with marks inserted/ between phrases or ideas/ so that they can be read/ or recalled/ by speakers looking directly at the audience. Others prefer to drop the long horizontal line and write out a speech in short lines with double spacing that can be easily assimilated, thus allowing the reader to look at the audience without losing his place and without leaving a finger on the appropriate line of text. With this technique, it is possible to underline or highlight key passages more easily, so that the necessary emphasis can be made.

If the speech is to be read, it must be written as it will be spoken. It is very difficult to sound natural if the speaker is reading written English which differs in style and structure.

The introduction

Great attention should be paid to the very first part of the presentation. This is the first chance to impress the audience and it may be difficult to recover from a poor start. Speakers should also listen carefully to their introduction from the chair in case there is something that they can use to advantage.

To secure immediate attention, an introduction may contain a captivating statement such as: *I believe that, if current trends continue, unemployment in our sector, and that means all of us, will soar. Let's consider the issues and see what we can do about them.* Sometimes, a speaker might start with something that catches the audience's attention because it is visual. It is unwise to begin with a joke, especially if it is not relevant and, at this stage, the speaker will not know the nature of the audience. Equally, a personal anecdote should be eschewed unless it is relevant, short and inoffensive.

A strong introduction, from leaving the speaker's seat to where he will be making the presentation, to the end of the first delivered paragraph, will increase confidence and indicate to the audience that the speaker is worthy of their attention. Experienced speakers do not hurry and may even pause whilst gathering their notes. This can attract attention more effectively than a rapid start, which so many speakers prefer, doubtless because their nerves induce them to begin with minimal delay. Should the presenter's introduction be received less enthusiastically than expected, the speaker should not be dismayed, as this disappointment could affect the remainder of the presentation. The reasons for the disappointing reaction may be outside his control.

Finally, when checking the final version of their notes, preferably on the day of the presentation, speakers should ensure that the latest newspapers, magazines or relevant websites do not contain something that could completely undermine their thesis. By the same token, both before the event and during the day on which individuals are scheduled to perform, they should ascertain whether any other speaker has mentioned their topic. If this has happened, it is important to determine what was said and the audience's reaction.

The text of the paper

Preparing a paper is at best an art form, but, as in all forms of communication, planning is essential. Most importantly, the speaker must decide the underlying purpose of the presentation and gear all else to this. Themes that are not relevant to the main thesis should be discarded as they will take time, divert audience attention and undermine their understanding and recollection. Presentations should have a lively, relevant start, which compels attention.

It is desirable to have a clear beginning, middle and end and to explain the logical approach. Equally, speakers should tell the audience what they are going to be told, then tell them and eventually tell them what they have been told. Vague generalities should be shunned and speakers should not be seen to be ignorant on a key fact as this could destroy their whole paper. The presentation should be structured so that the talk immediately seems relevant and it is useful to begin with a comment on the purpose of the talk and the route that will be taken. If the audience can see a logical path, their interest can be sustained. When moving from one aspect to another, it is useful to explain the "bridge" which also shows that the speaker is moving to a different but related topic. Some people, inevitably, fail to follow the speaker on the journey, so it is useful to reiterate the main points occasionally.

Where possible, speakers can bolster their case by citing authoritative sources but presenters' own experiences should be limited as too many positive tales induce boredom and could suggest that the individual is conceited. One trick favoured by experienced speakers is to use contrast for its impact. For example, *I would rather be deemed a failure by defending what I believed in than a success for supporting what I oppose.* Audiences, especially those who have paid, do not like flattery, so presenters should avoid glib comments like *I don't know what I can tell a knowledgeable audience like this anything they don't already know.* Similarly, speakers should neither apologise nor promise too much. One of the biggest sources of irritation for an audience is to be asked for its understanding for any flaw in the presentation and this, particularly, applies to badly presented visual aids.

The paper should allow for the repetition of the key themes so that they will be more easily recalled by the audience and speakers must show tact. "You won't know this, so I'll explain it" sounds much worse than "we all know this but let me just emphasise a few key points". Jargon and the excessive use of statistics should be avoided. When statistics have to be used, preferably very sparingly, skilled presenters put the data into a context. *Our road vehicles last year travelled the equivalent of 100 return trips to the moon, without a single accident.* All acronyms should be eliminated or explained. Clichés and puns must appear only rarely as one person's sense of humour is another person's incitement to violence. Wording is, of course, crucial so phrases like "to be honest" must never be uttered as it may imply that the speaker has not been truthful elsewhere. Speakers must eschew current fads, such as "you know" that litter public presentations. "At this moment in time" rather than "now" suggests that the speaker is playing for time or has no understanding of good communications. Unnecessary detail can derail a presentation and encourage the audience to cease listening. One potential hazard is an excessive use of negatives. One broadcast interviewer often used so many in his opening questions, such as *Would I be wrong in saying that you do not believe that * never happened* that interviewees did not know whether the response should be yes or no.

Finally, the presentation should have a clear and powerful conclusion. One politician, addressing his party conference, ended so weakly that the faithful did not realise that he had finished. Speakers should indicate that the finish is imminent as even a friendly audience will want to know when the next break is coming and, if possible, speakers should end with a short but pithy summary of their main points. One favoured by an experienced speaker on the economics of a key UK industrial sector was *whilst you have been listening to me talk about investment, some £50 million has been spent. It's time I left you to win your share.*

Physical presentation

Nature has endowed us all differently, physically and mentally, and many presenters lack charisma. Audiences understand that the lecturer is not auditioning for a key television role but, possibly, because television is so popular, they expect a very professional level of presentation.

An audience will appreciate a well-prepared, relevant paper, delivered confidently. By following certain rules, speakers can win and retain the attention of the audience. Furthermore, because so many business presentations are truly dreadful, those speakers who take the trouble to be more professional in their approach will please the audience. Before the presentation, the speaker should not consume alcohol or take any drink that will increase a sense of drowsiness or dryness, especially if he is nervous. Some speakers take up valuable time with a good and prolonged cough before beginning. Any throat clearance must be done in advance and in private.

The first challenge, as the presenter is about to perform, might be to ignore the remarks of the chairman. Consider, for example, this very rare but true example of "diplomacy". *This morning, we heard a frankly disappointing presentation from * * who showed that he was out of date with informed thinking. Now we have Mr.. * * whom we hope will interest us with more modern views.*

Speakers must not indulge in a detailed analysis of their performance whilst still on their feet as such introspection could undermine the remainder of their speech. They should always feel comfortable with their appearance and material. Audiences look at the speaker, as well as listening to his words and a strong visual performance is essential to support the speech. Clothes should be relevant to the audience or occasion, if only because something deemed inappropriate will deflect attention from the words. Speakers must feel confident and comfortable and the right, smart clothes will enhance a sense of well-being.

Even the walk from the seat to the podium will say something about the speaker. A slow shuffle, with eyes firmly fixed on the speaker's shoes, will be interpreted, usually accurately, as a lack of confidence or even enthusiasm for the topic. The performance starts when the speaker stands up, after the chairman's introduction, and then begins the move to the rostrum, not when he begins talking. Many speakers use a lectern as support and sometimes almost retreat from sight, implying that they fear attack from the audience. An experienced and confident speaker will move around the podium area, thus creating the opportunity to look directly at different parts of the audience.

On arriving at the position from which the paper is to be presented, many speakers immediately commit serious offences. One is to test the microphone by tapping it or blowing into it. The sound system should have been checked before the first presentation of the day and if it does not work, it will soon become apparent. Presenters sometimes think that the system is not working as only a high pitch sound is heard. Usually, this is feedback and is eliminated by the speaker retreating modestly from the microphone. The second crime is to ask whether everyone can hear the speaker. This has always seemed odd because if a section of the audience cannot hear, how do they know he is asking them?

Many speakers immediately thank the organisers for their invitation to present. Some include such a comment in their opening whilst others prefer to say something along these lines at the end. This can weaken what should be a powerful conclusion and some analysts maintain that the comment is redundant. Certainly, the company has been given a platform for its views but the conference organisation is seeking to make profits from the presenters who are seldom paid much to offset their time in preparation and presentation.

When speaking, it is legitimate, where appropriate, to use gestures but these should be carefully controlled, otherwise they detract from the point being made, rather than adding emphasis. Hand movement for their own sake should be avoided. Speakers should always seem relaxed and behave as if they were enjoying the experience, even if they are not. If a presenter loses his place, he should not mutter er, er erm and other grunting-type noises. The advice is to pause, find the correct place again and continue undaunted. Similarly, if the brain suddenly goes blank, the presenter should pause, repeat a key point and then move to a section that, it is recalled, is in the next part of the presentation.

Speakers must ensure that they and their words, together, are the sole focus of attention, so all nervous gestures, such as running hands through their hair, playing with change in their pockets or frequently taking off and putting on glasses, unless medically necessary, must be banished. Similarly, some speakers like to stand lopsided, shifting the load from time to time on each foot. This may intrigue the audience who are waiting anxiously, not for the next verbal gem but for the speaker's collapse.

A change in tone and volume and the discreet use of pauses are powerful tools not just to keep audiences awake but to stress important points. Equally, the speed of delivery is important. A taped rehearsal can allow an assessment of the correct speed. 160 words a minute is too quick and 110 is too slow. Looking around the audience and making eye contact with individuals is recommended. It not only makes them feel part of the presentation but denies the speaker the chance to study the carpet in some detail.

Visual aids

Some speakers are besotted with visual aids, especially those emanating from modern technology but the medium must not overtake the message. Others bombard the audience with visual aids emerging on two screens. This can complicate more than assisting understanding. Perhaps the worst offence is to show graphs or statistics which are complex and then remove the material before the audience can even detect what it is being shown, let alone understand it. Many presenters offer really busy visual aids and then apologise for the detail, as if they are surprised by what they see. If it is so busy, or difficult to read at a range of more than a metre, why is it being shown? Visual aids must clarify, not confuse, and be explained by the speaker who leaves them on the screen long enough for the audience to digest the details. Some speakers then stand in the way, so that parts of the audience cannot see the art work and others, shunning more professional or modern aids, use a pencil over a vu foil on the projector to point out salient details.

Another offence is the failure to put the visual aids, of whatever kind, in the correct order, later implying that some evil-minded gremlin is responsible for this unprofessional disaster. Similarly, equipment, whether operated by the conference staff or the speaker, must always be checked well in advance. Some presenters, ironically making presentations on technical matters, do not even know how to start a machine.

Little is achieved by reading out notes from a screen: the only function of visual aids is to assist in enhancing the audience's understanding and retention of a point. A declining number of lecturers prefer old-fashioned vufoils, claiming that they are more flexible, in that they can be discarded easily when time is short and nobody in the audience realises that the speaker has bungled on the timing and has to scrap part of the presentation. Audiences now expect a more professional approach and the era of vufoils is all but over.

Speakers should ask themselves whether they really want the hall plunged into gloom which might induce sleep and which certainly means at the very least, a temporary loss of eye contact with the audience. Nevertheless, the use of PowerPoint or carefully chosen slides can improve a presentation if they are relevant, uncluttered and clearly visible from all parts of the hall or conference room.

The room

All presenters must feel comfortable in the conference room and be aware of the geography. Where do intending speakers sit and where do those who have performed go to? Is the room too hot? Speakers are entitled to discuss all this with the chairman in advance, long before the actual presentation and this highlights the importance of arriving early. Apart from testing all the visuals and associated equipment, an early arrival enables the speaker to spend time sitting at the back of the hall to determine whether the visuals can be seen and whether a microphone needs to be used. Arriving early also permits a chat with the chairman, to discuss his stance on time keeping, and the system for taking and dealing with any questions. Where should the speaker be when taking questions and will comments and questions be taken after the individual's presentation or at the end of the session? Executives can also ensure that he has a copy of their biography, but it must be short. Few things antagonise an audience more than a long and boring bio followed by a lacklustre performance. It is also desirable to meet fellow speakers and to ensure that the presenters' position is not under a noisy air duct.

Presenters should determine whether there is a clock in the room, and, if there is, they should ensure that it reflects the same time as their own watch. If there is no clock, speakers must make sure that they can look at their own watch without being detected.

CHAPTER 20

CONCLUSIONS

The basic assumptions underlying all emergency planning are that nature is unpredictable, technology will not always work as intended and that humans can behave erratically, causing additional chaos. The resulting impact on people and the environment can be very severe and will be even more serious if organisations do not plan how to cope, not least in the dissemination of information.

These repercussions can be emphasised and even exaggerated by the media which are growing increasingly influential and which can even determine a company's prospects of survival. Consumer power, influenced by pressure groups and by media coverage, is also at unprecedented levels in some countries. Society not only demands higher standards in business, particularly in relation to safety and the environment, but expects organisations, whatever their size, that could be involved in an emergency, to have planned to minimise the adverse repercussions. It also expects organisations to be able to communicate and will immediately be suspicious of those which do not or cannot, as reported by the media, which will soon expose and possibly magnify any shortcomings.

It matters little that journalists may be ill-informed or wrong on occasions, especially when companies refuse to communicate. Organisations that effectively advance media incompetence as a justification for corporate silence will merely hasten their own demise. Meanwhile, the media will continue to flourish, pausing only to chalk up another victim on the scoreboard and wondering why a company had made no plans or refused to communicate on what it was doing.

No organisation can guarantee that it will not be involved in a crisis. Some, of course, are more at risk than others, but some groups pay inadequate attention to teaching executives on how to communicate effectively through the media. There is a widespread view amongst these companies that communicating effectively is some kind of automatic ability, given generously to senior executives, presumably through a system of management osmosis, granted on promotion. If the consequences of this view were not so potentially serious, shareholders might enjoy the joke.

The reality is that the media industry requires understanding by those who would seek to use its facilities to advantage. It is often said that the media offer a free resource in disseminating important information, especially during crises. That may be true but there is a price and a penalty. The price is the cost of understanding how the media work and setting up systems and teams that can assist journalists whilst simultaneously aiding the company. The penalty is that if this does not happen, and executives make serious errors or fail to communicate, the damage inflicted by the accident will be magnified as the impression gains ground that the organisation is incompetent because it either failed to communicate or did so inadequately.

Companies cannot hide, hoping that media interest in an emergency will fade if corporate silence is observed. Of course, this merely inflames the situation and encourages the media to investigate the reasons for the silence. Journalists expect companies to be able to explain themselves and to communicate, so when little or no information emerges from a company in an emergency, the immediate assumption is that there is something to hide. Of course, the reluctance to communicate may reflect other factors, such as fear of the media and the view that comment would merely make a bad situation worse. All that the outside world knows is that the company has ignored society, failed to express its regret and has not indicated what it is doing to mitigate the consequences of the emergency, which may or may not have been its fault.

Some general conclusions can be drawn on the basis of current trends. Emergencies will happen and reacting to the media is, in a sense, as important as dealing with the operational aspects. A proliferating and more powerful media will become more involved in emergencies and their presence must be handled sensitively and sensibly if the company is not to be overwhelmed.

Organisations must also make an effort to convey the essentials of their industry and operations, otherwise the media, frequently ignorant on such matters, may cover the emergency unfairly or badly. Currently, many industries make an inadequate effort to explain themselves and then wonder why their actions are misunderstood. Good communication must be a continuing process, not something to be taken off a dusty shelf in times of crisis. Some organisations still believe that the creation of an emergencies manual will ward off misfortune, whilst others have managements that fail to accept their own limitations. All this inspires a false sense of security and may even help to induce emergencies. Companies must regularly assess their systems, possibly fashioned to meet different criteria, to see if their style and organisation permits appropriate communication with the contemporary media which is, itself, evolving all the time.

In some relatively low key situations, a decision may have to be taken to determine the nature and extent of an organisation's response to the media. It might be wise, for example, at least initially, to adopt a relatively low profile, especially if another involved group is perceived as the "villain". However, the organisation must be fully prepared to respond more comprehensively if circumstances so dictate.

That said, communicating effectively with the media is compulsory for companies wishing to stay in business after being involved in a serious incident. Understanding the structure of the media and the necessary techniques, as outlined in this book, and undertaking training is a small price to pay for improving the prospects of survival if disaster strikes. Saving this small sum of money will seem a ludicrously bad decision when a supine, mean and unimaginative organisation involved in an emergency is forced out of business because of media pressure.

GLOSSARY

Crisis management has generated a modest jargon of its own. In this book, jargon, hopefully, is minimal but here are some phrases that have been employed.

Board writer: The person charged with the responsibility of ensuring that the latest information is written clearly on the white boards in the telephone media response team room.

Bridging: The skill, which must be employed with some subtlety, to avoid appearing crass, which is used during interviews, especially on television, and during telephone conversations, of moving from an area of little interest to the company, or which is negative, to a topic of greater interest or which is more positive.

Crisis management team: The group of senior executives who take responsibility for organising the overall response to the incident, from operational aspects to public affairs considerations.

Doorstepping: Journalists gathering outside an office or location occupied by a sought-after individual or organisation, or at the site of an emergency, hoping to talk to key participants.

Down the line: An interview, given to the press, radio or television, given down a telephone line.

Fact File: A document, giving background information about the company, compiled especially for members of the telephone media response team, to assist them in answering journalists' questions.

Holding statement: The initial press statement or release which confirms the basic details of an emergency and which is issued mainly to establish that the company is prepared to deal with media enquiries.

Hunting system: The telephone system used by many telephone media response teams which seeks out any line that is not engaged and connects the caller to the vacant line.

Log sheet: A sheet designed for telephone media team responders to indicate the identity and affiliation of the caller from the media and some basic and brief points on the conversation. Any allegations against the company should be noted on this form and passed immediately to the co-ordinator.

Media kit: A folder which will include background material about the company and its key personnel, possibly some photographs and a copy of the latest press release.

Media Response Plan: A plan which specifies the roles, duties and requirements of various relevant individuals and groups involved in external communications.

Pooling: The system used when many news organisations want interviews and when it is not practical to meet all the requests. One interview is given to one or more journalists but it is made available to all parts of the media.

Press briefing: A meeting convened by the organisation, for the media, and addressed by senior company officials. A new statement will be read by the officials after which they take questions from the media.

Press conference: A more usual name for a press briefing.

Press release: A formal and official comment from the company, on paper or in electronic form, that is distributed to the media to offer news and information about an incident.

Press statement: Another name for a press release.

Runners: Individuals who carry messages from the telephone media response room or the emergency control room to other locations, as requested by the telephone media response team co-ordinator or public affairs representative.

Soundbite: Often called a "quotable quote", a soundbite is a brief but memorable and appealing phrase that the media will be inclined to use.

Telephone Media Response Team: Trained company volunteers, or external specialists, who can be called at short notice to respond to the media's telephone enquiries. Team members are rarely members of the public affairs division.

Telephone Media Response Team Co-ordinator: The person charged with leading the team, who, ideally, has some knowledge of both the company and how the media operates.

White boards: The boards in the telephone media response team room on which the latest and approved information is written so that members of the telephone media response team can convey the information to journalists.

FORMS

Individual companies will have different requirements for the information that needs to be collected or disseminated during an emergency. What follows, therefore, is but a minimal guide and it only refers to the media-related aspects of the crisis.

Checklists

A checklist for all the different functions should be devised so that nothing is omitted in the chaos that characterises emergencies. They can be compiled from the information in individual chapters in this book. The functions could range from call out to dealing with requests for television interviews. An early checklist, concerned with call out, for example, might include:

- Notifying security staff, media telephone response teams and telephone operators, other responders, management, external advisers, staff, any affiliated companies and official organisations if that is the role of the media team
- Establishing outlines of what has happened, brief individuals and teams as necessary
- Ensuring media telephone response room is organised and equipment is working

- Organising despatch of on-site representative
- Preparing holding statement or press release one
- Ensuring that media coverage is monitored
- Noting time of key events, such as despatching press releases etc.

Media responders' forms

Some companies provide their media responders with two forms: one is used to record the name and affiliation of the caller and, briefly, the nature and tone of the questions. The second form may be employed to note any key questions for which currently there is no answer and which should provoke a response from the organisation because it is on a significant point. It should also be used to note any serious allegations. The form is then passed on to the crisis management team for action. However, some organisations use the "first" form for both purposes.

The white boards

What information is recorded will depend on the company involved and the incident but some common headings might include basic details of the incident, new information, weather, personnel and their disposition, response resources on site, the plan of action, progress achieved and telephone numbers of other involved organisations who can deal with questions that should have been directed to them.

Index

ALSO BY PHILIP ALGAR

WITH IMMEDIATE EFFECT- a satire on office life and business

What happens when an honest but bored, frustrated, inexperienced and unexpectedly-promoted office worker tries to cope with novel business and social changes? Millions work in offices but few novels reflect the humour of office life, managements' eccentricities or multinationals' behaviour and the world in which they have to operate. *WITH IMMEDIATE EFFECT* fills this gap and takes a wry look at smug politicians, weather forecasts, acronyms, tabloid newspapers, supermarkets, job advertisements, taxi drivers, management gobbledegook and much more.

Bored and frustrated at work and at home, 55 year old Henry Perkins just wants to survive to pensionable age. Suddenly, he is exposed to a new world of business and pleasure. How will he react, especially to the opportunity to compensate for his lost youth? We watch, as, relying on honesty and a sense of humour, he tries to cope with a major industrial accident, a television interview, an after-dinner speech, an annual general meeting and a major event that threatens to end his new life almost before it began.

Praise for *WITH IMMEDIATE EFFECT*

Highly amusing and perceptive, this original portrait of office life should be read by all wage slaves who are chaffing at their shackles. *Chris Hirst of The Independent*

Hugely enjoyable and hilarious. Insights abound. Worth several weeks of **management training and development courses.** *A former senior executive*

The text romps along, cutting swathes through the ridiculous, often in a manner deliciously short of political correctness. While there is a narrative line, arguably the book is less of a novel and more a **management guide**. It's all good fun. *A senior company executive and communications adviser*

An amusing read in itself, this book also acts as a highly instructive **management guide** to handling communications in high profile situations. Highly recommended. *Petroleum Review*

A barrel of laughs, a riveting and enjoyable read with the author's humour shining through. *Lloyds List*

A witty satirical novel. *Energy Economist*

See www.philipalgarbooks.co.uk for more information

Order direct from: Philip Algar,
                    PO Box 39,
                    Ottery St. Mary, Devon EX11 1WT

Price: £11.95 including postage and packing. Discounts are available for bulk orders.

Philip Algar, B.Sc. (Econ.), FCIJ, worked in the international oil industry, including a period when he was responsible for a large company's media relations. Subsequently, he became a writer, contributing regularly to publications in the UK, Norway and the US. He has participated in more than 500 broadcasts in the UK and North America and has experience of live interviews, phone-ins and debates. He has also written his own radio scripts.

Two of his earlier books on crisis management were published by the Financial Times. He has attended actual crises in the UK and Europe, as a company employee, journalist or consultant. Algar has trained some 150 organisations, in many different sectors, in more than 20 countries, on how to handle the media during emergencies and has participated in many hundreds of training days and exercises. He has also prepared crisis communication plans and manuals, written scenarios for training exercises, scripted videos and lectured at the UK's National Emergency Planning College and in the UK, Europe, Middle East, North America and Australia.